POSTCOLONIAL BIOLOGY

POSTCOLONIAL BIOLOGY

Psyche and Flesh after Empire

DEEPIKA BAHRI

University of Minnesota Press
Minneapolis
London

Published by the University of Minnesota Press
111 Third Avenue South, Suite 290
Minneapolis, MN 55401-2520
http://www.upress.umn.edu

The University of Minnesota is an equal-opportunity educator and employer.

Library of Congress Cataloging-in-Publication Data
Names: Bahri, Deepika, author.
Title: Postcolonial biology : psyche and flesh after empire / Deepika Bahri.
Description: Minneapolis : University of Minnesota Press, [2017] | Includes bibliographical references and index.
Identifiers: LCCN 2016047367 (print) | ISBN 978-0-8166-9835-6 (hc) | ISBN 978-0-8166-9836-3 (pb)
Subjects: LCSH: Commonwealth fiction (English)—History and criticism. | English fiction—History and criticism. | Cultural fusion in literature. | Postcolonialism in literature. | Biology in literature. | Race in literature. | Kunzru, Hari, 1969– Impressionist. | Rushdie, Salman. Midnight's children. | Barnes, Julian. Arthur & George.
Classification: LCC PR9080.5 .B34 2017 (print) | DDC 820.9/9171241—dc23
LC record available at https://lccn.loc.gov/2016047367

UMP LSI

CONTENTS

PROLOGUE

Oh! Calcutta!

No body, never mind.

—**ANTONIO DAMASIO**, *THE FEELING OF WHAT HAPPENS*

I did not want this revision.

—**FRANTZ FANON**, *BLACK SKIN, WHITE MASKS*

I GREW UP IN A CITY CALLED CALCUTTA, officially renamed Kolkata, its Bengali equivalent, with the advent of the new millennium. The two words, and arguably the two cities, had long coexisted. The sonic distinction between the two also pointed to matters of class and education. Those who called the city Calcutta—phonetically kæl'kʌtə, culminating in the retroflex /t/ instead of the softer palatal /T/ of Kolkata (coal-kata)—were most likely to be educated in "English-medium" schools founded by colonial missionaries. They/we were intended to be designer versions of Macaulay's minutemen, "a class of persons, Indian in blood and colour but English in taste, in opinions, in morals, and in intellect," as he describes them in his 1835 "Minute on Indian Education" (249). The making of this class, however, involved more than abstract interactions between empire and psyche; minute-made natives embodied this refashioning in the flesh as well. The *corporeal* commitment involved in pronouncing the Anglophone version of the city's name requires lingual, alveolar, and glottal orchestration. Tongue, teeth, breath, diaphragm, palate, mouth, and elocutionary training collaborate in the pulsive production of language lined with flesh. As he practices rolling his *r* for hours in his room after arriving in France, Frantz Fanon's aggrieved speaker in *Black Skin, White Masks* discloses the reason for undertaking this sort of labor: "I must take great pains with my speech because I shall be more or less judged by it" (20). It seems to me now that the Anglophone word "Calcutta," born of the concerted efforts of flesh and mind, was but one of many ways of *bodying* forth the piecemeal, "retail"-level refashioning implicit in the colonial civilizing mission, an early harbinger of the struggle for control over the body, its expressions, ingestions, and reformation in globalization (Foucault, *Discipline and Punish,* 137).

Fanon's observation, "not with impunity . . . does one undergo [colonial] domination" (*Toward the African Revolution,* 41), and Theodor Adorno's disconcerting insight, "it is part of the mechanism of domination to forbid recognition of the suffering it produces" (*Minima Moralia,* 63), point us to the problem of how to think from the standpoint of "damaged life" in the aftermath of imperial modernity. What should be at stake in postcolonial conversations today? This book aims to uncover the dually psychophysiological dimensions of hybridity and claims biology as a valid—indeed a *crucial*—area of interest for critical postcolonial studies in order to direct attention to the question of life lived in the psyche *and* the flesh after empire. The sociopolitical challenges of the twenty-first century require us to look beyond biologically deterministic conceptions of racialized difference to porous, pliable, and plastic bodies and psyches as critically embattled zones of conflict in the wake of imperial modernity. Global capital's inheritance of imperial designs on the psyche and the flesh is part of a long season of the production of what I call "postcolonial biology" in an attempt to draw attention to power over life and lifeways in the relay from colonialism to a late capitalist, consumption-driven world under new forms of empire.

INTRODUCTION

Plasticity, Hybridity, and Postcolonial Biology

> These creatures you have seen are animals carven and wrought into new shapes. To that, to the study of the plasticity of living forms, my life has been devoted.
>
> —**H. G. WELLS**, *THE ISLAND OF DR. MOREAU*

> Man's first and most technical object . . . is his body.
>
> —**MARCEL MAUSS**, "TECHNIQUES OF THE BODY"

Hybridity Redux

Salman Rushdie's *The Satanic Verses* opens with Gibreel Farishta and Saladin Chamcha tumbling earthward after their London-bound flight AI-420 explodes with a "big bang" over the English Channel. As they fall toward "the slow, congealed currents of the English Sleeve," Farishta breaks into a popular Hindi film tune, "translating the old song into English in semi-conscious deference to the uprushing host-nation": "O my shoes are Japanese . . . These trousers English, if you please. On my head, red Russian hat—My heart's Indian—for all that" (5). The jingoistic jingle from the 1955 film *Shree 420* (Mr. 420) establishes a meaningful gap between surface appearance and core identity by confining what is foreign to the sartorial drag. Easy on, easy off. The irony of "semi-conscious" translation into English eludes Farishta as he chants Bollywood's nationalist fantasy of essential inviolability. The narrator, however, likens the English Channel to a "birth canal . . . the appointed zone of their watery reincarnation," even if the two tumblers "did not become aware of the moment at which the processes of their transmutation began" (4–5). The terms "reincarnation," "mutation," and "big bang" suggest that the relationship between mimicry, hybridity, and performance—in other words, form and content—requires closer scrutiny of assumptions about the nature/culture divide. Rushdie's references to 420—the section of the Indian Penal Code involving crimes of cheating and deception—in the flight number as well as the film title pointedly intertwine singer, song, and swindle, asking us to look out for a major fraud requiring further investigation.

In the same novel, Rushdie traces the making of the "English-medium" Indian to Thomas Macaulay's 1835 Parliamentary "Minute on Indian Education," a doctrine founded in similar suppositions of deterministic difference and inviolable core, but nonetheless invested in certain forms of Anglicization: "We must at present do our best to form a class who may be interpreters between us and the millions whom we govern, a class of persons, Indian in blood and colour, but English in taste, in opinions, in morals, and in intellect" (*The Satanic Verses,* 58, 249).[1] "Colonial mimicry," as Homi Bhabha explains the project, "is the desire for a *reformed,* recognizable other" who would remain other (*The Location of Culture,* 86; emphasis added). What made this reformed other recognizable? What were the building blocks of this reformation? Although mimicry arguably magnified racial divides, the civilizing mission was designed to allow the English to distinguish the minute-made subject of the civilizing mission from millions of others under colonial rule. However poorly defined or understood by both colonizer and colonized, and however contested, fetishized, and partial in form, ideas of "English . . . taste, opinions, morals, and intellect" were nevertheless translated into recognizable behaviors and judgments loosely associated with Englishness, and thereby with modernity.[2] Moreover, in identifying taste as the first in a list of modifiable attributes, Macaulay was unwittingly blurring the nature/culture boundary. If taste, according to Pierre Bourdieu, governs "all forms of incorporation, choosing and modifying everything that the body ingests and digests and assimilates, physiologically and psychologically," and it is "culture turned into nature, that is *embodied,*" we need to account for what it means to accord with practices and lifeways connected to Englishness (*Distinction,* 190).[3] I submit that colonial hybridity, robustly conceptualized in postcolonial theory to challenge essentialized notions of identity in favor of a third space of encounter and translation, nonetheless also involved significant interference in the colonized native's *biological* and physiological being. A full reckoning with the biophysiological dimensions of hybridity requires us to confront the implicitly *reincarnative* politics of the so-called civilizing mission in imperial modernity.

In the wake of the repudiation of deterministic racial differences in the life sciences today, I revisit the concept of hybridity in this book to include consideration of biological plasticity and epigenetic factors in evaluating the significance of intercultural contact. On the understanding that sex is only one mode of bodily penetration and reproduction, biological hybridity implies forms of mixture that are neither confined to sexual congress alone nor rooted in essentialized racial differences. If the racist science of its time assumed that genetics locked in the differences between races, the invitation to colonial mimicry, I argue, implied an as-yet scientifically unverified but implicit belief in human bioplasticity and aesthetic reformation. Colonial investment in racial border patrol based in ideas of deterministic difference was complicated by imperial designs on impressionable, *plastic* body-minds at the level of ideology as well as the micromanagement of the subject's bio-physiology, or what author Hari Kunzru calls the "grammar of behavior, a social language" (*The Impressionist,* 335). For better and for worse, the imperial civilizing mission would not only recalibrate knowledge systems but also bodily aesthetics and comportment in matters as fundamental as how to eat, speak, sit, shit, or spit. The reincarnative logic of the civilizing mission discloses itself even in a cursory survey of practices associated with "Englishness." Those related to diet, bearing, ingestions, or forms of evacuation are more obviously bodily, whereas others—pertaining to language, speech, and accents, for instance—seem less so, but language, too, is lined with flesh.[4] Incarnate moments of speech unfold in the coordination of breath, diaphragm, lip, palate, head tilts, eyebrow lifts, vocalization, airflow, and hand gestures.[5] The touted notion of identity as performance of forms also requires psychic, physical, muscular, and neuronal conjunction, pointing clearly to the biopoetic entailments of hybridity and mimicry. The twisting of tongues into a second language, regulation of plosive breath to produce prestigious versions of the English accent, the muscular labor of mastering new postures, the altering of body chemistry through the ingestion of new foods or the application of new products, and scores of other corporeal revisions speak resonantly of the incarnate, physical scene of hybridity.[6] Human biology interacts with forms, ideas, objects, things, and commodities pushed upon and into the body and mind, with and without the subject's awareness, demanding a theory of performativity and a conception of hybridity attuned to the indissociability of "matter and meaning" (Barad, *Meeting the Universe Halfway,* 3).

The physical scene of hybridity involves the sensate, biological body interacting with a world founded in dominative rationality. Adorno frequently turns to the "incarnate moment" (*leibhafte Moment*) of experience because it reveals the extent to which our behaviors as well as our instincts and urges have been socially regulated (*Negative Dialektik,* 201; translation mine). I translate *"leibhafte Moment"* as the "incarnate moment" instead of the more commonly used "physical moment" in order to emphasize the involvement of the carnal, life-filled sensorium in experience.[7] Attention to these moments discloses the neurophysiological load of acculturation. Parsing the grammar of "comportment," from the Latin *com-* (together) + *portare* (to carry), reveals the burdens of hybridity and mimicry: what the body must endure to become more becoming (*Oxford English Dictionary Online,* s.v. "comportment"). The incarnate moment directs us, moreover, to a realization of the extent to which our behaviors and our judgments of the world, our selves, and others are animated in the flesh, and the ways in which ideology and the mind itself are "body-minded," as neuroscientist Antonio Damasio describes it. In the relay between "racism's two logics, the biological and the cultural," and in moments when form impinges on cognition and flesh takes form, human plasticity, mimicry of privileged aesthetic forms, the development of habits, and the carnal foundations of knowledge, behavior, and motivation emerge as key factors in thinking about what makes us human (Said, "Always on Top," 6).

This book returns to the figure of the racial hybrid—long designated the biological hybrid through historically generated categories—to put pressure on traditional notions of biological hybridity in light of today's understanding of plasticity and body-minded cognition. Writ large in the figure of the racial hybrid is the drama of the inherited *and* malleable body in the permeable border between nature and culture. The signature themes of this book, pursued through readings of the sociocultural worlds of hybrid characters in Julian Barnes's novel *Arthur and George,* Hari Kunzru's *The Impressionist,* and Salman Rushdie's *Midnight's Children,* derive from vexing the question of the biological and physiological dimensions of hybridity in particular and the question of the human in general. Although their genealogical histories are distinct, and the differences between them are simultaneously maintained and denied in postcolonial studies, what racial and nonracial cultural hybrids potentially share is the experience of the body-mind under revision at the porous borders between race, biology, and culture in the sociobiological laboratory of empire. By implication, then, paged by history and inseminated by the logic of imperial modernity, cultural and racial hybrids are *both* biologically reincarnated. Located in a complicated subcontinental context, the figure of the hybrid disclosed in this book demonstrates various kinds of psychophysiological formation in excess of the fact of racial mixture. These include adaptive behaviors in response to the struggle for recognition by superiors and the need to distinguish the self from those deemed inferior. Comportment in accordance with privileged aesthetic forms inadvertently reveals the sedimented logic of civilizational, racial, classist, and species hierarchism.

A turn to the plasticity of living forms brings the eternal braid of biology, culture, and aesthetic forms back into renewed focus. Taking into consideration "the thinking of the body" (William Butler Yeats's phrase) as simultaneously biological and historical returns the salience of race to culture, culture to race, and civilization and its aesthetic preoccupation with form and the formation of plastic minds and bodies to both. In this reading, hybridity emerges as the bio-logic of identity crafted for successful passage in the modern world, defined by a state of war against nature, and a modification of behaviors that remind us of our biological, animal being. The displacement of biologically deterministic forms of racial thinking into new formulas for adjudicating bio-social evolution based on the grammar of comportment and behavior as social language directs attention, moreover, to the politics of hybridity and mimicry *among* the colonized. Together, these readings reappraise the postcolonial concept of hybridity and explore its persistent salience in globalization.

Despite the origins of "hybridity" in botany and zoology in reference to mixture between species, and subsequent use in debates about race in anthropology and biology, the term began to take a culturalist and linguistic turn after the conclusive exposure of race as fiction.[8] The postcolonial turn in discussions of hybridity is most closely associated with the work of Bhabha. Mikhail Bakhtin's conceptualization of hybridization *(gibridizacija)* as "the mixing, within a single concrete utterance, of two or more different linguistic consciousnesses, often widely separated in time and social space," supplied the structural formula for resistance within language, subsequently acquiring a poststructuralist gloss in Bhabha's work (*The Dialogic Imagination,* 429).[9] These departures from traditional usage have been indispensable for exposing the ruse of purist essentialisms, turning hybridity into a master trope for investigating intercultural contact.[10] The subsequent appropriation of hybridity as the *Lieblingswort* (favored term) of globalization, however, threatens to reduce the term to banality at a global moment driven by the tendency to subsume difference in sameness.[11] Disregard for the relationship between word and history, moreover, also signals impatience with history *tout court.*[12] In the wake of this semantic gerrymandering, a term that invites direct engagement with questions of biology and flesh has increasingly moved away from both, thereby successfully avoiding the associated whiff of essentialism, but also discouraging further interest in alternative conceptions of biological hybridization at the very moment they are most needed.[13] In this book's advised return to the intercourse of biology, culture, and the body, colonial contact emerges as a salient, instructive precursor to the nexus of capital, corporation, and the biopolitics of hybridity in the global present. Hybridity may well be "the cultural logic of globalization," as Marwan Kraidy's book title suggests, but it must also be understood as the covert *bio*-logic of the rule of capital and corporation. On this understanding, the pliant, bio-mentally plastic and permeable body is a battlefield no less worthy of our urgent attention than the biologically deterministic body of bad science and worse politics that long served as the traditional focus of antiracist discourse.

In one of the first substantial volumes on human variability and plasticity in the life sciences, D. F. Roberts suggests that the concept of plasticity is applied in "widely differing biological situations" that include "overall body form" as well as "details of body composition, soft tissue distribution, and the structure of the bony skeleton." Biological plasticity can extend from the postnatal stage to adulthood and senescence, involve the impact of adaptive changes in one part of the body to others, and effect "greater changes in one individual than can the most intensive genetic selection of hereditary variation over many generations." Roberts's conclusions suggest *an extra evolutionary mechanism* that is "additional to natural selection" ("The Pervasiveness of Plasticity," 12), with intriguing implications for a return to the politically and biologically vulnerable body in postcolonial reckoning with hybridity. In the humanities, Catherine Malabou's sustained engagement with the Hegelian idea of plasticity as "a capacity to receive form and a capacity to produce form" has initiated a significant dialogue "between the role of genetic nondeterminism at work in the constitution of the brain and the possibility of a social and political nondeterminism, in a word, a new freedom, which is to say: a new meaning of history," to use her own words.[14] Along with mounting interest in biological plasticity in the life sciences, research in embodied cognition now routinely foregrounds the physical and affective machinery involved in realizing cognitive processes, requiring us to reengage with the role of the senses in encounters with difference.[15] Related developments in extended cognition, moreover, prompt a reconceptualization of the idea of the human body-mind as coextensive with the physical, social, and cultural environment, revealing the significance of prosthetic and technological dilations attached to adaptable biological beings, and therefore of the impact of goods, products, and lifestyles introduced by empires old and new.[16]

If our inherent plasticity rescues us from a biologically deterministic fate, it also makes us a favored site for projection, manipulation, and product placement. Imperial "goods" such as new kinds of food, music, medicines, pills, drugs, contraceptives, sanitary regimes, and grooming materials not only transform cultures in contact in the abstract but also living bodies through taste transfer and new commodity aesthetics. The potential bidirectionality of the exchange of products and ideas does not cancel out the structural inequalities that characterize colonial relations. Underwritten by the civilizing mission, culture is at once dislocated and sedimented in a sensuous, pulsing fiction worked over by imperial history: *habemus corpus*.[17] In *Alimentary Tracts*, Parama Roy has argued persuasively for an understanding of the "grammar of ingestion and avoidance" as germinative for an understanding of the ways in which "colonial transformation" is "situated simultaneously in theaters of the flesh and of the psyche, rather than the latter alone" (29). With its organic specificity, pliable musculature and neurology, environmental adaptability, susceptibility to authority and epigenetic factors, as well as its eminently revisable practices of ingestion, evacuation, and consumption, the plastic body-mind stands at the intersection of history, culture, and biology as an embattled embodiment of the dialogue between form and flesh.[18] Not only does our biological plasticity make us pliable and manipulable, but otherwise neutral observations about the continuum between society, culture, technology, and the individual in theories of extended cognition imply that pejorative judgments about our bodily techniques and prosthetics predispose us to mimicry of privileged forms, as well as to the adoption of commodities associated with positive evaluations and power. In this reading, the biological scene of transformation emerges forcefully in incarnate moments as we revise our behaviors and habits in response to social evaluation, pointing to an additional evolutionary mechanism that involves sociogenic and epigenetic factors as well as forms of species supremacism inherent in the civilizing mission of imperial modernity.[19] In sum, form is sedimented content.

Reclaiming human biology as neuropolitical and biocultural, *Postcolonial Biology* examines unsettled postcolonial subjectivities and new hierarchies born of the union of ideology, aesthetic forms, and power structures working through ductile, mutable body-minds in the imperial theater. This line of inquiry becomes more urgent as we confront "colonialism in its new forms," in Fanon's prescient words (*The Wretched of the Earth*, 235). The struggle for control over aesthetic forms associated with advanced civilization and modernity—in other words, the biopoetics of forms of living—continues in the disjunctive relay from colonialism to the rule of capital and corporation in globalization. In the name of global citizenship, a range of subject effects is being produced today through the global culture industry's advertorial regimen, commodity aesthetics, and profit-minded body politics. The long season of the manipulation of biologically volatile subjects continues well after colonialism has ended. Then, as now, Empire reaches us where we live, all the way down to our gut. With this understanding, the "postcolonial" of

Postcolonial Biology must be understood as what follows after colonization, albeit disjunctively—rather than as a particular moment of political decolonization. *Postcolonial Biology,* then, is the name we might give to the intersection of power, capital, and supremacist thinking expressed through the body-minded cognition, categorization, and manipulation of human life from early modern colonialisms to their newest season in globalization. In other words, it is the name we might give to the largest-scale ongoing experiment in human lives in history.[20] When the different come to fear their own difference, when an appliance manufacturer can commandeer the idea of the good life in its logo, LG ("Life's Good"), when the numbers of the wretched of the earth grow beyond counting, we are obliged to ask whether there is still time to reopen the horizon of history. In place of the perversion of life and lifeways by new and old empires that exalt capitalist personhood and supremacist behavior to an art form and not only tolerate but promote inequality, perhaps we might think of postcolonial biology as the name we might give to something different, to a utopian desire for imaginatively richer forms of good life as a shared but as-yet unrealized horizon of human longing.

In the main, this project responds to Davis and Morris's "Biocultures Manifesto," and its call to "join the biological and cultural" in a productive intersection of culture, history, and biology (411). More broadly, it is also responsive to Ian Baucom's call to imagine "a new set of inquiries" in critical postcolonial studies, since "questions arising from the contemporary life sciences," especially "biology, biomedicine, cognitive neuroscience, genomics, genetics, and ecology," are "breaking the boundary walls of the humanities" (6).[21] However, it draws its inspiration as much from a current interdisciplinary paradigm as an earlier tradition in critical theory that recognizes the birth of aesthetics in the body; invests in explorations of "the good life"; and conceives of human biology as the study of life lived in physically incarnate moments that are profoundly historical, for they are delimited by the structural conditions of the very possibility of experience (Adorno, *Minima Moralia,* 15). If "aesthetics is a discourse born in the body" as Terry Eagleton claims,[22] and meaning is made in the "body-minded mind" as Antonio Damasio declares (putting a tradition associated with William James and Thomas Dewey into dialogue with experimental neurobiology),[23] postcolonial studies have the opportunity to reconvene aesthetics, somatics, and cognition in a productive matrix to understand how the tyranny of aesthetic forms and the educability of plastic body-minds have been instrumental in the production of civilizational hierarchies in the past, as well as how they collude in the persistence of racial prejudice and the production of new divides in the present.[24] The field's traditional preoccupation with the intersection of culture, power, and politics, I argue, must urgently extend now to consideration of the politics of life as it is lived in the body and the mind.

The turn from race and biology to culture in most contemporary discussions of hybridity has obscured the historical entwinement of these terms. "The racial was always cultural," Robert J. C. Young notes (*Colonial Desire,* 28).[25] Although it would require a suppression of the historical relay between race and culture as each other's understudy, as well as a disregard for the role of biology in underwriting both, implicit in the twentieth-century drift from the former to the latter was an increasing abstraction of the idea of culture as elusive and pluralistic, and a discursive narrowing of the idea of biology, promoting the confinement of body as organism to the laboratory, and an understandable legacy of caution regarding any language linking race, culture, or difference with biology.[26] Despite the accepted understanding in the humanities that words are contested and concepts hijacked, we are inured to surrendering not only the word but also the concept of "biology" to science, thus instating a false divide between biology and culture on the one hand, and race and culture on the other, as if the former were the circumscribed preserve of science, and therefore objective and stable, while the latter was to be embraced as the legitimate province of the humanities, since it can be assumed to be less rigid, less categorical, and more open to interpretation. In fact, the move from race to culture in uses of the term "hybridity" offers no asylum from matters of the flesh since both deploy the discourse of our biological and "animal" prehistory, rely on sensory perception for evaluating individual and collective form, share the language of civilization and aesthetics, ally the idea of civilization with control over biological functions in one way or another, and deploy the mind–body split variously. Moreover, research in the health sciences increasingly exposes the fiction of race while investigating the ways in which the sociopolitical can nonetheless become biological.[27] The sundering of the arts and the sciences, and segregated modes of body-talk in the soft arts and the hard sciences, with territorial entrenchments in language or the laboratory, are no less my target in calling for a bastard history of hybridity that crosses these disciplinary boundaries so we can acknowledge the mutual imbrications of culture, race, and biology in the making of human life today.[28]

The Incarnate Moment

I turn to writings by Frantz Fanon and Theodor Adorno for an elaboration of the sociophenomenological production of experience and life under the yoke of Empire and Capital.[29] In my reading of the ramifications of intercultural contact, hybridity emerges as a zone of contestation tied to the question of the good life, a topic Adorno explored at some length in *Minima Moralia* and adumbrated elsewhere in his writings, often with direct reference to social control over the body. Fanon's ruminations on the colonized body in various writings constitute a politically situated, racially conscious response to Maurice Merleau-Ponty's theories of the phenomenological body and its corporeal schema.[30] Adorno, not traditionally thought of as a philosopher of the body, frequently turns to somatic considerations—in response to the Holocaust, for instance, or in exploring the commodification of the body under the rule of capital and instrumental rationality in *Negative Dialectics, Minima Moralia,* and with Max Horkheimer in *Dialectic of Enlightenment.* Adorno's thoughts on the repression and distortion of the fleshy *leibhafte Moment* of experience and Fanon's on a racially charged *l'expérience vécue* inform my investigation of colonial and neocolonial theaters of interaction, revealing undertheorized biophysiological dimensions of hybridity and mimicry (*Negative Dialectics,* 203; *Negative Dialektik,* 201; translation mine). Fanon makes an elaborate case for the sensory foundations of racism in his works, as well as the relationship of sensory cognition to the moral economy of the animal in colonial relations. Adorno, sometimes in conversation with Horkheimer, argues for sensation as "the crux of all epistemology"; the emergence of physicality "at the ontic pole of cognition, as the core of cognition"; and the repression of the sensory and corporeal as the product of a "conniving consciousness" (*Negative Dialectics,* 193–94; *Metaphysics,* 117). Cognition, experience, judgment, aesthetic evaluations of form, and dominative rationality are joined for Adorno in the living, incarnate moment that often goes unacknowledged. Although ideas, beliefs, and unconscious impulses are understood to belong to the psyche, "all mental things," according to Adorno, can also be understood as "modified physical impulses" that begin with an urge (*Negative Dialectics,* 202). Adorno contends that in attending to these moments, we veer closer to knowledge about the human condition. His meditations on species supremacism and the role of the animal in philosophical considerations of the human supplement his scattered but frequent references to physiological and biological being as related concerns. In writings by Fanon and Adorno, the biological apparatuses involved in societal and intercultural contact become apparent, effectively recasting the theory of mind in terms that emphasize *body*-minded sensation and cognition.[31] Together, they amplify the role of the senses and body-minded cognition and categorization, and the associated discomfort with animal being as the pretext of the urge to civilize.[32]

Horkheimer and Adorno invite us to examine the mechanics of the civilizing process, arguing that "all more recent culture," by which they mean modernity, is colored by a "love-hate relationship with the body" (*Dialectic of Enlightenment,* 193). A problematic relationship to the biological body, its sounds, odors, excretions, urges, emissions, and expressions, informs the civilizational project. The relationship of the colonial civilizing mission to the politics of the plastic body becomes clearer if we place it within the larger context of the European civilizing process, which is characterized by discomfort with reminders of animality in our biological functions and the subsequent suppression, administration, and regulation of the sensorium as well as the mimetic instinct, with the consequent production of dominative relations on the basis of an aesthetics of sociality developed through these repressions. A long history of Cartesian dualism, the racialization and feminization of the senses, and an excessive identification of the native with the body and its crude biological functions in colonial accounts are part of a complicated biopolitical complex that also produced others *within* Europe.[33] The *leibhafte Moment* of experience takes place within this extensively overdetermined structural logic of repression and reformation of both psyche and flesh.[34]

Pointing out that "the *menace* of mimicry is its *double* vision which in disclosing the ambivalence of colonial discourse also disrupts its authority," Bhabha concludes that the "final irony" of mimicry lies in the fact that there is no "presence or identity behind its mask," only "empty form" and "partial representation" (*The Location of Culture,* 87–88).[35] This convincing explanation of the deconstruction of essential identity through the menace of mimicry strikes a necessary body blow at illusory notions of the integrity of differential identities. But more is demanded of us. Because "the most forgotten alien land is one's own body," as Walter Benjamin writes in his reading of Kafka, and the body conceals its workings from us, we are apt to overlook moments of hybridity and mimicry rooted in the flesh (*Illuminations,* 132).[36] I argue that mimicry not only menaces the colonizer with reminders of this repression, but more alarmingly, it also begins a process of biological sclerosis and rigidification in the colonized mimic precisely through "empty form" as performance. We fail at our own peril to recognize "empty form" as the sclerosed version of a life that once lived more freely before it became rigid through repression. For Adorno and Horkheimer, civilization begins a process of sclerosing instinctive urges, expressions, and their moral possibilities. Fanon recognizes the peculiar manifestations of this process under conditions of imperial domination. Horkheimer and Adorno claim, "only culture treats the body as a thing that can be owned, only in culture has it been distinguished from mind, the quintessence of power and command, as the object, the dead thing, the *corpus*" (*Dialectic of Enlightenment,* 193). Culture, Adorno reminds us, has always been bound up with administration and relations of domination and control (*The Culture Industry,* 108, 113). Collective civilizational goals have always included education in aesthetic modalities of being in the world. The civilizing process, however, involves not only the grand arenas of expression—sculpture, painting, music, and civic structures—but also prescriptions and proscriptions involving the individual body's expressions, behaviors, and dilatory extensions; the latter are key elements in assessing fitness and success in civilized society. The clash of civilizations therefore extends to questions of form in the kitchen and the bathroom (or bush) as much as in temples, museums, concerts, and courts.[37]

Mimicry and Eumemics

Sensory and aesthetic education—the terms of colonial mimicry and the cultivation of taste—and the adoption of cultural prosthetics and appropriate techniques of the body are part of cultural administration in every society. From Aristotle's disquisition on the topic to Adorno and Benjamin's, and to today's neuropsychological research, imitation learning emerges as the engine of the "big bang" or "the great leap forward" in human evolution, casting mimicry simultaneously as a mode of cultural and biological subject formation.[38] In his essay on the mimetic faculty, Walter Benjamin accords a primary role to mimesis in human existence:

> Nature creates similarities. One need only think of mimicry. The highest capacity for producing similarities, however, is man's. His gift of seeing resemblances is nothing other than a rudiment of the powerful compulsion in former times to become and behave like something else. Perhaps there is none of his higher functions in which his mimetic faculty does not play a decisive role. (*Reflections,* 333)

Crucial to the development of sociocognitive skills, the regulation of an inherent capacity for mimesis plays a vital role in the process of civilization, *tahzeeb,* or *sabhyata,*[39] however differentially these ideas are conceived in diverse cultures.[40] Mimicry is a mode of assimilation into any culture, *including our own.* Indeed, we are hybridized no less by our *own* culture—its ideals, thoughts, foods, proprietary aesthetics, and other bodily codes of movement and rest—than that of others.

When asked if Parsis are "characteristically Hindu or Muslim," Bhabha describes them as a "hybridized community" ("their rituals pay formal respect to Hindu customs and rituals while articulating their own religious and ethnic identity"), and adds,

> I don't think it's a deferral to think that the question of what it means to be Parsi is an open question; but supposing somebody said that, I would say that Parsis come together most communally over the dining table. Our cuisine is important to us—as you know from the hours I spend in my kitchen. (Quoted in Mitchell, "Translator," 80)[41]

Indeed, the dining table with its commensal regime, foods, manner of eating—plate or banana leaf, utensils or with hands—may well be one location of culture.[42] To grow up in a culture is to incline to its practices through habit and repetition.[43] The body as both embodiment and interpreter of culture in a mutually dynamic relationship is never static, but it nonetheless tends toward compliance with its affiliational groups. Variously acculturated, the human body is a voluble, fleshy text that speaks both its common humanity and its distinction from others. As acculturated beings, we are guided by kinesthetic, vestibular, and muscle memory, so aptly captured in the idea of *inclination*—that which we habitually incline to—as we enact ourselves through dispositions sedimented by habit, even as we are vulnerable to new forms of acculturation.[44] Marcel Mauss's arguments for an understanding of difference through the techniques of the body, subsequently developed in the work of Norbert Elias and Pierre Bourdieu, demand recognition of bodily acculturation and orientation through habit, contextual reinforcement, and reward.[45] Beyond differences in skin color, the kinetic, postural, and aesthetically expressive body presents a complicated text of cultural lifeways. The body that speaks of its civilizational standing is flesh that is stylized. Its expressions in its arts as well as its behaviors, postures of sitting, eating, or defecating, verbal comportment, forms of work and play, and management of its emissions and effluences are performed and experienced in accord with aesthetic and sensory training. Whether individual or civilizational, aesthetic evaluations and judgments hinge on diverse notions of being well formed. An argument for acknowledging differences in variously stylized flesh undoubtedly carries the danger of suggesting that biological and bodily differences are part of cultural difference—hypostatizing biological difference anew—but why should our models of humanity rely on sameness rather than difference as their foundational premise?

Part of the paideia of the individual from childhood on, rewards and punishments associated with mimicry of privileged forms, as well as repression of devalued ones, influence subject formation in every culture, even though these forms may vary greatly in different parts of the world. The invitation to sanctioned mimicry comes from many quarters in our lives, with the most dominant and powerful most likely to gain our compliance. The human sensory apparatus joins with the body-minded mind in the evaluation of our own and other bodies in part as a consequence of our aesthetic training, one based on the preferred eumemic forms controlled by those variously in power. Mimicry—the copying and internalization of ratified forms of comportment and avoidance of those prohibited in a culture or prohibited to certain groups within a culture—operates as a form of "passing" implicit in the process of acculturation.

Mimicry, regulated by its prescriptive and proscriptive logic, is the engine that produces subject groups as well as their boundaries. Horkheimer and Adorno inject the short fuse of dominative rationality into these supposedly universal mechanisms across cultures, while Fanon introduces that of racial difference to Merleau-Ponty's proposals regarding the allegedly universal phenomenological body. In the contact zones, conflict emerges over better or worse cultures and civilizations. Fanon's adumbration of the colonizer's judgmental evaluation is crucial to an understanding of colonial mimicry. Postcolonial concern with unmasking the disorder of colonial authority should not overtake due consideration of those who suffer its dominative, if anxious and unstable logic. In the subsumptive logic of empire, Fanon tells us that native "language, dress, techniques, are devalorized," as "expropriation, spoliation, raids, objective murder, are matched by the sacking of cultural patterns" (*Toward the African Revolution,* 33). The colonial "enterprise of deculturation," informed by the intertwined texts of race and sexuality, casts the native as intellectually and emotionally primitive, to be derided by psychologists through the symptomology of deviance detected in "a way of speaking, of walking" tantamount to aesthetic disability (31–33). Fanon unmasks the relationship between racism and culture, and the profound impact of the colonizer's "pejorative judgment with respect to [the native's] original forms of existing" (38). Dismissive of "the values borne by the culture, *incarnated* by men," colonial subjugation "makes the native an object" in the hands of the occupying nation—"an object man" whose "desire to live, to continue, becomes more and more indecisive, more and more phantom-like" (34–35; emphasis added).

Revising ideas that first appeared in a speech before the First Congress of Negro Writers and Artists in Paris in September 1956 (later published in *Toward the African Revolution*), Fanon goes on to outline the connections between biology, racism, and culture in *The Wretched of the Earth:* "every effort is made to bring the colonized person to admit the inferiority of his culture which has been transformed into instinctive patterns of behavior" and "in the last extreme, the confused and imperfect character of his own biological structure" (236). Fanon reminds us that "it is not necessary to be wounded by a bullet in order to suffer from the fact of war in body as well as in mind" (290). Sensing the reaction of the white boy to his "[skin as] uniform" in *Black Skin, White Masks,* Fanon decides that it is "indeed ugly," going on to ask, "who can tell me what beauty is?" (114). In response, Fanon implies that the native is prompted to undertake an ambitiously scaled reformation, as the black man's "metaphysics, or, less pretentiously, his customs and the sources on which they are based, were wiped out because they were in conflict with a civilization that he did not know and that imposed itself upon him" (*Black Skin, White Masks,* 110).

The native body split apart under imperial eyes is reenvisioned as a multiply disabled, dysplastic body, lacking in the collective and individual graces of civilization. Fanon's knowing black speaker reveals this conjunction:

> I was responsible at the same time for my body, for my race, for my ancestors. I subjected myself to an objective examination, I discovered my blackness, my ethnic characteristics; and I was battered down by tom-toms, cannibalism, slave-ships, and above all else, above all: "Sho' good eatin'." (*Black Skin, White Masks,* 112)

Fanon's reference is to a *tirailleur* (African soldier in the colonial infantry) declaring his enjoyment of a heavily marketed French breakfast food in an advertisement. "Y a bon Banania," he is imagined to say, in an uncouth version of the more standard, "C'est bon Banania." Of all that offends, "et surtout, et surtout" (above all, above all), repeated twice, this comment on an offense to linguistic as well as euphagic etiquette brings colonial contempt to rest in the buccal cavity, demanding a recognition of the politics of prejudice in its retail, fleshy particulars.[46] Ingestive and expressive regimes are both underwritten by colonial intervention; the mouth and word of mouth together incriminate the *tirailleur.* Crude of speech, aesthetically disabled, the *tirailleur* is a figure in need of superior nutrition and ameliorative prosthetics—bodily, lingual, and mental. The description discloses the figure of an absent judge and the sensory foundations of racism; it hints, moreover, at the motivations of a future subject who will seek to disarm prejudice by recalibrating behaviors and speech patterns to lessen the sensory impact of difference from imperial aesthetic norms.

In a sensitive reading of the black body's muscular tension in Fanon's writing, Darieck Scott explores his interest in "how to read the [blackened] double-body's flinches at the moment that the external stimulus which cleaves it in two flicks across its boundaries" (*Extravagant Abjection,* 64). According to Scott, "the muscles, in contraction or tension, are a metaphor referring to some reservoir of resistance to the colonizer's acts of subjugation and enslavement" in what amounts to a bodily performance of "*political* 'refusal'" (64–65, 70). Fanon recognizes the fact of "the native's reticence, the expression in muscular form of his rigidity and his refusal with regard to colonial authority" (*The Wretched of the Earth,* 291). At the same time, the muscular tonus and corporeal torsions of the twitchy native in a state of compliance with Western lifeways that have triumphed aggressively over native forms of existence constitute an important, alternative text, I argue, in our reading of Fanon's muscles. While Fanon claims that the "native's muscles are always tensed" because "he is not convinced of his inferiority," it is also the "impulse to take the settler's place" that "implies a tonicity of muscles" (53). Fanon's well-known claims about the native's envious dream of "putting himself in the place of the settler" indicate active desire, but in an earlier text he emphasizes the anxieties that precede and inform it (52): "The racialized social group tries to imitate the oppressor and thereby to deracialize itself. The 'inferior race' denies itself as a different race. It shares with the 'superior race' the convictions, doctrines, and other attitudes concerning it" (*Toward the African Revolution,* 38). Under "the name of assimilation," "the oppressor . . . manages to impose on the native new ways of seeing, and . . . a pejorative judgment with respect to his original forms of existing" (38). The native's self-revision and the neuroses precipitated by it manifest in his mentality as well as his bodily comportment, posture, emotional expression, and sensorial recalibration: "Having judged, condemned, abandoned his cultural forms, his language, his food habits, his sexual behavior, his way of sitting down, of resting, of laughing, of enjoying himself, the oppressed *flings himself* upon the imposed culture with the desperation of a drowning man" (39). In the same essay, Fanon speculates on the selective return to nativist traditions, but his stance there, as in *The Wretched of the Earth,* is to scrupulously avoid false nostalgia for an earlier, romanticized native culture while nonetheless bemoaning its sclerosis. It is not surprising that the dreams of muscular prowess, the native's resistance, and "the tonicity of muscles" implicit in "the impulse to take the settler's place" in *The Wretched of the Earth* are part of the same dialectic. Fanon's muscles, therefore, suggest both subjugation and resistance in a conflicted response to the power and style of the colonial civilizing mission (53).

Bhabha's expansive range of choices for the native constitutes a species of evasion when he asserts, "it is difficult to agree entirely with Fanon that the psychic choice is to 'turn white or disappear.' There is the more ambivalent, third choice: camouflage, mimicry, black skin / white masks" (*Black Skin, White Masks,* 100; *The Location of Culture,* 120). This ambivalent, third choice is understood as subversive for three reasons: first, because it "disrupts" the authority of colonial discourse by disclosing "its ambivalence"; second, because "mimicry marks . . . moments of civil disobedience within the discipline of civility: signs of spectacular resistance"; and finally, because "mimicry conceals no presence or identity behind its mask" (*The Location of Culture,* 88, 121, 88). While Bhabha initiates a legitimate quarrel with essentialism, one wonders why he downplays the significance of what Fanon describes as the "social structures" that are the "real source of the [black man's] conflict" with regard to the choices available (*Black Skin, White Masks,* 100). Moreover, if we understand mimicry of preferred aesthetic forms as a means of learning through repetition, and if we understand color as code for multiple attributes of identity, mimicry for the colonized group is a sort of turning white through repeated muscular and neuronal training. Bhabha, otherwise alert to it, makes too little of the imbalance of power between white and black in the passage quoted above, and discounts the creeping suspicion of the "inferiorized group . . . that its misfortunes resulted directly from its racial and cultural characteristics," as Fanon explains (*Toward the African Revolution,* 38). Fanon is intent, in other words, on exposing the affective register of shame and anxiety that prompts the desire for whiteness, initiating revisions that are not merely formal but more profoundly transformative. Fanon's ultimate objective is "to put . . . [the black man] in a position to choose action (or passivity) with respect to the real source of the conflict—that is toward the social structures . . . *once his motivations have been brought into consciousness*" (*Black Skin, White Masks,* 100; emphasis added). It is, after all, the inferiorized group that more consistently dons the mask and resorts to mimicry, however subversively it does so. Mimicry of native forms is rare among colonizers. In *Indian Traffic,* Parama Roy describes the colonizer gone native as someone who "put a dangerous distance between himself and the cultural appurtenances of the west, particularly 'civilization' and Christianity" (30). Until the unlikely reversal of dominative rationality and "the real source of conflict," the native's repudiation of "his own cultural style" and "his total and unconditional adoption of the new cultural models" made available by colonization have momentous implications for hybridity lived in the flesh as much as in the mind (*Toward the African Revolution,* 38–42). In this understanding, mimicry becomes the site of bodying forth a response to the imperial call to flesh and psyche, amounting to a bioformal conversion narrative. The conversion is undertaken in the hope of disarming colonial prejudice—or reducing it—as well as in the hope of reward and recognition for becoming a perceptibly reformed other distinguishable from other natives. Fanon describes the anxious Martinican immigrant to Paris who practices "rolling his R": "suspicious of his own tongue—a wretchedly lazy organ—he will lock himself into his room and read aloud for hours—desperately determined to learn *diction*" (*Black Skin, White Masks,* 21). The *bodybildungsroman* of colonial hybridity and mimicry turns out to be a violent text made poignant by its longing for acceptance and recognition.

Metonymic Aesthetics

Bhabha suggests that "partial," "incomplete," and "virtual" representations strain the idea and authority of Englishness, making colonial mimicry "at once resemblance and menace"; in this disruptive mode, "hybridity is heresy" (*The Location of Culture,* 86, 226). Bhabha's conception of mimicry as camouflage against a mottled background, drawing on Lacan and a zoological example, emphasizes its partial and fragmented nature (90, 121). This exposure of the deception of essential, whole identities, however, does not clarify sufficiently the politics of a *metonymic aesthetics* of identity. That pejorative judgment and mimicry *both* operate on the logic of the partial offers no immunity from the particular burden of hybridity borne by those with underprivileged positions on the civilizational and aesthetic ladder. A metonymic aesthetics of identity—patched together from multiple, incomplete, and piecemeal representations of "Englishness"—nonetheless produces the pulsive fiction that we recognize as the Westernized or Anglicized postcolonial subject. Although colonial hybridity does not add up to an English self, it generates a series of subject effects that nonetheless cobble together an alternative sociogenic category among the colonized, that of the Anglicized subject whose corporeal schema and vestibular orientation have been recomposed in contact with empire. In a bid to reintroduce consideration of the body politics of hybridity, I have emphasized the idea of *hybridity in the flesh* as implying something biological in a sense that is other than or beyond sexual mixture. The logic of the partial challenges the ruse of the whole, but it is also pernicious because it is the very engine of the civilizing mission, which targets the body in its piecemeal, *retail* particulars at the level of muscle, tongue, glottis, viscera, and myriad administrations of the sensorium and bodily expression.

In *Black Skin, White Masks,* the look of the white man, falling upon black skin, inaugurates a simultaneous session of a "thousand details, anecdotes, stories" (111). Prejudice and native reform both involve the metonymies of presence: tom-toms, "nigger underwear" with "nigger smell," big feet, white teeth, poor speech. Grounding his remarks in an epistemology of the senses rather than in a rational Enlightenment project, Fanon understands that the triggers of prejudice lie beyond reason for "*in vivo* and *in vitro* the Negro had been proved analogous to the white man . . . with the same morphology [and] histology as the white man" (119). It has long been understood that it is not enough to understand or combat racism by challenging its genetic bases in biology. Fanon stakes his arguments to the biological dimensions of cultural body politics as he coimplicates the societal and discursive idea of race with sensory cognition. In more recent memory, one recalls that French president Jacques Chirac's notorious speech against immigrants in 1991 when he was the mayor of Paris referred pointedly to their "noise" and "odor" ("le bruit et l'odeur") as the last straw in testing the limits of French tolerance, highlighting the link between sensory and affective triggers in prejudicial judgments. Addressing a crowd of supporters on France's emergent immigration issues, Chirac thundered, "What happens when a hardworking French worker" finds as neighbors "a piled-up family with a father, three or four spouses and twenty children earning 50,000 FF via benefits?" He concluded with his punch line, "If you *add* to that the noise and the smell, well the French worker, he goes crazy."[47] Sensory triggers—music, smell, food, posture, accent—are incarnate forms of stereotypes and clichés under pressure in regimes of assimilation focused precisely on small parts of identity.

In the long run—and it is the long run that is of consequence—today's discourse of assimilation, which is a sanitized version of the older "civilizing mission," tacitly builds its case on the grounds of reducing perceptions of difference from the mainstream sensorium through retail therapy and remediation—deodorants, accent reduction, and so forth—as much as opinions, morals, and intellect. The fetish of the skin is multisited, pointing not only to color, but also to postural, phonetic, and scented identity, with every retail particular available for judgment, control, and emendation. Colonial mimicry, then, is no less pernicious because it is based on the logic of the partial or focused on metonymic aesthetics. The microphysics of imperial power—vestibular reorientation and a renovated corporeal schema—necessarily take place bit by bit, as it were, in simultaneously ideological and motor actions that can become habitual through repetition over time. In *Discipline and Punish,* Foucault quotes eighteenth-century criminologist Joseph Michel Antoine Servan on the importance of inculcating the habitual conjunction of ideas to enforce compliance. I would suggest that this form of social engineering is founded in manipulating the subject's neurobiological plasticity: "On the supple fibres of the brain is founded the most stable of Empires," because new neural pathways develop as the subject is exposed to ideas and forms associated with privilege and reward, and discouraged away from those that elicit punishment or prejudice (Servan, *Discours sur L'Administration,* 35; translation mine).[48] In a project that is simultaneously aesthetic and political, the "subtle coercion" of the civilizing mission operates through a manipulation of the hybrid body's "movements, gestures, attitudes"—a reformation, I argue, that extends from thought to neural firing, glottis to gut, and neural substrate to muscular micromovement (Foucault, *Discipline and Punish,* 105, 137). The biopolitics of the civilizing mission relies on a metonymic aesthetics that withholds the satisfactions of integral identity and fixates instead on bits and parts in a synecdochic mode—targeting psyche and flesh together to produce neurobiologically altered mimics copying the norms of an order that disdains the native, but disdains some natives more than others. Even though it cannot change color, the colonized body can become more becoming through the adoption of regimes of regulation invested in making alien bodies more bearable to the overlords while investing them more visibly with power among their own. For the exclusive few who were chosen and rewarded in colonial times, others would have continued even more obsessively, driven by an unpredictable, variable schedule of rewards while enduring the contempt colonizers often reserved for the native who tried too hard.

The politics of *discriminatory eumemics*—the biosocial indoctrination and engineering of others in matters of good form to make a better, more civilized body defined by those in power—is part of the new shape taken by racial thinking in modernity. The invitation to eumemics, the mimicry of allegedly good form, exploits the body-mind's plasticity as well as its search for reward. The mimicry of the dominant by the dominated must thus be understood multiply: as an attempt to mimic and thus experience the enjoyment of those in power; as enjoyment located in forms of comportment associated with those in power; and finally, as instrumental mimicry driven by the desire for advancement and the neurosocial rewards of assimilation to the dominative order, at first through the selective, if unpredictable, approval of the colonizer, and later by a postcolonial nation that continues to be enamored with the aesthetic forms of comportment associated with those who ruled over them. "The not quite / not white" minute-made postcolonials, often mocked for their hysterical overcompliance with Anglophilic aesthetics in colonial literature, nonetheless go on to reap the rewards of assimilating to forms associated with the colonizers (Bhabha, *The Location of Culture,* 92).

Manufactured piecemeal by empire, a certain class of persons has gone on to reproduce the hierarchical structure and aesthetic logic of the civilizing mission within the nation, while serving as its recognizable, modern representatives abroad, albeit with variable success. Arguably, the acquisition of aesthetic forms associated with modernity and the brandishing of goods and prosthetics associated with success permit forms of passing not necessarily as white but as a "better" sort of native in interactions with others as well as among their own. Moreover, it is not unusual for this elite to acquire, along with these dissembled semblances, disdain for those unconverted within the nation, so that colonial contempt is replicated and naturalized in the social discourse of the colonized. In time, cultural, aesthetic, and comportmental memes associated with power and status filter down through the mediators without necessarily erasing old or new divides. Bhabha reads "signs of spectacular resistance" in the native's "masque of mimicry" in the "realm of discourse . . . as a form of defensive warfare" (*The Location of Culture,* 121). In the logic of relations within the postcolonial nation and among the colonized more generally, mimicry of privileged forms can also be understood as a form of offensive warfare. Fanon spots the propensity of the colonized to surpass and dominate their own others, those "less intelligent than I, blacker than I, less respectable than I" (*Black Skin, White Masks,* 211).

Hysterical compliance with privileged aesthetic forms derived from colonial contact therefore has a corollary: disgust for the unassimilated among the colonized. Those seen as enjoying the earthly rewards of assimilation to such norms subtly reinforce the command to assimilate, to become less other to the mainstream, and more sensually and comportmentally compliant with the expressive forms of the regnant order.

Animal Prehistory and Postanimal Aesthetics, Prosthetics, and Technics

If whiteness as a norm constitutes the big Other of postcolonial subject formation, a silent other is the animal—and animal prehistory as part of biotic, bodily being. In *Dialectic of Enlightenment,* Horkheimer and Adorno argue for an understanding of civilization as the repression and redirection of practices associated with our shared "biological prehistory" or "animal prehistory" (148, 156). In their work, the urge to formulate the self beyond the conditions of *Nur-lebenden* (merely living) animal existence emerges as the engine of history. They remind us, "In popular fairy tales the metamorphosis of humans into animals is a recurring punishment. To be imprisoned in an animal body is regarded as damnation" (205). Horkheimer and Adorno repeatedly interpellate the body and its animal prehistory as the object of discipline in the course of Europe's civilizing process and prejudice in encounters with others, including their own others. Dominion over the animal self and over nature, they suggest, is on a continuum with the domination of humans by humans. "The animal to be devoured," Adorno says, is evil, for it is the "not-I, *l'autrui*" that "reminds us of nature" and so "is inferior." "The unity of the self-preserving thought," he says, "may thus devour" the "not-I" reminiscent of the evil animal "without misgivings" (*Negative Dialectics,* 22–23). If Derrida's elaboration of *l'animot* directs attention to human propriety in terms of speech and *techne,* their work appends a consideration of human propriety explicitly with regard to a *postanimal* state reliant both on the suppression and disguisement of biological being and the call of nature, as well as the acquisition of tools, weapons, and things.

Along with an investment in postanimal aesthetics and technics, the idea of the human conceptualized as postanimal manifests variously in the following ways: in upright man's posture; Cartesian dualism; the projection of animality, emotion, and sensory excess onto different others; prejudicial cognition of others parlayed into intellectual theory and racial science; and the impulse to civilize those whose difference appears disgusting and intolerable as a sensory reminder of our crude, biological being.[49] The microhistory of racism is nestled within a long history of the simultaneous significance and devaluation of the senses in the struggle against the animal self and bare life. Allying perception and projection, Horkheimer and Adorno explain that the "projection of sense impressions is a legacy of [our] animal prehistory, a mechanism for the purposes of defense and obtaining food, an extension of the readiness for combat with which higher species reacted actively or passively to movements, regardless of the intention of the object" (*Dialectic of Enlightenment,* 154). If mimesis is inherent and innate, so too is "the blind instrument of hostility . . . in animal prehistory," which continues to fight the rest of nature (156).[50] The trained postanimal uses sensory apparatuses and animal instinct to turn on the other who demonstrates insufficient control over biological being or differently stylized ways of living in and through the body. The blind hostile organ of animal prehistory is activated when "in the sickness of the individual," a "sharpened intellectual apparatus is turned once more upon humanity." The sick individual relates to others "just as within humanity, the more advanced races have confronted the more primitive, the technically superior nations the more backward" (156–57).

The colonial experiment is a potent arena for animal studies founded in examination of the multiple ways in which the animal and animality are adduced in the discourse of the civilizing mission. In my assessment, not only does this mission derive its aesthetics of form and formation from the capacity for sensation and perception that is part of the biological apparatuses of the humanimal but it also categorizes the difference of the other as defined by the inability to rise above bare animal life because the other lacks recognizably postanimal aesthetics, prosthetics, and technics. In a graphic metaphor that exposes the dominative politics of those in possession of the supposedly right prosthetics, Horkheimer and Adorno ask why, "in this epoch . . . machines, chemicals and organizational principles" should "not be seen as a part of it [the human species] as teeth are a part of the bear, since they serve the same purpose and merely function better?" (*Dialectic of Enlightenment,* 184). Although technologies, techniques, and prosthetics feature prominently in discussions of the posthuman, the Frankfurt School thinkers prompt us to consider their role in conceptualizing the human through postanimal subject formation; this modern subjectivity, they argue, is typified by instrumental rationality, control over bodily expressions, emissions, and behaviors, as well as the making and possession of things. "Things and their makers," as Shiva notes in *Midnight's Children,* "rule the world," while things and their possession drive history (307). By extension, at the intersection of empire and capital, aesthetic reformation takes place in the process of taste transfer in the dual arenas of formal and commodity aesthetics.

Aesthetic forms developed out of uneasiness with bare, biological animal life, the ensuing program of sensory repression and redirection in the civilizing process, and the obsession with good form—in forms of government and sociality in the nation as much as those of individual comportment—emerge forcefully in colonial metrics of civilizational and human status at home and abroad. Colonial manipulation of the capacity to receive and generate forms of thinking and living—colonial mimicry and hybridity, in other words—must therefore be located within a preceding history in which upright stature had come to define the human, creating a tacit backdrop for the mind-body split, the denigration of those seen as less cerebral or closer to nature and the earth, and the projection of socially taboo behaviors associated with *Nur-lebenden* animal life from subject to object. Reminders of animal nature—smell, hairiness, dirt, closeness to the ground in postures of sitting—or physical features that remind people of any of these—noses or lips perceived as large, or short stature (with darker, shorter people perceived as closer to the earth)—can constitute triggers to prejudice. In noting the distinction between "squatting mankind and sitting mankind," Mauss points to the markings of sociocultural, economic, and political status on the body in relation to the biological echoes and effects of postural form and comportment ("Techniques of the Body," 81).[51] In his discussion on the possibility of the disappearance of distinctions between the races of man through hybridization, Darwin dwells on the mixture of Aryans with others, citing Mr. Hunter's description of the Santali, or hill tribes, of India in an implicit valorization of the taller, nobler of the two types after several years of mixture in the Indian subcontinent: "hundreds of imperceptible gradations may be traced 'from the black, squat tribes of the mountains to the tall olive-coloured Brahman, with his intellectual brow, calm eyes, and high but narrow head;' so that it is necessary in courts of justice to ask the witnesses whether they are Santalis or Hindoos" (*The Descent of Man,* 241). Color, stature, and squatting ally the former with those closer to the ground and the lighter and taller with rationality, intellect, and calm.[52]

In surveying the violent march of history, Horkheimer and Adorno assign a foundational role to civilization's unease with the body and its animality:

> The compulsion toward cruelty and destruction stems from the organic repression of proximity to the body, much as, according to Freud's inspired intuition, disgust came into being when, with the adoption of the upright stance and the greater distance from the earth, the sense of smell, which attracted the male animal to the menstruating female, fell victim to organic repression. In Western civilization, and probably in any civilization, what pertains to the body is tabooed, a subject of attraction and revulsion. (*Dialectic of Enlightenment,* 193)[53]

Horkheimer and Adorno draw a direct connection between suspicion of the flesh and humankind's developmental progress:

> The phobias and idiosyncrasies of today, the character traits which are most despised and derided, can be deciphered as marks of a huge advance in human development. From the disgust aroused by excrement and human flesh to the contempt for fanaticism, idleness, and poverty, both spiritual and material, a line connects behavioral forms which were once adequate and necessary to those which are abominated. This line is at once that of destruction and of civilization. (*Dialectic of Enlightenment,* 72–73)

A long history links civilization, domination, and the suppression and redirection of the mimetic faculty. The desire to become other—to cede the self to the object—has been under sustained assault in the course of civilization: "Civilization has replaced the organic adaptation to others and mimetic behavior proper, by organized control of mimesis. . . . Uncontrolled mimesis is outlawed . . . leading finally to the kind of teaching which does not allow children to behave as children . . . [as] the condition of civilization" (*Dialectic of Enlightenment,* 180). Signs of tabooed mimetic traits appearing in others invite disgust and mockery in modes that conceal unconscious desire, and recognition that "what repels . . . as alien is all too familiar" (148–49). Michael Taussig claims, "racism is the parade ground where the civilized rehearse this love-hate relation with their repressed sensuosity" (*Mimesis,* 67). Repressed and distorted, the mimetic urge becomes a source of some of the anxieties that bedevil interpersonal encounters, resulting in relations of dominance. Confronting the brutality of fascism, Horkheimer and Adorno claim that anti-Semitism was based on a false projection, "a pathic character trait" related to repressed form (*Dialectic of Enlightenment,* 154). In other words, repressed urges, desires, and sensory needs become available for projection on the weaker and relatively powerless objects of the evaluative gaze: "impulses which are not acknowledged by the subject and yet are his, are attributed to the object—the prospective victim" (154). In their view, "the nucleus of all civilizing rationality" involves "the denial of nature in man for the sake of domination over non-human nature and over other men" (54). The war on the self precedes the domination and war on the other. Given this history of mimetic and sensory repression, the sensory enjoyment of cultural others can simultaneously evoke longing and cruelty, a response born of the repressions that seem to forbid the subject a similar enjoyment. In this understanding, mockery of the expressive forms of the weak by the powerful conceals the latter's desire for mimicry, that is, the longing to become other and surrender subjectivity to experience "extimacy," the condition of repressing the other in the self in projectional fantasies.

In his essay on extimacy, a concept derived from Jacques Lacan, Jacques-Alain Miller explores alterity within the subject through the category of jouissance. It is precisely the other's enjoyment, and the other's *way* of enjoying, he argues, that elicits hatred: "We may well think that racism exists because our Islamic neighbor is too noisy when he has parties. However, what is really at stake is that he takes his jouissance in a way different from ours. Thus the other's proximity exacerbates racism" ("Extimité," 79). Referencing Miller, Žižek emphasizes that "what really bothers us about the 'other' is the peculiar way he organizes his enjoyment, precisely the surplus, the 'excess' that pertains to this way: the smell of 'their' food, 'their' noisy songs and dances, 'their' strange manners" (*Tarrying with the Negative,* 203). Chirac's snuffling nose and raised antennae for "le bruit et l'odeur" of the immigrant is an example of the repressive logic that defines extimacy. Resentful of the other's undeserved *plus-de-jouir,* or what Žižek calls "the surplus" or "excess," the subject turns repressed desire for pleasure into hatred for the other's access to it. It is in "the confrontation of incompatible modes of *jouissance*" that intolerance festers (Miller, "Extimité," 80). Bourdieu suggests that in the civilizational register, disgust is "the ambivalent experience of the horrible seduction of the disgusting and of enjoyment which performs a sort of reduction to animality, corporeality, the belly and sex" (*Distinction,* 489). Objects that impose consumption and enjoyment on us arouse disgust with reminders of our fleshy animality. Sensational reactions of disgust at the other's way of living and being result from the long history of repressive sensory administration associated with the idea of civilization, according to Adorno, who describes "the system in which the sovereign mind imagined itself transfigured" as rooted in a "primal history in the pre-mental, the animal life of the species." The other's seemingly unregulated indulgence of behaviors long repressed in the self creates psychic dissonance through the recollection of "the animal life of the species" shared with the object of judgment and derision. Projecting evil on the "not-I" and raging at "all that reminds us of nature," rage at the victim "is rationalized by projection . . . in the advance to humanity," prompting Adorno to conclude, "the system is the belly turned mind" (*Negative Dialectics,* 22–23). Primal hunger, redirected anger, projectional fantasies, and rational man's investment in the primacy of his intellect collude to produce a system marked by dominative rationality and a tortured relationship with the animal.

The imposition of the conceptual mind's dominance on biological urges and physiological life is the very stuff of civilization, and its long history of oppressing those who invoke the "not-I" in the "I" struggling to imagine itself as "the sovereign mind" (*Negative Dialectics,* 22). Adorno directs us to "the dialectic of culture and barbarism" (*Prisms,* 34), which is also resonant in Benjamin's proclamation that "there is no document of civilization which is not at the same time a document of barbarism" (*Illuminations,* 256) to recall the imbrication of primal history with the productions of the rational animal and its claims to exclusive breeding and culture. Sexual repression and the mortification of the flesh, part of the civilizational process, and according to Marcuse in *Eros and Civilization,* of capitalist production and Christian asceticism, are part of the history of civilization as well as that of antimiscegenation legislation and its regulation of desire in the colonial context. In almost every culture, civilizational norms invest heavily in recommendations and prohibitions related to sexual behavior so as to control sexual expressions and bodily positions, even within alleged heteronormativity, not to mention homosexual, transgender, or other sexual practices. The *zoon politikon* who becomes recognizable as a civil subject bearing the right to freedom is paradoxically born out of a "primal history" that it continues to suppress (*Negative Dialectics,* 22). Domination of the other turns out to be part of the repression of the self.[54]

In mapping the distance of the human from the animal in the realms of consciousness, psychology, and being in the world, it is the biological core of being that is increasingly suppressed as the alterity within. This version of the institution of speciesism in conceptualizing the human becomes spectacularly visible in passages of *écriture excrément* (scatology) in two "primal" scenes in the jungle in Kunzru's novel *The Impressionist.* The first features a gathering of high-ranking British colonial officers and local princes on a tiger hunt. The second is located in Fotseland, an "almost pristine" site in West Africa, where an assorted group of geographers, surveyors, and others are gathered under the aegis of Fotse expert and Oxford anthropologist, Professor Chapel. Both sites present the opportunity to explore the intricacies of intercultural contact in venues that are remote from the amenities of civilization and niceties of cultural (and toilet) training as the parties are stricken by diarrhea. In these liminal spaces of encounter, one might read not only the third space between cultures but also that between civilization and what it must repress to produce human culture. In *Midnight's Children,* Rushdie depicts the Sunderbans as a space marked by a similar suspension of civilizational norms in the jungle, the locus classicus of premodernity associated with the animal.

The ambivalence of the human-animal relationship is not limited to disdain of bare life, the suppression of the life-filled incarnate moment, the warmth of feeling, or the inculcation of postanimal aesthetics and acquisition of technics and things. In the colonial encounter, it also surfaces in the paradoxes of habitual, unquestioned carnivory among the colonizers; the categorization of native meat eaters and vegetarians using the language of muscular prowess or weakness, and the colonial sport of the hunt alongside investment in wildlife preserves; the inclination toward pastoral care, and even love, of animals; and the condemnation of those, especially different others, who do not treat animals well. It surfaces in anxieties about humane slaughtering practices alongside the slaughter of indigenous populations. A kind of love of the animal combines with hatred for the animal other as one of the many paradoxes of dominative rationality. "The precondition of the fascists' pious love of animals, nature, and children," Horkheimer and Adorno remind us, "is the lust of the hunter"; "the idle stroking of children's hair and animal pelts signifies: this hand can destroy" (*Dialectic of Enlightenment,* 210). Adorno indicts Kantian ethics, "which accords affection, not respect to animals," and can only "muster disdain" for a morality founded in the imperative: "to try to live so that one may believe himself to have been a good animal" (*Negative Dialectics,* 299). Arguably, the civilizing mission might be understood as an attempt to resolve these ambivalent impulses partially by "caring" for the underdeveloped other through pastoral care and indoctrination in postanimal sensibilities and technologies of living that include a conflicted stance regarding animals simultaneously as pets, protein, and tools in service of humans. These themes come dramatically to light in *Arthur and George,* Julian Barnes's retelling of the real-life story of the indictment of a half-Indian lawyer, George Edalji, on charges of animal mutilation in turn-of-the-century England, and the role Sir Arthur Conan Doyle played in real life attempting to clear George's name of guilt for a crime unimaginable to animal-loving Englishmen.

The love–hate relationship with the body, its animality, and indeed the animal, also take more straightforward forms in projecting the other as animal. On a biocultural evolutionary scale, the production of bourgeois enlightenment subjectivity has invested in a suppression of features associated with the animal and the feminine, and disdain of cultural groups associated with effeminacy and insufficient distance from bodily nature.[55] Founded in a Cartesian dualism that predates Descartes, the association of the body, emotion, and sensory excess with women and other lesser human animals is a powerful strand in the production of colonial difference. Relations of domination under empire thus prevail within a complex set of factors: fear of nature, animal, and woman; belief in the body as other to the rational mind; and contempt for those who are thought to bear a retarded relationship to modernity.

Fanon's repeated exposure of the casting of natives as animalistic, biological, and beastly in *Black Skin, White Masks* and his refusal of this casting in *The Wretched of the Earth* introduce the peculiar difference of race into the long history of the making of the human, that is, the *zoon politikon* born for meaningful citizenship.[56] Fanon's oft-cited passage in the latter outlines the colonial project of recasting human others as animals:

> The terms the settler uses when he mentions the native are zoological terms. He speaks of the yellow man's reptilian motions, of the stink of the native quarter, of breeding swarms, of foulness, of spawn, of gesticulations. When the settler seeks to describe the native fully in exact terms he constantly refers to the bestiary. (42)

In the former, he repeatedly refers to the "Negro" as the bringer of biology, one who "symbolizes the biological" (167). Elsewhere, he explains how the native is depicted as an animal-child, an embodiment of repressed urges to the white colonizer, incapable even of understanding his own experience of pain: "Whereas the doctors say: 'The pain in their case is protopathic, poorly differentiated, diffuse as in an animal, it is a general malaise rather than a localized pain'; The patients say: 'They ask me what is wrong with me, as if I were the doctor'" (*A Dying Colonialism,* 127). Fanon cites Carothers of the World Health Organization: "The African makes very little use of his frontal lobes," being most akin to a "lobotomized European" (302). In a much-quoted statement from *The Wretched of the Earth,* Fanon outlines the native's resistance to this characterization: "For he knows he is not an animal, and it is precisely when he recognizes his humanity that he begins to sharpen the weapons with which he will secure his victory" (43).

Such is the impact of investing in a conception of the human through post-animal subject formation that the colonized subject is left bewildered and conflicted about a proper response to the logic that entraps him as animal other. The regnant order obliges the native to embrace a formula in which bodily being, emotion, and all alleged signs of the animal self, including ways of eating, laughing, feeling, and enjoying life, must be erased in the quest to achieve the status of human. In the metaphysical schematics of the colonized, becoming human relies on becoming not-animal using models of subjectivity defined by enlightenment and imperial modernity. Fanon's response to colonial violence is charged with a rueful irony in its rejection of the animal, a move that he replicates in his discussion of emotions versus reason in a Manichean racial scheme. Fanon's writings document the colonial stage of the making of the modern subject conflicted and troubled by the overheated expression of emotions. Susan Buck-Morss writes that "Kant's transcendental subject purges himself of the senses which endanger autonomy not only because they unavoidably entangle him in the world, but, specifically, because they make him passive ('languid' [*schmelzend*] is Kant's word) instead of active ('vigorous' [*wacker*]), susceptible, like 'Oriental voluptuaries,' to sympathy and tears" ("Aesthetics and Anaesthetics," 29–30). Fanon's deeply ambiguous response to colonial descriptions of the "Negro" as emotion embodied, and the celebration of emotion and bodily being by writers of the negritude movement, is symptomatic of the politics of the body/mind divide put in place by Cartesian and colonial logic. Seeming to mock it, Fanon instantiates and uncovers values that have stood against reason in racist science. Fanon's double gesture—his recognition of attempts made by writers such as Aimé Césaire and Leopold Senghor to write black values and bodily affect back into a civilizational register, and his ironic distance from the language in which such a move is made possible—compel us to confront the dilemma of the postcolonial subject caught between two equally conflicted modes of being: an affectively charged emotional being that has been discredited or a valued intellectual subjectivity that has overcome the heat of emotion but has also lost the warmth of the humanimal. Fanon rewrites colonial descriptions of the "Negro" as primitive with arch references to Senghor: "Yes, we are—we Negroes—backward, simple, free in our behavior. That is because for us the body is not something opposed to what you call the mind. We are in the world. And long live the couple, Man and Earth!" (*Black Skin, White Masks,* 126–27). The romanticism of this coupling, celebrated elsewhere in German and English romanticism without the discomfort that accompanies Fanon's restatement, is followed by a borrowed clip from Senghor: "Emotion is completely Negro as reason is Greek" (127). In Fanon's rehearsal of different responses to the denigration of the black man, at one stage this "Negro" is a poet, a feminized creature not afraid to be allied to something like the animal that is one with nature, and at others even a reminder to mechanized whites of the humanness of all humanity glimpsed through the lens of the biological animal (129). But he cannot forget that these features are seen as "typical of people that have not kept pace with the evolution of the human race. Or, if one prefers, this is humanity at its lowest" (126). "I had to choose," he declares, and then questions himself, "What do I mean? I had no choice" (126). The tortured text of the self is torn between unviable polarities, hunted and haunted by a history in which the possibilities are prematurely foreclosed and every option denies the "Negro's" humanity, even when the West turns to him for inspiration and rehabilitation in a cold world from which neither emotion nor reason offers deliverance.

An additional strand connecting Fanon's work with that of the Frankfurt School thus involves what I would describe as the thermal dynamics of the making of the human—and its less human other—on the basis of a sliding scale between the human as cognitive being and animal being. Here I adduce the idea of the heat of emotion against the ideal of a temperate character. In a move that is suggestive for postcolonial studies, a thermal dynamics of race, sex, and class relations in the production of the civilized subject leads Adorno to formulate the notion of "bourgeois coldness," a subjectivity developed through a calculated distance from the warmth of the bodily being, the ardor of emotions, and susceptibility to affect, especially in response to suffering. Those insufficiently converted to this temperamental coolness suffer opprobrium: "Anyone who is not cold, who does not chill himself as in the vulgar figure of speech the murderer 'chills' his victims, must feel condemned" (*Negative Dialectics,* 347). Fearing that the body and its sensual being will interfere with a developmental project founded in instrumental rationality, the bourgeois subject becomes a thing that does not feel the suffering of others or of the self, sits in judgment of others, and preaches a creed dependent on rationalizing suffering as inevitable to grander civilization aims. Senses, emotions, feelings, and animal warmth are anathema to the rational Enlightenment subject.

Playing it cool is playing dead; repressing the merely biological, animal instinct and turning away from suffering, the hollowed subject suppresses the impulse to respond to suffering and rationalizes the suppression. The colonial civilizing mission offers the native a model for modern subjectivity that approximates a form of death. In its final irony, colonial mimicry is tantamount to *Mimesis ans Tote* (mimesis of death) as the mimetic impulse is channeled into rigid, repressed forms founded in self-alienation from nature in the production of a repressed, deadened, sclerosed subject in whom "there is life no longer" (Adorno, *Minima Moralia,* 15). In a bootless attempt at attaining full humanity, what the native mimics is a dead, concept-driven object, more *körper* (corpus as object to be possessed) than *leib* (living body). "The reason that represses mimesis . . . is itself *mimesis: of death*" (*Dialectic of Enlightenment,* 44; emphasis added). "Imitation enters the service of power when even the human being becomes an anthropomorphism for human beings" producing a subject who, instead of seeking a happy life, mimics forms associated with the exercise of power, aping a model who has already sacrificed the longing for a fulfilled life to become the privileged subject produced by mastery over nature (*Dialectic of Enlightenment,* 45). The biosocial consequences of this exercise entail a conflicted state of morbid scission, a *Haßliebe* (love–hate) relationship with the body, and "compulsive aversion" toward everything that seems to exceed the purposeful and reminds us of our animal nature because it "has not been absorbed into utility by passing through the cleansing channels of conceptual order" (*Dialectic of Enlightenment,* 148). Colonial mimicry of empty forms turns the body into an object for control. "No matter how trained and fit it may be," the body under the power of instrumental and dominative rationality "remains a cadaver. . . . [Its] transformation into dead matter, indicated by the affinity of *corpus* to corpse" is a "part of the perennial process which turned nature into stuff, material" (194). Postcolonial mimic-men are destined to join the processional of decomposing modern subjects in whom "life does not live" at the end of history.[57] They are, like their modular predecessors, "victims of the same conditions and the same disappointed hope" as the ghosts of the past, as Horkheimer and Adorno conclude in their theory of ghosts (*Dialectic of Enlightenment,* 178), uncanny reminders of the death that the allegedly sovereign, "thoroughly emptied subject" has already suffered (Žižek, "Hegel," 222). In *Midnight's Children,* it is the dispossessed twin Shiva who notes that "the world . . . is things," and "today, what people are is just another kind of thing" (307). In the end, Adorno and Fanon's is not an argument for the recovery of a pristine self in the search for freedom but an explanation of the process of individuation and socialization under imperial modernity as mimicry of empty forms associated with false ideas of a good life, even as the colonized object man's desire to live becomes more and more "phantom-like," in Fanon's memorable phrase (*Toward the African Revolution,* 35).

If aesthetics is the capacity for sensation and perception, human self-making defined by mimicry of postanimal aesthetics unwittingly entails a deadening and perversion of these faculties. Susan Buck-Morss points to the senses as our "biological apparatus," claiming that aesthetics has intrinsically less to do with beauty, art, or truth, and should be placed instead "within the field of animal instincts" ("Aesthetics and Anaesthetics," 6–7). The emptying of the subject implies the repressive regulations of the animal capacity for sensation and bodily feeling in the course of a process of anaesthetization on the one hand and the perversion of instincts and the sensorium on the other. In the current stage of global capital and its attendant regime of neoliberal hybridity, the thermal dynamics of personhood finds expression in a contradictory logic: what is hot is what is cool and vice versa. Drawn increasingly to dead forms and the cold comforts of capitalist personhood and its commodity culture, today's cool subject presents a conjunction of person, commodity, and empty forms. "Personality," Horkheimer and Adorno note, "means hardly more than dazzling white teeth and freedom from body odor and emotions" (*Dialectic of Enlightenment,* 136). The "compulsive imitation by consumers of cultural commodities" is a mark of "the triumph of advertising in the culture industry" (136). Along with a display of formal aesthetics signaling cultural and social capital, the better sort of human is also identified by the acquisition of capital qua capital in imperial modernity in a world of "things things things" (*Midnight's Children,* 526). The conjunction of personhood with empty forms and dead commodities as markers of more human identity in the developmental regimes of modernity furnishes rich material for an object-oriented postcolonial studies sensitive to race and class differences.

Hybridity, Internal Colonialism, and Globalization

The politics of colonial hybridity as simultaneously racist, classist, neuropolitical, and biocultural is broadly applicable. Examples of spectacular mimicry and characters hybridized by the taste transfer of commodities and forms can be readily adduced in literary representations ranging from Chimamanda Adichie's *Americanah,* Hanan Al-Shaykh's *Only in London,* Jill Ker Conway's *The Road from Coorain,* Tsitsi Dangarembga's *Nervous Conditions,* Andrea Levy's *A Small Island,* Arundhati Roy's *The God of Small Things,* or Jhumpa Lahiri's stories about immigrants in the United States, to select texts randomly for a course one might teach on postcolonial or "global" women writers. Many a literary text on metropolitan migrant identity today will expose the biopoetics of assimilation as the long shadow cast by a body-minded colonial civilizing mission founded in preemptive notions of beauties of body and mind.

Historical variables nonetheless complicate wholesale generalizations about the civilizing mission and its contemporary forms. As I explain in the following chapter, there are instructive lessons in attending to the particular complications of the civilizing mission and colonial hybridity in an allegedly "once great civilization," namely, India (Goetz, *The Art of India,* 205). A serious reconsideration of the politics of hybridity requires a reckoning with the politics of race and class among the colonized and not simply between colonizer and colonized. Attention to the dynamics of hybridity among the colonized reveals new forms of hierarchical thinking in modernity in particular sociopolitical contexts to better illuminate the problem of class inequality on a global scale.

With stray references to a few comparative examples, this book focuses on fictions concerned with India and Indians to explore the differential politics of hybridity between and among colonized peoples beyond the usual lens of white and other. This focus allows me to locate intercultural traffic within particular histories of race, class, and chromatism. References to *the* civilizing mission are apt to obscure its local variations. Along with race as the distinctive postcolonial dimension of the Western project of biopolitics and anatomo-politics described by Foucault, native hierarchies—of class, caste, and civilizational standing in India, for example—present specific, historically contingent variables of the civilizing mission. Colonial racial hybridity, moreover, demands analysis not only of usual problems with racial typology, but also confusions peculiar to subcontinental theaters of mixture.[58] Although the Indian Constitution attempts to stabilize colonial interraciality under the nominal "Anglo-Indian," this is a notoriously complicated category.[59]

Postcolonial Biology does not attempt to excavate the history of Anglo-Indians at any length, or stake a claim to "Anglo-Indian literature" as its province of study as such,[60] although particular moments in the novels chosen for this study turn to this history to examine the concepts of diaspora, nation, mimicry, and hybridity, from the vantage point of the racial hybrid.

The differential politics of race in discourses of hybridity deserves special attention. In *Slavery and the Culture of Taste,* Simon Gikandi has demonstrated that "the establishment of a realm of taste, or even the valorization of ideals of beauty, depended on systematic acts of excluding those considered to be outside the systems of explanation that were being established as social norms" (37). Gikandi's identification of the figure of blackness as a counterpoint to ideas of aesthetic beauty is pertinent to this study, I argue, even though it involves characters not considered black in usual typology, because of the particular role of blackness in the racial politics of hybridity and mimicry in South Asian identity politics. Blackness may well be the magnetic pole of differentiation from whiteness, but it is not unusual for accounts of race to be formulated along the axis of a desire for whiteness without a consideration of how this desire maps itself directionally with regard to blackness. The role of brown bodies in the consolidation of colonial racial hierarchies aside, anxiety among nonwhite, nonblack individuals about being confused with blacks surfaces in all the novels under discussion in this book. The desire for Englishness in the brown/white encounter is belied by anxieties about the *not quite / not black* casting of the Indian, exposing blackness as an underreported polarity in colonial relations in the subcontinental scene. In this dispensation, the presentation of brownness as a more acceptable form of blackness illuminates a differential calculus of race founded in part on skin color and in part on the logic of aesthetic form and a display of what I have called postanimal prosthetics and technics on a civilizational ladder. As Vivek Bald demonstrates in *Bengali Harlem,* among the options for passing as other than African American in the American South was passing as Hindu: "for those who were darker skinned, posing as 'Hindu' or 'East Indian' was a recurring and prominent theme." Bald admits that "we will probably never know which black southerner first employed this ruse, first discovered that it was possible to move across from the line between 'Negro' and 'Hindoo,' from a denigrated to an exotic otherness, from an unacceptable to a nominally acceptable blackness," but he speculates that Bengali peddlers in the South probably demonstrated the advantages of displaying a civilizationally better shade of black, at least before Jim Crow altered the circumstances substantially (50).

Apart from racial hierarchies, the peculiarities of class composition in particular historical contexts present further challenges to an understanding of the colonial civilizing mission. Because of the particular complications of class and caste,[61] this study of the impact of the colonial civilizing mission resists any suggestion that it may have produced a singular ideological and biological subject. The earlier discussion of mimicry and discriminatory eumemics highlights the fact that the civilizing mission invested from the beginning in reproducing the hierarchies that characterized its own disjunctive formation. Macaulay's minute not only legislated a built-in class hierarchy, it was *founded* by it. It is well understood that the representatives of empire were themselves divided by reasons of class, ethnicity, status, education, and rank. Colonial whiteness was defined by "a class of superior settlers" negatively circumscribed against subordinate classes of poor whites who were also flooding into India (Mizutani, *The Meaning of White,* 21, 24).[62] Farwell writes that in the diverse composition of the British Army, the

> "other ranks"—the warrant officers, non-commissioned officers and privates were so different [from the higher-ranking officers] . . . that they seemed to be of two different races . . . their accents (even language in some cases), their habits, manner, tastes and, of course, financial circumstances were far apart. The British army operated on what was basically a caste system. (*Mr. Kipling's Army,* 79)

Buettner explains that "behaviour and lifestyle made possible mainly by wealth . . . determined racial categorization as much as, if not more than ancestry" ("Problematic Spaces, Problematic Races," 281). Whiteness in colonial India was a cultural category overdetermined by various factors beyond skin color. Economic and social mobility were prominent among them, in addition to behaviors and lifestyles associated with class privilege, factors that were also salient in evaluating and categorizing the native population. Furthermore, given the conflicted but powerful colonial belief in a shared Aryan heritage, the civilizing mission in India was developed in conversation with native hierarchical structures, while nonetheless reinforcing racial divisions.

Two conclusions follow from this understanding of internal diversity among colonizers and colonizeds. First, that existing class and caste privilege in the colony was refreshed and reconsolidated by the additional accretion of perceptible forms of modernization in lifestyle and thought *while also contributing to their formation.* Second, that *aesthetic form*—underwritten by a long history of the administration of the sensorium—and the display of postanimal aesthetics, prosthetics, and technics repeatedly emerge as the alternative logic of judgment and categorization in perceptions of difference between colonizer and colonized, even if racial differences have never been insignificant. The multiple sources, contexts, and contradictions of the civilizing mission and its impact notwithstanding, complex and interlocking hierarchies based on race, class, lineage, bodily comportment, and aesthetic form have nonetheless become part of the legacy of empire and its contribution to additional modes of social striation based on bioaesthetics. However uneven this process, aesthetic forms associated with colonial power have left their impression on plastic bodies and minds in a disjunctive but perceptible legacy in the arena of bodily habits, sensory lives, and corporeal inclinations as much as in ideology and psychology.

Fanon's muscles, Adorno's desensitized bourgeois subject, squatting Padma's musculature, Saleem's cultivation of pure accents, the art form of the spitters in *Midnight's Children,* Pran's exercises in producing the labial-dental fricative *v,* Lily's warnings against head waggling and squatting in *The Impressionist,* George's ultimately failed training in the metonymic aesthetics of Englishness and Horace's success in *Arthur and George,* and the unrelenting seduction of "things things things" and capitalist personhood are coimplicated in an ongoing drama in the politics of empire, psyche, and flesh. Fanon notes that "vulgar racism in its biological form corresponds to the period of the crude exploitation of man's arms and legs" (*Toward the African Revolution,* 35). Moreover, he adds, "the perfecting of the means of production inevitably . . . [camouflages] the techniques by which man is exploited, hence of the forms of racism" (36). Fanon's comments prompt renewed consideration of imperialism as a key stage of capitalism, first in its exploitation of native resources, labor, and markets, and subsequently in its neoliberal phase in the alliance of person and capital through patterns of hyperconsumption on the one hand and disguisement of continued exploitation on the other. In the newest season of the nexus of empire, capital, and globalization, and the persistent assault on animal, biotic being, *Postcolonial Biology* calls for a theory of the human that can address the continued manipulation of plastic body-minds in the name of the very prospect it compromises: that of the "good life."

1 "NO ESCAPE FROM FORM"

Saleem's Spittoon, Padma's Musculature, and Neoliberal Hybridity in Salman Rushdie's Midnight's Children

Beyond language was the plain bodyness of it.
—**SALMAN RUSHDIE**, *THE MOOR'S LAST SIGH*

You can distinguish squatting mankind and sitting mankind.
—**MARCEL MAUSS**, "TECHNIQUES OF THE BODY"

IN HIS 1981 *NEW YORK TIMES* REVIEW, Clark Blaise notes that Rushdie's tour de force novel *Midnight's Children* sounds "like a country finding its voice." Whose voice is this and how does it come to be the voice of the nation? The country's voice box is located in the person of a certain Saleem Sinai, who delivers his peculiar, hyperbolic history of modern India and its complex inheritance with suspicious self-assurance and presumptuous confidence. The voice of the country, as Saleem's audience figure Padma discovers to her scandalized horror, is "an Anglo," a racial hybrid born of an afternoon's passion between two unlikely partners: William Methwold, departing British proprietor of Methwold Estate, which is to become the Sinai family's new home, and Vanita, impoverished street singer Wee Willie Winkie's wife.[1] Saleem is not, after all, "Babar ki aulad" (son of Babar, founder of the Muslim Mughal dynasty in India), as the current anti-Muslim fundamentalist rhetoric in India would have it, nor the legitimate heir of a well-to-do Muslim family, but someone who was destined for the slums as the unacknowledged heir of a colonial overlord. How does such an individual come to command the stage as the nation's amanuensis and spokesperson, albeit self-appointedly so?

Vanita's brief encounter with Methwold points to a more substantial trail of historical bread crumbs.[2] Named after an early factor (commercial agent) at the East India factory at Masulipatam who subsequently became president of the factory at Surat in the 1650s, the word "Methwold" invokes colonial history and its pervasive legacy. The historical Methwold presided over Surat, a city held and sacked by the Portuguese in the sixteenth century, during the heyday of its Indian adventures. During his time as factor, Methwold is reported to have bemoaned the practices of his English company servants: "Their private whorings, drunkennesse and such like ryotts," he complained in a letter, "have hardened the hearts of the inhabitants against our very names" (quoted in Dalrymple, *White Mughals,* 25). Part of this history includes interracial encounters that produced a group colloquially referred to as "Anglos." This undercover, secreted history comes to light briefly in Saleem's disclosure of Vanita's seduction by Methwold, her silent incubation of midnight's Anglo-Indian heir, and her dying in poverty and neglect while delivering him into the world.

How does someone with this provenance become the voice of his people, much less the nation?[3] The answer is twofold: he does not speak for his people—even if the novel includes several sympathetically depicted Anglo-Indian characters;[4] and he does not become the voice of the nation in his *propria persona* as an "Anglo-Indian." Given their systematic exclusion by prejudicial colonial policies that restricted opportunities for higher education and advancement, Anglo-Indians as a group were not equipped by the colonizers to yield leaders of the nation, even if major national figures such as Frank Anthony belie this history as significant exceptions.[5] Moreover, as Rukmini Bhaya Nair explains, "no historian disagrees with the patent conclusion that the Anglo-Indians were deliberately erased as a community—first by the British and then, collusively, by the elite and caste-conscious Indian administrators who took over the governing of the country after 1947" (*Lying on the Postcolonial Couch,* 32). Setting aside the fact that Saleem is deluded in assuming that he speaks as the voice of the nation or has a pivotal role in the national narrative, this fantasy would not so easily have been harbored by an impoverished bastard born in the charity ward of the same hospital as Amina and Ahmed Sinai's real heir, Shiva. Originally destined for the slums where his doppelgänger Shiva languishes as a child, Saleem was never intended to be the voice of the nation, which is to say that he would never have had the luxury of enjoying the illusion of being its rightful representative.

In *A Critique of Postcolonial Reason,* Gayatri Spivak cites an East India Company document on criteria for the employability of Anglo-Indians. Apart from proof of European ancestry—"the stipulated qualification of *legitimate birth*"—the candidate must furnish proof that he "has had the benefit of a liberal Education," a "clinching requirement" in Spivak's words (document quoted 166–67). Spivak's identification of the specific terms of "the right of access to a white world administering the black" is poignantly resonant for a postcolonial world reconjugating indigenous preoccupations with birth and cultivation in conversation with those introduced by colonial modernity (167). When "the empire writes back"—to use Rushdie's phrase—it does so courtesy of the legacy of an expensive, exclusionary colonial education designed to form "a class of persons, Indian in blood and colour, but English in taste, in opinions, in morals, and in intellect," in Macaulay's aforementioned words (Rushdie, "The Empire Writes Back," 8, 249). Pointing to the relay between colonial and postcolonial hierarchies, Rushdie writes, "those who were made powerful then remain, for the most part, powerful now" (8). Midnight's impoverished bastard child was never invited to join this class, but "thanks to the crime of Mary Pereira," Saleem tells us, "I became the chosen child of midnight" (*Midnight's Children,* 135). Saleem's panoramic history discloses the politics of hybridity and mimicry not only between the colonizer and the colonized but also *among* the colonized in the aftermath of empire, and the displacement of anxieties about race and civilization into a range of bioformal aesthetic practices that converge with the politics of class and caste in what some colonizers considered a "once great civilization" (Goetz, *The Art of India,* 205).

Colonial interaction with India and Indians was complicated by multiple factors: the presence of a powerful Mughal empire when the Europeans first arrived in India; the status of Muslims in a majority Hindu nation; the odd racial sanctuary granted to its Parsi population; a usually ignored African diaspora;[6] complex caste divisions; and a population comprising various others, including diverse, multilingual aboriginal populations. Despite the presence of this perplexing diversity, several prominent Orientalists believed that Indians belonged to a once great civilization and shared a racial prehistory with a group that came to be known as Indo-Aryan.[7] Judgments of "the wonder that was India" in A. L. Basham's eponymous history and in Friedrich von Schlegel's passionate assertion that "everything, absolutely everything, is of Indian origin" exerted a complicated influence on both sides (quoted in Bernal, *Black Athena,* 230).[8] Trautmann claims that in the British vision of India, "the Aryan idea always has the function of being a sign of the kinship between the two nations" (*Aryans and British India,* 15). Max Müller declared the East Indian "our Aryan brother" (quoted in Sreedharan, *A Textbook of Historiography,* 424); Indian leaders such as Keshab Chandra Sen believed that "in the advent of the English nation in India we see a reunion of parted cousins, the descendants of two different families of the ancient Aryan race" (quoted in Thapar, *India,* 16); and Mahatma Gandhi claimed that "both the English and the Indians spring from a common stock, called the Indo-Aryan" (quoted in Steger, "Mahatma Gandhi on Indian Self-Rule," 133). These comments suggest a bidirectional racial sense veering on racial pride that abides in displaced forms to this day.

Gradually, however, imperial ambassadors of a civilizational mission that also devalued its own poor, underclass, and female populations, began to favor the doctrine of degeneracy over the narrative of kinship. David Arnold concludes that in colonial estimation, "some Indians might be deemed to have European-like complexions or physiques, they might even be regarded as fellow 'Caucasians' or 'Aryans,' but that did not signify a shared ethnic identity in the present nor a common social and political destiny in the future" ("Race, Place, and Bodily Difference," 273).[9] Darwin attributed the dilution of the race to mixture:

> The singular fact that Europeans and Hindoos, who belong to the same Aryan stock and speak a language fundamentally the same, differ widely in appearance, whilst Europeans differ but little from Jews, who belong to the Semitic stock and speak quite another language, has been accounted for by Broca through the Aryan branches having been largely crossed during their wide diffusion by various indigenous tribes. (*Descent,* 240)[10]

Hybridity and degeneracy are linked in the assessment of the native population even before mixture with the European colonizer. Degeneracy and difference from Caucasian cousins, moreover, are also ascribed to the "external influences of high temperature, and corresponding habits of life and diet" according to J. R. Martin, a nineteenth-century surgeon in India who concludes that "these general causes, together with the premature development of the generative function, produce an excitability of the nervous system, diminished volume, enervation, and relaxation of the muscular system as compared to Europeans" (*The Influence of Tropical Climates on European Constitutions,* 212–13). Martin's observations on physiological differences between Indians and Caucasians in a text published in 1856 introduce epigenetic considerations in the development of biological differences despite the fact that Indians are described as being "of Caucasian origin" (212). Martin is also alert, moreover, to the internal diversity among Indians, who "are moulded by a great variety of climates, localities, habits of life, diet, occupation, &c., so as to constitute in reality a people varying exceedingly in moral and intellectual qualities, in physical powers and appearances" (212).[11]

Why, then, did the idea of a shared Aryan heritage persist? Determined to uproot what he calls "the racial theory of Indian civilization"—the belief that "India's civilization was produced by the clash and subsequent mixture of light-skinned civilizing invaders (the Aryans) and dark-skinned barbarian aborigines (often identified as Dravidians)—Trautmann acknowledges that it "has proved remarkably durable and resistant to new information" (*Aryans and British India,* 4). The durability of the Aryan idea might be attributed in part to its dual serviceability for colonizer and colonized: for a Europe seeking a civilizational vintage for its own stock *and* for India in tracking relative civilizational distance from Africans, who were cast as the former's *absolute* other and India's *relative* other. Scholars have suggested that the myth of a shared Aryan heritage may well have been at the fulcrum of racial theories in the nineteenth century, putting India at the center of the production of hierarchical racial thought in modernity.[12] Arguably, Africa and blackness as the polar opposite of whiteness could not have been constructed without the conception of India as a degraded Aryan civilization in a hierarchical chain of being.

After Bhabha's important work on the production of difference in the enunciative context of encounter gained currency, a fairly sustained focus on the interdictory "desire for colonial mimicry" in postcolonial criticism has allowed us to investigate a desirous colonized subject who is "not quite / not white" and "*almost the same but not white*" (*The Location of Culture,* 86–87). Along with the historical, cultural, and phenotypic diversity of the colonized subjects of the British-Indian encounter, I argue that an extra vector must be confronted: for colonizer and colonized alike, the Indian subcontinental subject triggers additional anxiety on *both* sides about a people *almost the same but not black* and yet *not quite / not black.* Gandhi's aforementioned appeal to a shared Aryan heritage was marshaled to protest what he perceived as British degradation of Indians in South Africa "to the level of the raw Kaffir whose occupation is hunting and whose sole ambition is to collect enough cattle to buy a wife with and then, to pass his life in indolence and nakedness" (quoted in Steger, "Mahatma Gandhi on Indian Self-Rule," 134). It is not my intention to expose Gandhi as a racist through this cursory reference so much as it is to suggest that this is an example suggestive for exploring the ways in which the rhetoric of race can be displaced into lifestyle features mapped on a civilizational scale defined not only by a colonial mind-set but an *indigenous* one in which cultural, chromatic, and other hierarchies hold considerable valence. Both rely on evaluative judgments founded in the criterion of the inadequate formation of plastic bodies or their actual *de*formation, producing mirror images of native and imperial notions of hierarchy, without erasing the structural inequalities implicit in the latter. It was in reference to aboriginals that "the most extreme language of race, especially the physicality of race, was employed, with the supposedly debased physical type of 'the Negro' (rather than that of the allegedly elevated 'Caucasian') as the principal guide" (Arnold, "Race, Place, and Bodily Difference," 266).[13] The drama of plastic bodies in the Indian imperial scene thus plays out on a stage more crowded than we normally credit; it includes not only diversely brown bodies against unmarked, indefinable whiteness as the norm, but also the absent black as an instructive, negative model.

Midnight's Children introduces us to South Asian pigmentocracy through the figure of Saleem's "mother" Amina, who was born Mumtaz and changes her name at her husband Ahmed's request. Born "black Mumtaz," albeit with "luminous skin" (57), she "who had come out of her mother's womb as black as midnight" (59), and whose "dark skin stood between her and the affections of her mother" (56), was "the blackie whom she [her mother] had never been able to love because of her skin of a South Indian fisherwoman" (60). Years later, soon after she and Ahmed are living in Delhi after their wedding, his coquettish cousin Zohra looks in on the young couple, and flirts openly with the young Ahmed, "then in the high-summer of his charm" (77): "Oh look, pink! But then you are so fair, cousinji! . . . Just like me, don'tyouthink? . . . Lovely pink babies we'll have, a perfect match, no, cousinji, pretty white couples?" (77). With Amina out of sight, Zohra continues: "How awful to be black, cousinji, to wake every morning and see it staring at you, in the mirror to be shown proof of your inferiority! Of course they know; even blackies know white is nicer, don'tyouthinkso?" (77). Spying Amina, who has just walked in, Zohra cries: "'Oh, present company excluded, *of course!*' just in case, not being sure whether she's been overheard or not, and 'Oh, Ahmed, cousinji, you are really too dreadful to think I meant our lovely Amina who really isn't so black but only like a white lady standing in the shade!'" (78). Amina's mother's and Zohra's prejudice against Amina's dark complexion calls out a widely shared dislike of dark skin in the subcontinental psyche. "Black" and "blackie" are derogatory terms routinely used by many characters in the novel, *including* Amina. "'Saleem, you've dubashed [messed up] your room again, you black man!' Mary would cry" (151), while Amina scolds the young boy thus: "'You black man! Goonda!'" (151, 194). "When I spilt 7-Up on the carpet or sneezed into my dinner," Saleem confides, "the worst my uncle would say was 'Hai-yo! Black man!'" (289). At the same time, the text makes explicit reference to "fair-skinned northerners reviling Dravidian 'blackies'" and Pakistanis cursing Bangladeshi fellow Muslims as "blackies" (306).

Rushdie goes to some lengths to underline the shame of darkness through numerous references to his dark mother and to his father's pleased response to being afflicted by vitiligo because it lightens his skin.

> [Ahmed] was secretly rather pleased when they [doctors] failed to explain the problem or prescribe a cure, because he had long envied Europeans their pigmentation. One day . . . he told Lila Sabarmati at the cocktail hour: "All the best people are white under the skin; I have merely given up pretending." His neighbours, all of whom were darker than he, laughed politely and felt curiously ashamed. (212)

Skin, "the most visible of fetishes," and the implications of being "white under the skin" are reconjugated in Rushdie's literalization of hybridity as biological transformation (Bhabha, *The Location of Culture,* 78, 212). Rushdie then goes a step further by hitching color and its submerged nod toward race and to other more clearly social and *economic* texts: Ahmed's is not a solitary condition: "The businessmen of India were turning white" (212). In alloying color with the ostensibly dephenomenalized character of capital, moreover, Rushdie yokes together color, capital, and colonialism.

In addition to enshrining civilizational hierarchies among racially diverse colonized people, colonialism and the civilizing mission also fortified hierarchies intraculturally and intranationally, exposing internal fissures and creating new ones. Saleem's father, Ahmed, who is marginal in a Hindu national narrative and belittled in a colonial one, is described as bedeviled by the question of origins and fabricates "fictional ancestors" in a bid to rival William Methwold's pedigree (128). Simultaneously victim of a civilizational hangover and a colonial concussion, Ahmed, "anxious to impress the departing Englishman," "apeing Oxford drawl," had laid claim to "Mughal blood": "Wrong side of the blanket, of course, but Mughal certainly" (127). "To hammer his point home," Ahmed invents a family curse that will haunt him in years to come, proving that one can be haunted by fiction as much as by the truth. His fictional claim to a sort of hypergamy, even if illegitimate, comes with no reward, not even the temporary psychological solace of having passed off a tall tale as truth, because the departing colonizer responds insultingly with "a veiled hint of amusement in his eyes" (127). In a free India, his assets frozen, Ahmed is enveloped in "the old aroma of failure which hung about him from the earliest days," steeped, like others living in fictions of the self in the nation, in a "Djinn-sodden" history plagued by ghosts and the unfinished business of the past (242). Saleem's accidental primus inter pares status as the chosen midnight's child born in a bourgeois family is thus haunted at the outset not only by the suppressed history of Anglo-Indians but also by an anxious Muslim identity also seeking its own secure genealogy within the text of a Hindu majority nation born in a bloodbath while the colonizers have got off scot-free.

Postcolonial scholars, Bhabha prominent among them, have labored to develop theories of hybridity that challenge the ruse of origins. Rushdie's repeated confrontations with the problem of race suggest that interstitiality, or indeterminacy, of identity is nonetheless no armor against racism. Colonial encounter may well have compounded anxieties about origins, not only through its politics of divide and rule but also through its reanimation of the Aryan thesis.

Along with the usual racial politics associated with colonialism, an additional vector of imperial biopower is the mirroring of colonial prejudices toward those seen as inferior in its own population and the development of prejudicial structures in the colony in dialogue with indigenous prejudices and divides. Classist and other diversities of expression *within* cultures reinforce the hierarchies implicit in the civilizing project, even if they are routinely overlooked to produce the ideological average in discussions of intercultural encounter. If colonial aesthetics produced (menacing) subjects "*almost the same but not white,*" they also produced a class of persons distinct from the rest of the native population, as Macaulay's minute had promised all along (Bhabha, *The Location of Culture,* 86–87). English, at once an adjective and a noun, must be understood simultaneously as language, culture, *and* class. English is a "class act." Along with caste, financial status, and other existing hierarchies, colonial education and the anatomopolitics of the civilizing mission introduce an additional mode of class formation in the subcontinent. A recombination of *native* markers of elite status with the comportmental aesthetics associated with Englishness introduce a new bioaesthetic fault line evidenced not least in new techniques of the body associated with the "better sort" of natives: liberal education, posh accents, and the brandishing of commodity aesthetics, grooming practices, and so on (Rushdie, *Midnight's Children,* 147). What I have earlier referred to as the moral economy of the animal, moreover, is another, underreported text that underwrites the psychocorporeal transformation of the "better" sort of postcolonial humanimal under the aegis of the civilizing mission.

Saleem is one of a host of "Bleddy Macaulay's minutemen" in Rushdie's fictions. In *The Moor's Last Sigh,* Vasco Miranda points to the distance between this secular elite and the rest: "Bunch of English-medium misfits, the lot of you. Minority group members. . . . Country's as alien to you as if you were what's-the-word lunatics. Moon-men. You read the wrong books, get on the wrong side in every argument, think the wrong thoughts. Even your bleddy dreams grow from foreign roots" (165–66). Vasco Miranda does not mention the remaking of flesh implicit in the revision of daily motions and functions, but they include, as Saleem's mother Amina notes, British-style bathrooms, with "no water near the pot" and the unbelievable practice of "wiping . . . bottoms with paper only!," a practice that is widespread in today's India with squat toilets gradually disappearing from newer constructions in urban locations (110).

The list of "bleddy Minutemen" includes Saladin Chamcha, who "prayed for an English victory" when the English team played India, a proclivity admittedly rare in postcolonial India (Rushdie, *The Satanic Verses,* 37). Postcolonial minutemen, sold on an English-medium understanding of the meaning of progress, development, and self-election as superior, were designed to continue the legacy of the former rulers in their polished accents. In a corpus that teems with aspirational cultural hybrids, Chamcha discovers the traps that lie in a return home, as memory, place, and earlier training threaten to overturn the careful cultivation of better form. In a fit of jet-lagged stupor, he finds himself reverting to an Indian accent when awakened by the flight attendant on his way back to London from India:

> *Something to drink, sir? A drink?,* and Saladin, emerging from the dream, found his speech unaccountably metamorphosed into the Bombay lilt he had so diligently (and so long ago!) unmade. "Achha, means what?" he mumbled. "Alcoholic beverage or what?" And, when the stewardess reassured him, whatever you wish, sir, all beverages are gratis, he heard, once again, his traitor voice: "So, okay, bibi, give one whiskysoda only." (*The Satanic Verses,* 34)

Chamcha has spent a long time learning to manage his bodily emissions and effluences—its sounds and its fluids—in accord with English taste and "civilized" society, and what I have earlier referred to as the civilizational code of postanimal aesthetics. Chamcha's relapse occasions "a nasty surprise" and fear that he will regress into the discredited ways of the uncultivated native:

> How had the past bubbled up, in transmogrified vowels and vocab? What next? Would he take to putting coconut-oil in his hair? Would he take to squeezing his nostrils between thumb and forefinger, blowing noisily and drawing forth a glutinous silver arc of muck? Would he become a devotee of professional wrestling? What further, diabolic humiliations were in store? He should have known it was a mistake to *go Home,* after so long, how could it be other than a regression; it was an unnatural journey; a denial of time; a revolt against history; the whole thing was bound to be a disaster. (*The Satanic Verses,* 34)

Chamcha's list of "diabolical humiliations" includes a host of practices Fanon would have described as the native's "original forms of existing" (*Toward the*

African Revolution, 38); in the subcontinent, grooming with hair oil, cleaning out phlegm in the manner Chamcha has come to loathe, and the love of indigenous wrestling have been cast into the narrative of tradition at best and regression at worst.

Chamcha's fears of regression stem from a fear of being seen as inadequately postanimal in his speech as well as other bodily expressions. As he fears, the labor of this assimilated immigrant can be undone in a minute, as history bursts through a weak moment on the part of the mimic, or a strong one on the part of the Enoch Powells of the world. On his way to the detention center for other immigrants with less polished accents, Chamcha will learn that he is one among many perceived as "all the same . . . animals [who can't be expected] to observe civilized standards" (*The Satanic Verses,* 159). Chamcha is incredulous: "This isn't England. . . . How could it be, after all; where in that moderate and common-sensical land was there room for such a police van in whose interior such events as these might possibly transpire?" (158). A failure to study the sources of one's subscriptions can be dangerous. Outside the colonized nation that has also placed its trust in these borrowed Enlightenment values despite its collective experience of racism, scores of immigrants confront the limits of ideas that promise equality in principle but withhold it in the breach. In postcolonial Ellowen-Deewon, as *The Satanic Verses* elaborates at length, voice-over artist Saladin Chamcha, minuteman and mimic par excellence, confronts what writer Amitav Ghosh has described as "the +R," the racism of the English, which scans him as incorrigible despite years of self-delusion and whole-hearted subscription to a liberal ideology that was to have delivered him to a utopia above race, color, and tribe because he was liberal, secular, and enlightened.[14]

In a conversation with the historian Dipesh Chakrabarty, Amitav Ghosh insists that "Race [+R] is the unstated term through which the gradualism of liberalism reconciles itself to the permanence of Empire. Race is the category that accommodates the notion of incorrigibility, hence assuming the failure of all correctional efforts (and thus of tutelage)" ("Reflections," 152). Signing on to the program of modernity, Ghosh insists, enjoins a denial, repression, or outright erasure of memories of humiliation and shame in the colonial past. Indeed, the inculcation of bourgeois civility as an effect of colonialism may well have served to repress postcolonial anger at the debasement of native forms of existence. Ghosh suggests that intellectuals "flinch" at the juncture between racism and liberal tutelage because it "contaminates that aspect of liberal western thought in which *our own hopes of social betterment* . . . are often founded." But then he goes on, "don't we have to ask also, at what point does our aversion to this subject become either complicity or denial?" (154; emphasis added).[15] Chamcha's fears may well be founded in anxieties about falling out of favor in English society and its civilized standards since he has hoped to pass as a "better sort of native," but it is worth noting that they are also occasioned by his fear of being thought lacking by an *Indian* flight attendant on an expensive journey usually reserved for the better sort of Indian among other Indians during the period of time described in the novel. While the novel dwells at length on the humiliations of being thought incorrigible by the English, it also seems to matter to Saleem that the flight attendant not confuse him with lesser Indians.

It is the fate of the ordinary masses—the unconverted, unpolished hoi polloi—that Saleem is supposed to be spared by "the crime of Mary Pereira." Mary is Saleem's nanny, formerly a midwife at the nursing home where Saleem and Shiva are born (*Midnight's Children,* 135). Saleem's not-so-immaculate conception requires a Joseph for his Mary: "Like every Mary she had her Joseph" (119). A disorderly orderly at the hospital, Joseph D'Costa is a radical class activist, a figure for the troubled masses whose ghost will become Rushdie's tongue-in-cheek reference to the Marxist idea of the specter of communism. To curry favor with Joseph's subversive credo and thus, she hopes, to gain his love, Mary impulsively commits "her own private revolutionary" act of switching the name tags of two infants born at Doctor Narlikar's nursing home at the same hour, sealing their fate by "giving the poor baby a life of privilege and condemning the rich-born child to accordions and poverty" (135). Shortly after this domestic-scaled version of class reversal, Joseph, the champion of the people, is captured with his homemade bombs and killed by the police (174). Saleem is reborn as the "little laad-sahib [English Lordship] . . . from the big rich hill" in a "world cocooned in money and starched white clothes and things things things" on account of Mary's unconsummated love for Joseph (228, 526). Mary furnishes the precondition of Saleem's presumptuous self-selection as the voice of the nation *after* the lowborn racial hybrid has been repositioned in an outlandish Bollywood-style story of babies switched at birth, a passer *malgré lui.* Saleem, never intended to be its voice, is class-positioned by Mary, and therefore saved by "education or class-origins," as he puts it, allowing him to tell the story of the nation by "a show of erudition . . . and the purity of my accents" (254). Class position, liberal education, a show of erudition, and purity of accents, Rushdie suggests, successfully shame Saleem's fellow Indians into "feeling unworthy of judging" a man whose tale not only strains credibility but the bounds of sanity.

Accordingly, Saleem is processed through the laboratory of missionary education at the "Cathedral and John Connon Boys' High School run 'under the auspices' of the Anglo-Scottish Education Society" (192). Originally, India's European schools were not "nurseries for the ruling race," and "placed an individual within the racially *amorphous* realms of the 'country born,' which included both domiciled Europeans [poorer whites] and Anglo-Indians" (Buettner, "Problematic Spaces, Problematic Races," 286). Gail Coelho suggests that mingling with lower British classes, Anglo-Indians would have learned English informally through exposure "to less prestigious BrE dialects" ("Anglo-Indian English," 568). Coelho cites Spencer on perceptions of accent: "British attitudes towards the accent also appear to have been absorbed by many middle-class Indians. It is not uncommon . . . to find a middle-class Indian mother rebuking her child for picking up a chee-chee accent as a result of attending an Anglo-Indian school" (568). Buettner explains, "just as accent was an important marker of class, cultural, and regional background in Britain, in colonial India 'chi chi' English was widely viewed as a sign of social and racial 'contamination'" ("Problematic Spaces, Problematic Races," 284). Among the many names designating the group—"Mestizo," "Oolandez," "Wallendez," "Mustees," "Metis," and "Fringy," among others—was the nominal *Chee Chee,* a sound bite of disgust in turn regrafted upon the racially mixed body. Yule and Burnell define *Chee Chee* as

> a disparaging term applied to half-castes or Eurasians . . . and also to their manner of speech . . . said to be taken from "chi" (Fie!), a common native (South Indian) interjection of remonstrance or reproof, supposed to be much used by the class in question. The term is, however, perhaps also a kind of onomatopoeia, indicating the mincing pronunciation which often characterizes them. (186)[16]

Buettner reports, "a girl enrolled at Auckland House School in Simla reassured her parents that 'I try to talk carefully, and I don't think we'll come home speaking chee-chee'" ("Problematic Spaces, Problematic Races," quoted 288–89).[17] By the time Saleem gains admission to it, the missionary school would have acquired its second life as an exclusive source of education for the well-heeled, yielding some of Mumbai's most prestigious alumni.

At the young age of nine, "washed and brushed every morning, I stood at the foot of our two-storey hillock, white-shorted, wearing a blue-striped elastic belt with a snake-buckle," says Saleem as he prepares for his exclusive education (*Midnight's Children,* 181). Saleem's will be a voice full of money, convent-educated accents, and things. A turn down the lane leading to

Saleem's childhood home discloses Reader's Paradise, the bookstore where he must have bought his Superman comics, Chimalker's Toyshop, and Bombelli's the Confectioners, with their cake and "One Yard of Chocolates!" in a brief glimpse of this privileged upbringing and the coming explosion of commodity culture after the liberalization of India's economy in a world already full of things in the "hillock-top world" (526).[18] One of Saleem's proudest possessions is a globe bearing the legend, MADE AS ENGLAND (319). The voice of the nation is not only a product of the class-sensitive "crime of Mary Pereira" for her Joseph, but something like a crime wave, one in which we might include the crimes of colonialism that produced the empire, educated it in the English language, now rewards it lavishly for writing back in the former master's tongue, and creates new hierarchies based on language, education, things, and the "purity of accents." The acquisition of capital qua capital as well as cultural capital through bodily reform, commodity aesthetics, liberal education, gadgetry, and other prosthetics furnish the biosocial weapons for primacy in the new jungles of civilization and modernity.[19]

In yet another unreported crime, we learn that Shiva's true parents, the Sinais, never once "set out to look for the true son of their blood," a failure Saleem ascribes to a "lack of imagination," while acknowledging that "worse interpretations" were possible, "such as their reluctance to accept into their bosom an urchin who had spent eleven years in the gutter" (360–61). This belated speculative admission might explain why, as Saleem alleges, "when we eventually discovered the crime of Mary Pereira, we all found that it *made no difference!* I was still their son: they remained my parents" (136). As it turns out, the revelation *does* make a difference. Saleem is exiled and his father's tenuous hold on reality and sanity are strained to the breaking point, triggering a return of paranoid anxieties about origins and belonging. And yet, Saleem tells us, "if you had asked my father (even him, despite all that happened!) who his son was, nothing on earth would have induced him to point in the direction of the accordionist's knock-kneed, unwashed boy" (137). Beyond this family-scaled anxiety about origins is a nation's paranoia about making its voice heard on the world stage of modernity in the cultured accents of liberal education. Saleem's parents have little interest in their real son, who is impoverished, uneducated, and prone to violence. While Saleem is positioned to stand in for the metaphorical hybridity of all of India, Shiva, equally midnight's child, could never be the voice of the nation, although he is recruited as its hammer with his powerful knees. Moreover, Saleem's own dislike of Shiva, the true heir of the Sinai family, is founded not only in guilt at having stolen his heritage but in his perception of the "crudity of his ideas," as well as "the roughness of his tongue" (271). Crude, raw, impoverished, and undereducated, Shiva has learned the language of violence, ironically directed not least upon those who remain in the slums in which he himself has been raised.

What Rushdie calls "the Rhesus factor," which betrays Saleem's true heritage with fateful results, is also an arch reference to those parts of liberal ideology that inseminate postcolonial thought, leading to delusions of representative government, in the name of which those not born to its privileges can be treated as less than human. That most "mysterious of sanguinary attributes, known as rhesus, which is also a type of monkey" (*Midnight's Children,* 271) points its unanswerable finger at those whose accidents of birth make them available for bestialization, sterilization, and displacement in the name of development, their homes razed in the name of urban beautification during the Emergency.[20] Authorized by the son of the prime minister, the slums that house the midnight's poorest children are declared "a public eyesore" and razed under a "Civic Beautification programme" (511) that begs comparison with the civilizational re-formation of the nation's chosen class of persons, the ones who get to define what it means to be classy, and entail in this self-definition contempt for the ugliness of those who are déclassé because they have been left behind in the underserved, malodorous, unhygienic slums of a progressive history that does not confront the ugliness of its own contaminated logic:

> From the vans there poured a stream of finely-dressed young ladies of high birth and foreign education, and then a second river of equally-well-dressed young men: volunteers, Sanjay Youth volunteers, doing their bit for society . . . but then I realized no, not volunteers, because all the men had the same curly hair and lips-like-women's-labia, and the elegant ladies were all identical, too . . . standing in the chaos of the slum clearance programme, I was shown once again that the ruling dynasty of India had learned how to replicate itself. (*Midnight's Children,* 511)

In what is tantamount to biological warfare on those obliged to live closer to a state of nature, the slum-dwellers are led to vasectomy tents in the name of a civic, civil project of beautification that targets its poorest hut-dwellers for culling. The erasure of a slum "where cockroaches spawned, where rats made love, where flies gorged themselves on pie-dog dung" resurrects the figure of the animal even as civic beautification begins to look like pest control (465). To Ghosh's appending of "+R" to liberal ideology, we might then add, "+C" and "+A," which is to say class and the Rhesus factor that recalls the specter of unredeemed animal being.

The unexpected rise of Saleem's historical twin, Shiva, once a slum-dweller, offers further indictment of the ironies of melioration and social betterment. Shiva explodes onto the scene at the same time as "India's arrival . . . at the nuclear age" (486). Harnessing his hopes for social betterment to war, Shiva becomes one more example of the ways in which "war and war only can set a goal for mass movements on the largest scale while respecting the traditional property system," as Walter Benjamin observes (*Illuminations,* 241). Benjamin notes that the aesthetics of war appears as follows: "If the natural utilization of productive forces is impeded by the property system, the increase in technical devices, in speed, and in the sources of energy will press for an unnatural utilization, and this is found in war" (242). This is why, as the Futurists note, war is beautiful, for humankind's "self-alienation has reached such a degree that it can experience its own destruction as an aesthetic pleasure of the first order" (242). The pipeline from a position of class immobility into the army is a familiar one in many nations. Rushdie's alertness to the mobilization of its poorest for the nation's defense from its foreign others, as well as the others within, becomes evident in his exploration of Shiva's career as enforcer within the nation as well as its martial arm without.

Shiva's fortunes rise in the Bangladesh war of 1971, as legends of his exploits "leaped into newspaper and into magazines, and thus insinuated themselves into the salons of the well-to-do . . . so that Shiva found himself elevated in social status as well as military rank" (*Midnight's Children,* 487). Shiva subsequently becomes known as a ladies' man, "a cuckolder of the rich; in short, a stud" (487). He also develops a reputation for deserting "the bedrooms of all who bore his children" (488). Among those he impregnates and abandons are Parvati from the slums and Roshanara from the elevated social circle to which he has been admitted as a war hero. Horrified at his impregnation of Parvati, Shiva confronts "a balloon-fronted slum girl, who now seemed to him to represent everything he most feared—she became the personification of the slums of his childhood, from which he had escaped, and which now, through her, through her damnable child, were trying to drag him down down down again" (492).

Shiva's intercourse with the rich, however, had never been other than tenuous. Roshanara, the spurned society woman, exacts her revenge in terms of the very ways of being Shiva has learned to be ashamed of:

> Callously she whispered that it was so funny, my God, the way he strutted around in high society like some kind of rooster, while all the time the ladies were laughing at him behind his back, O yes, Major Sahib, don't fool yourself, high-class women have always enjoyed sleeping with animals peasants brutes,

> but that's how we think of you, my God it's disgusting just to watch you eat, gravy down your chin, don't you think we see how you never hold teacups by their handles, do you imagine we can't hear your belches and breakings of wind, you're just our pet ape, Major Sahib, very useful, but basically a clown. (489)

Shiva's cruel education in the caprice of meliorative aesthetics and liberal tutelage is worth quoting in full:

> After the onslaught of Roshanara Shetty, the young war hero began to see his world differently. Now he seemed to see women giggling behind fans wherever he went; he noticed strange amused sidelong glances which he'd never noticed before; and although he tried to improve his behaviour, it was no use, he seemed to become clumsier the harder he tried, so that food flew off his plate on to priceless Kelim rugs and belches broke from his throat with the roar of a train emerging from a tunnel and he broke wind with the rage of typhoons. His glittering new life became, for him, a daily humiliation; and now he reinterpreted the advances of the beautiful ladies, understanding that by placing their love-notes beneath their toes they were obliging him to kneel demeaningly at their feet . . . he learned that a man may possess every manly attribute and still be despised for not knowing how to hold a spoon. (489)

Language, technics, prosthetics—the attributes of the human that are refused to the animal—furnish the scale from which civilized taste draws its authority. Shiva's failure by the rubric of civilization, where empty forms overtake all other considerations, fuels his hatred against those in power as well as those without it, like himself. Saleem claims that he knows that this is why Shiva grabbed the chance at power when offered the chance by the Emergency—a project that will turn his violence loose upon his own.[21]

In yet another twist in the narrative, the same war that makes Shiva a hero reduces Saleem, for a short period, to preverbal, macrosmatic existence as a sniffer man-dog in service of CUTIA (meaning "bitch" in Hindi), the Canine Unit for Tracking and Intelligence Activities deployed during the Bangladesh War. Deprived of speech, the defining attribute of the human in contradistinction to the animal in most philosophical traditions, he is an object of derision and abuse. Both children of midnight are pressed into service in the war machine, Shiva on the Indian side and Saleem on the Pakistani. The redirection of this "nasal inheritance" from its powerful uses as the instrument of a "nasal ethics" that allows him to sniff out "the olfactory incompatibility of Islam and socialism, and the inalienable opposition existing between the after-shave of Sind Club members and the poverty-reek of the street-sleeping beggars at the Club gates" points to the perversion of a sensory capacity for sniffing out injustice and inequality in favor of prejudicial, and indeed violent, uses (*Midnight's Children,* 380). Classen's observation that the "Latin word *sagax* (sagacious), meant both a keen sense of smell and a shrewd mind," suggests a body-mind relationship that would change over time to divorce the two and repress humanity's biological and animal prehistory (*The Color of Angels,* 59). The uses of the nose for pleasure, too, have come to be restricted.[22] Elias shows "how the use of the sense of smell, the tendency to sniff at food or at other things, has come to be restricted as something animal-like" (*The Civilizing Process,* 17). Even though "in terms of the numbers and sizes of sebaceous and apocrine glands, man has to be considered as quite by far the most highly scented ape of all" (Stoddart, *The Scented Ape,* 51), Alain Corbin explains

> Sniffing and smelling, a predilection for powerful animal odors, the erotic effect of sexual odors—all become objects of suspicion. Such interests, thought to be essentially savage, attest to a proximity to animals, a lack of refinement, and an ignorance of good manners. In short, they reveal a basic failure at the level of social education. The sense of smell is at the bottom of the hierarchy of senses, along with the sense of touch. Furthermore, Kant disqualified it aesthetically. (*The Foul and the Fragrant,* 7)

Corbin concludes that "Kant excluded it [smell] from aesthetics . . . Freud assigned it to anality" (229).[23] So successful were the psychosocial mechanisms used to reeducate the senses and produce models for civilized comportment that Jews being led to the gas chambers were led to believe that they were going into a bathroom where they would be free "from lice, dirt, and the stench of human sweat and excrement. Rational people will go quietly, meekly, joyously into a gas chamber, if only they are allowed to believe it is a bathroom" (Bauman, *Modernity and Holocaust,* 203).

Saleem's conscription as a man-dog tracker of other humans occurs after he is brained by an airborne spittoon—in the family since it was given as a gift to his mother, Amina, and her first husband, Nadir—in the explosion that annihilates his whole family in Karachi. Delinked from a legitimating bourgeois family apparatus, Saleem devolves into an amnesiac man-dog without the power of speech in a bizarre sort of species reversal. During months of training as a tracker of undesirables, he sits under a tree, hugging the silver spittoon, "with a foolish smile on his lips—as if he were actually happy that he'd lost his brains" (*Midnight's Children,* 419). He has taken, moreover, to "the art form of the masses" (535); his teeth and gums are stained with betel juice: "'Ekkkhh-thoo!' (He spits)" into his beloved spittoon (417). Raised in a home where children were chided for "bad table manners," Saleem now sits on the ground, heedless of the conventions of modern civility (180). Later, bemoaning its loss when the spittoon is bulldozed in the civic beautification of his slum, Saleem's observation on a gestural object redolent with past ways, albeit unhygienic, is as follows: "you should never underestimate a spittoon" (535).

The spittoon is an overloaded symbol in the text: sometimes it points to the past and memory, and at others to a yonic receptacle for phallic projection, as in Saleem's regretful failure to "hit [Padma's] spittoon" (39). In attending, additionally, to its material use for expectoration—the spittoon is a "lost receptacle of memories as well as spittle-juice"—the narrator alerts us to the confrontation between outmoded ways of managing bodily fluids and their newer expressions in ways that are deemed more proper to modern times (535). Coverage of Margaret Thatcher's meetings with Deng Xiaoping over the fate of Hong Kong in 1982 make repeated reference to the latter's liberal use of a white enamel spittoon, sometimes photoshopped out of press photographs, with the practice drawing comment in almost all media coverage of the meeting. "There has been a lively debate," one British official is reported as saying, "about whether Deng's habit of spitting while receiving visitors is done for effect, or whether he really is a vulgar old bugger" ("Hong Kong History"). Once used in the West outside bars and other public houses, spittoons are rarely found now, although cuspidors—from the Portuguese "to spit" / "place for spitting" (*cuspir/cuspidouro*)—are used by wine tasters under an opaque sobriquet that seems to sanitize the activity, in part because it now serves the instrumental purpose of testing, tasting, and grading wine rather than the idle pastime of old men sending out long arcs of betel juice "further and further from their squatting place" (45). Long before his beloved spittoon is bulldozed in Delhi, Saleem tells Padma the story of a "prince, or Nawab, [who] believed passionately in progress." "It grieved him," Saleem says, "that his subjects, who had become used to using the roads of Kif for purposes of social intercourse, quarrels and games of hit-the-spittoon, refused to get out of [the] way" of his Rolls-Royce motor car. The prince issues a "proclamation explaining that the car represented the future, and must be allowed to pass." Subsequent notices alert his subjects that "the car would henceforth run down anybody who failed to obey its horn." By the time Saleem's sister, Jamila the singer, comes to visit, she is able to pass smoothly from border to palace; "the Nawab said proudly, 'No trouble; the car is respected now. Progress has occurred'" (*Midnight's Children,* 383). Once an art object, "pukka [proper, first-class] goods," as Saleem's fellow soldier describes it in the screenplay version of the novel, the spittoon is now what stands in the way of the future as a reminder of the vulgar, bodily past that must be overcome in a nation anxious to restore its claims to modernity.

At the same time, aesthetic norms are also subject to revaluation as previously acceptable practices can be discredited and later recredited. In the early days of British presence in India, several Englishmen are described as having taken to the ways of the Mughal court. William Kirkpatrick is described as smoking a hookah, sporting Indian-style "mustachios," with his "fingers dyed with henna" (*White Mughals,* 90). William Dalrymple reports that "moreover, James had taken on the Eastern habit of belching appreciatively after meals," in addition to making "all sorts of other odd noises" while clearing his throat and his nostrils "in the enthusiastic and voluble Indian manner" (90). Mauss recounts the tale of the shah of Persia eating with his fingers as a guest of Napoleon III. Refusing his host's offer of a golden fork, he said, "You don't know what a pleasure you are missing" ("Techniques of the Body," 84). By the standards of today's polite society, eating with one's hands and fingers is a dubious practice. In a 2012 article in the *New York Times,* Amitav Ghosh wrote that "he doesn't go to Indian restaurants in London and New York because eating with hands is discouraged." Ghosh speculates that "Indians don't want non-Indians to see them eating with their hands and . . . Westerners don't want to see it either" (quoted in DiGregorio, "Mind Your Manners"). In the same year, the *Huffington Post* reported that Indians were outraged by Oprah Winfrey's remark, "I heard some Indian people eat with their hands still" during her special on India ("Oprah's India Special"). Veteran Indian journalist M. J. Akbar chose to adopt a very matter-of-fact tone in response: "History confirms that the major power of an era determines what becomes socially correct within the penumbra of its influence" ("Oprah's India Special"). In "Mind Your Manners," DiGregorio noted a new trend in utensil-optional restaurants, citing Korean American chef Roy Choi's comment, "I hope that people let their guard down and throw out some of the rules we have regarding etiquette and connect like animals." The association of traditional forms of eating, expectoration, and postures of evacuation with poor taste and animal behavior that came with the rise of imperial power reminds us that the jewel-encrusted spittoon is not only an overvalued symbol of the past and old traditions—with their own regimes of aestheticizing bodily practices and announcing their class status—but a reminder of their inevitable supercession by new aesthetic forms defined by those in power.

Before its conclusive destruction during the Emergency civic beautification program, however, man-dog Saleem was able to carry the spittoon with him into jungles "so thick that history has hardly ever found a way in" as he deserts the Pakistani army and its ruthless eradication program (*Midnight's Children,* 429). His violent participation in the war finally leads Saleem "into the history-less anonymity of rain-forests," where the unit members confront their misdeeds and are led "towards a new adulthood" in a negation of their narrowly walled concept-driven identities (431, 436). The jungle echoes with the lamentations of those they have hunted, and the men are forced to attune their senses to the suffering of others. Adorno famously avers, "the physical moment tells knowledge that suffering ought not to be, that things should be different" (*Negative Dialectics,* 203). In palpable encounters with a history that hurts, the clamor of lamentation reaches them in fleshy, incarnate moments of sensation and perception, try as they might to stuff mud in their ears. In the jungle, Saleem and the others feel the shame and guilt that one would like to think of as some of the better attributes of the human conscious of the suffering of others, perhaps more so than the language, technics, and prosthetics of the civilized human world. The possibility of a new adulthood looms in this turn toward suffering, only to recede as the group leaves the jungle. Saleem's subsequent history suggests that these moments of knowledge will not survive his brief encounter with the history-less sanctuary where raw instinct still serves a feasible purpose: that of drawing attention to one's own suffering and that of others. What he has known as his old life awaits, and will reclaim him as he returns to the urban spaces of civilization and history.

Overturning Mary's insurrectionary class reversal, Saleem's magical return to India places him in the slums of his original destiny. A long way from "the big rich hill" (*Midnight's Children,* 228), Saleem lives for a while with the wretched of the earth, finding magical possibilities there that the nation-state cannot recognize. No longer one of the "better sort" but part of the very dregs of the nation, he suffers their indignities and their fate until he betrays the midnight's children to ensure his own freedom because he has been "forced into treachery by the treason of another" (517). Shiva's treason triggers his own; they both undergo vasectomies, led into a chamber where, "because we are not savages, sir, air conditioning units had been installed, and a table with a hanging lamp, and doctors nurses" (522). Their generative potential is effectively neutered under the logic of the Emergency, a state, Benjamin reminds us, that "is not the exception but the rule" if we pay attention to "the tradition of the oppressed" (*Illuminations,* 257).

Saleem is spared a prolonged share in the fate of the wretched of the earth, once again through the offices of Mary. The end of (Saleem's) history takes him home to "the only mother I had left in the world" (*Midnight's Children,* 545), but his way there is facilitated on the one hand by "Businessism . . .

India's other true faith" (474), and on the other, by his genetically fortuitous nasal competence. Saleem will smell and taste his way home, thanks to "that impossible chutney of memory" made by none other than Mary Pereira, whose potentially misleading assumption of a pseudonym, "Braganza Pickles (Private) Ltd . . . best in Bombay, everyone knows," fails to throw Saleem off the scent (544). Mary's choice of Braganza for her pickle label establishes a direct line of descent from the colonial context that brought the islands of Bombay to the British crown through Catherine of Braganza's marriage to Charles II; Mary "has stolen the name of poor Queen Catherine who gave these islands to the British" (547). By this time, Mary's fortunes have changed. Mary and Alice, once more conventionally employed for "anglos" as nurse, secretary, nanny, have now become proprietors of the globally marketed Braganza Pickles, with Alice, former Coca-Cola girl, controlling the finances as respectable "Mrs. Fernandes," even if she, Saleem suspects, "still has her little liaisons" (548).[24] Mary, "the criminal of midnight," is now "Rich Mary, who never dreamed she would be rich" and who now "drinks sixteen Coca-Colas a day" as a sign of her arrival in a society that prizes things and spectacular forms of consumption (547).[25] She has consequently lost her teeth—defanged in her postanimal incarnation, one is tempted to conclude—and occupies with her sister an apartment in almost the exact same space as that vacated years before by the then-prosperous Sinai family in a since demolished palace.

Places have once again been traded: the criminal of midnight is now a respectable proprietor in the same space "where once . . . she slept on a servant's mat" (546), and in command of the prospect of the "Bom bahia," or "good harbor," which prompted the Portuguese to give the city its name, according to Saleem (106). Mary has fulfilled her early promise as a champion place-swapper in a peaceful, private class reversal through businessism in a contemporary, Indianized version of the career of her distant Portuguese ancestors: the spice trade that had set them sailing hundreds of years ago, and ostensibly inaugurated the dawn of modernity and the age of global corporations. Joseph D'Costa, instigator of her first, pivotal crime, would have been proud of her success, albeit on a scale of one, at most two, counting Alice, or three, including Saleem, who is, after all, a fellow Anglo-Indian, or four, counting Aadam, his son who is not his son, and is left to be raised in Mary's household. In a biographic, bibliographic vein, one notes that Rushdie dedicated an earlier draft of the novel to his family, and to his real-life nanny, "Mary Menezes who will never read it" (*Midnight's Children,* draft, Box 16, Folder 2). The published version of the novel dedicated the novel to his son who is his son, Zafar. In a psychobiographical mode, one might speculate that Rushdie's wishful culmination for the Mary Menezes figure in the novel serves to emphasize the poor odds of this kind of class mobility, even if the allegedly rising tide of economic liberalization after 1991 has arguably lifted a few boats. In *The Moor's Last Sigh,* which is arguably the sequel to *Midnight's Children,* the story of postliberalization India begins to be told. In it, Aadam will be reborn as Adam Braganza, "that twenty-first century kid," adopted—readopted as it were—legatee of Abraham Zogoiby's corrupt corporate empire in Bombay (359). By this time, the specter of communism seems to have receded almost entirely. At the end of history, in an India where the capitalist juggernaut is on a roll, the question in question may or may not be "who are you?" but rather, "how much are you worth?" In the new age dubbed liberal, Rushdie writes that "money . . . was breaking all the shackles on its desires" (*The Moor's Last Sigh,* 343).

In *Midnight's Children,* the impact of independence on the less privileged is measurable in terms at once historical, economic, and affective, through the Breach Candy pool, one of Rushdie's literalized metaphors for the nation. Saleem's retrospective on the fate of the Breach Candy Swimming Club in Bombay, where in colonial times "pink people could swim in a pool the shape of British India without fear of rubbing up against a black skin," furnishes an apt example of the transformation of colonial racial divides into postcolonial class divides (108). In the early years of Indian independence, this is what baby Saleem observes from his hill-top sanctuary:

> Here is India's first swimmer of the English Channel, Mr. Pushpa Roy [modeled after the real-life Brojen Das], arriving at the gates of the Breach Candy Pools. Saffron bathing cap on his head, green trunks wrapped in flag-hued towel, this Pushpa has declared war on the whites-only policy of the baths. He holds a cake of Mysore sandalwood soap; draws himself up; marches through the gate . . . whereupon hired Pathans seize him, Indians save Europeans from an Indian mutiny as usual, and out he goes, struggling valiantly, frogmarched into Warden Road and flung into the dust. (147)

The sight of the famous swimmer being denied access to the watery medium where he excels, evicted like a splayed-out lesser amphibian, punctuates Saleem's days throughout his childhood. In a curious anachronism, well after independence, the Breach Candy Swimming Club maintained a whites-only policy. In 1964, it began to admit nonwhites once a week (Memon, "Twenty Million People"). Saleem observes, "In the end his [Pushpa's] indomitable campaign won a victory, because today the Pools permit certain Indians—'the better sort'—to step into their map-shaped waters" (*Midnight's Children,* 147).

At the narrative end of the swimmer's saga, Pushpa, champion swimmer and the nation's standard-bearer in a competitive world, however, remains insufficiently reformed and capitalized; perhaps insufficiently pure of accents, he "does not belong," we are told, "to the better sort; old now and forgotten, he watches the Pools from afar" (147).

In its final consummate irony, the novel repeatedly offers a visual illustration of the material circumstances attending the story's composition, searing the following image of the nation's incarnate divides into the reader's imagination: Saleem, now a manager in Mary's pickle factory, composes his Anglophone confessions at his desk in a pool of "anglepoised light" in a posture befitting upright man, while "Dung-goddess" and audience surrogate Padma sits in his "shadows" at his "feet" (90, 141, 254). Saleem insists, "Padma is what matters—Padma-muscles, Padma's hairy forearms, Padma my own pure lotus" (353). Instead of an implied reader, we are given a living, breathing auditor written into the narrative as implausible witness. Like his real-life nanny, "Mary Menezes who will never read it," Padma will not be the reader because she is not a beneficiary of the liberal education the narrator has received up on the hill. She serves him well, however, as she tends to his many needs, not least to be listened to and to respond to his narrative. "The dance of her musculature" keeps him "on the rails" because he can detect in "her fibres the ripples of uninterest" (325). Saleem claims that his "squatting glimpser" is "captivated" (142).

But there is more to Padma's musculature than its function as a sign of her rapt attention to or distraction from Saleem's tale. If Fanon's discussion of the tonicity of the native's muscles indicates a complicated state of readiness to supplant the settler as well as compliance with the aesthetic regimes of the colonizer who has discredited his ways of existing, Padma's musculature reveals a body that has evolved very differently from Saleem's. "How I admire the leg-muscles of my solicitous Padma!" Saleem exclaims: "There she squats, a few feet from my table, her sari hitched up in fisherwoman-fashion. Calf-muscles show no sign of strain; thigh-muscles, rippling through sari-folds, display their commendable stamina. Strong enough to squat forever, simultaneously defying gravity and cramp." Saleem's admiration "extends also to her arms . . . her biceps and triceps [and] uncomplaining thews" (324–25). Padma's is the laboring body of someone who "stirs a bubbling vat all day for a living" alongside an "army of strong, hairy-armed, formidably competent women" (21, 197). Hers is the bodyness of differences that are acquired by conditions of class, work, and labor. She squats in a position that modern civilization has associated with supplication, defecation, and debasement. "Thick of waist, somewhat hairy of arm," she is squat, as suggested by the adjectival form of the word, and someone, moreover, who does not amount to squat, if we were to pursue another connotation of the term in its association with the worthless by-product of digestion. Beyond the confined orbit of yoga studies (which Mauss advocated early in the twentieth century), the "civilized" world has come to view squatting with suspicion. A nineteenth-century French physician's account of this bodily difference is rendered thus: "Savages squat whereas Civilized people sit, explained the doctor. A Batak, because of this, is akin to a monkey" (Regnault, quoted in Rony, *The Third Eye,* 3). Mauss explains in "Techniques of the Body": "The child normally squats. We no longer know how to. . . . It is a very stupid mistake to take it away from him" (77). Infants are believed to naturally adopt this posture for elimination until schooled away from it. Common to primates and man alike, it is a posture both for relaxation and a traditionally natural posture for efficient defecation.[26] Associations of the posture with primitive evolutionary functions have gradually led to a civilizing away from a position otherwise thought beneficial to the human body.[27] The renewal of biomedical interest in its benefits notwithstanding, squatting is associated with lower-class bodies even in societies where it has been customary for centuries. With increasing globalization, postures of sitting, ablution, and defecation accord more and more with Western ways, until the body itself has been bent out of the natural shape into which it had developed through millennia of evolution.

Padma's musculature is a vivid illustration of the bodyness of differences, muscular incarnation of the nation's divides. Saleem's plaintive plea to remember that "Padma is what matters—Padma-muscles, Padma's hairy forearms, Padma my own pure lotus" is belied by a history in which a rigid dividing line continues to separate those who sit and those who squat (*Midnight's Children,* 353). Handcuffed to history but also harnessed by it, midnight's minute-made child is a victim but also an agent of its exploitative, dominative rationality, reliant on the labor of his "solicitous Padma," his tale of the nation's history and its divides underwritten by his squatting auditor (*Midnight's Children,* 324).

2 SHIBBOLETH

Hybridity, Diaspora, and Passing in Hari Kunzru's The Impressionist

> The circumcision of the word must also be understood as an event of the body. . . . It is in the body, by reason of a certain impotence coming over their vocal organs, but an impotence of the body *proper*, of the already cultivated body, limited by a barrier neither organic nor natural, that the Ephraimites experienced their inaptitude to pronounce what they nonetheless knew ought to be pronounced *shibboleth*—and not *sibboleth*.
>
> —**JACQUES DERRIDA**, *SOVEREIGNTIES IN QUESTION*

> "Eric Cartman, you respect other cultures this instant!"
>
> "I wasn't saying anything about their culture. I'm just saying their city smells like ass."
>
> —***SOUTH PARK***

Chapattis or Bread? Alter-Natives

Urdu writer Saadat Hasan Manto's 1955 short story, "Toba Tek Singh," an allegorical retelling of the Indian partition that occurred in 1947, explores the dilemmas of identity in the wake of the traumatic division of countries and populations:

> Two or three years after Partition, it occurred to the governments of Pakistan and Hindustan that like criminal offenders, lunatics too ought to be exchanged: that is, those Muslim lunatics who were in Hindustan's insane asylums should be sent to Pakistan, and those Hindus and Sikhs who were in Pakistan's insane asylums should be confided to the care of Hindustan.

Along with an elaborate parody of political processes, the story lampoons that other staple of modernity: the nation, and with it, ideas of language, home, and belonging, issues that Indian historiography usually addresses with reference to Hindus, Sikhs, and Muslims. Among the motley crew of lunatics, however, Manto mentions those whose dilemma at the moment of India's independence and partition remains poorly recorded in mainstream history:

> In the European ward there were two Anglo-Indian lunatics. When they learned that the English had freed Hindustan and gone away, they were very much shocked. And for hours they privately conferred about the important question of what their status in the lunatic asylum would be now. Would the European Ward remain, or be abolished? Would breakfast be available, or not? Instead of proper bread, would they have to choke down those bloody Indian chapattis [unleavened flat bread]?

The focus subsequently shifts to the story's eponymous Sikh protagonist, but the passing nod to two players with bit parts in Indian national history—racially and culturally hybrid Anglo-Indians—invites consideration of the plight of those for whom the idea of a mother country was differently complicated than it might have been for Muslims, Hindus, and Sikhs at the time of independence. It dramatizes, moreover, the conjugation of identity and belonging through the problem of daily bread. "Proper bread," both an ingestible staff of life and a metonymic reference to colonial whites *and* their hybrid progeny, becomes an overloaded totemic symbol that is put into crisis by a consideration of the history of Anglo-Indians, the very differently "not quite / not white" subjects of colonialism, derogatorily referred to in Hari Kunzru's *The Impressionist* as "half-baked bread" (43).

In the chapter "By Bread Alone: Signs of Violence in the Mid-Nineteenth Century" in *The Location of Culture,* Bhabha examines the role that rumors played concerning the mysterious circulation of chapattis before the 1857 rebellion against the British in India. In his account of the rebellion, subaltern historian Ranajit Guha has examined the semiotics of the chapatti as opaque to the British but newly salient to the rebels in terms of an alternative language of insurgency. For Bhabha, the circulation of chapattis transforms the site of rebellion into one of cultural hybridity:

> The organizing principle of the *sign* of the chapati is constituted in the transmission of fear and anxiety, projection and panic in a form of circulation in-between the colonizer and the colonized. Could the agency of peasant rebellion be constituted through the 'partial incorporation' of the fantasy and fear of the Master? (*The Location of Culture,* 206)

Bhabha locates the "archaic, awesome, terrifying" turn in the "old and familiar symbol" in the *circulation* rather than the ipseity of the chapatti in the traffic between colonizer and colonized as part of the historical event of the 1857 rebellion (202). He goes on to suggest: "The margin of hybridity, where cultural differences 'contingently' and conflictually touch, becomes the moment of panic which reveals the borderline experience. It resists the binary opposition of racial and cultural groups, sipahis and sahibs, as homogeneous polarized political consciousness" (207). Parama Roy, in a more corporeal turn, has located the chapatti story within the "digestive troping of rebellion and counterinsurgency" (*Alimentary Tracts,* 32).

The valence of "proper bread" and chapatti clearly vary with the enunciative context in question, a point that Bhabha correctly emphasizes. Guha notes that rumors were also circulating before the 1857 rebellion to the effect that natives of all ranks would be obliged to feed upon "the most impure of all food, 'English bread'" (*Elementary Aspects of Peasant Insurgency,* 263). The significance of bread as the staff of life with a key role in the Christian mass, moreover, imbues the leavened product with considerable historical heft, adding a biospiritual dimension to the reasons why the rebels massacred converted Christians and half-whites along with whites during the mutiny. The subscription to "proper bread," as articulated by Manto's latter-day Anglo-Indian lunatics, therefore, would have functioned as an alternative sign during the rebellion. The somatic and alimentary logic of the rebellion, and the *ipseity* of the chapatti is of obvious interest here, with the proviso that the existence of a community caught between *sipahi* (soldier) and *sahib* (master) complicates the reading of cultural hybridity in a mode that can only deconstruct readily available binaries. Absent from the record is the quandary of racially mixed Eurasians with divided loyalties in the mutiny. According to historical accounts, some Eurasians joined the rebels, others were killed along with Europeans, and those that were either dark enough or fortunate enough to have a native, usually Muslim, name in addition to a Christian one, managed to evade the wrath of the rebels.

In the context of these excluded characters caught in the middle, chapatti and bread signify as dually *unheimlich* in doubly discursive and biobodily terms. And yet, as Freud concludes, "*heimlich* is a word the meaning of which develops in the direction of ambivalence, until it finally coincides with its opposite, *unheimlich. Unheimlich* is in some way or other a sub-species of *Heimlich*" (*Standard Edition,* 219). In the dissolution of categorical difference, the historically neglected Eurasian draws attention to contact zones *within* the nation, where bread and chapatti would have had variable salience, and we may have to confront the notion of a diaspora that never leaves home.[1] The Eurasian Anglo-Indian and the converted Christian who sometimes passed as racially mixed constitute the excluded middle in the usual traffic between binaries, asking for a reckoning with hybridity that can cope with the experience of a community caught between them in ways that disturb the notion of a third space reliant on binaries for agential and political charge.

Bhabha's stance on hybridity is perhaps clearest in some of the most widely quoted words on the topic in an interview with John Rutherford:

> All forms of culture are continually in a process of hybridity. But for me the importance of hybridity is not to be able to trace two original moments from which the third emerges, rather hybridity to me is the "third space," which enables other positions to emerge. This third space displaces the histories that constitute it, and in its place sets up new structures of authority and political initiatives. ("The Third Space," 211)

Hybridity as third space, resident in the crisis of signification, becomes the *navette* in the encounter between colonizer and colonized, reworking the effects of the colonial encounter as the production of hybridization "rather than the noisy command of colonialist authority or the silent repression of native traditions" (*The Location of Culture,* 112). However, the deconstructive, paleonymic shift in the understanding of the term "hybridity"—once used for racial hybrids—obscures a historically and discursively generated category of subjects in-between. Lost in the shuffle is *their* anxiety, *their* labor in crafting a livable cultural form, *their* stance toward chapattis as opposed to bread, no less born of the encounter between colonizer and colonized than hybridity as heresy.[2] It is this group, moreover, that instructively troubles the staples of the postcolonial theoretical register—nation, hybridity, mimicry, and diaspora—both to underscore the deconstructive lessons we are already familiar with *and* to illuminate the limitations of binary thinking that persist even in deconstructive readings of these concepts.

At the moment of the coeval independence and partition of India, the question "Chapattis or Bread?" encapsulates a multivalent code. To a people "divided to the vein," in Derek Walcott's evocative phrase, the logic of national belonging founded in jus soli, jus sanguinis, or in religious affiliation, the ostensible premises for nation formation, would have been equally irrelevant (*Collected Poems,* 17). Given restrictions placed by the colonial government on migration to England, an option made available exclusively to the few who could afford the cost of the passage and subsequent board and lodging, claims to a home in the mother country were belied by classist colonial policies.[3] Recognized neither in the national discourse of the former colony nor called to come home with the departing British, this was not a group that knew where home was as the sun set on the empire. While theories of the minus in the origin of the nation, critiques of its "linear narrative," and arguments about "the liminality of the nation-space" describe their situation as well as that of many others, in the moment of decolonization Anglo-Indians were not offered even the fiction of national belonging (Bhabha, "DissemiNation" 301).

For all the complexities of nation, culture, identity, and belonging, Manto's lunatics unwittingly grasp the core problem posed by the historical date, August 14/15, 1947, in metonymic terms that are also material to survival: "Would breakfast be available, or not? Instead of proper bread, would they have to choke down those bloody Indian chapattis?" The problem of leavened or unleavened bread, memorably connected to the Jewish diasporic experience, moreover, is part of a narrative that draws attention to ingestive, spiritual, and cultural practices as conjointly consequential in understanding the abstract concept of identity. Chapatti or Bread? The question turns upon practices of ingestion, commensality, and arguably corporeal commitments that attend them, constituting the stuff and staff of life through habit, repetition, and familiarity in concrete "forms of existing" (Fanon, *Toward the African Revolution,* 38). If cultural practices of dress, food, worship, language, and other habits of behavior comprise "the very stuff our identities are made of" (Žižek, "Tolerance," 679), Anglo-Indian fictions of community are sometimes expressed in terms of cultural homogeneity with regard to these staples of group identity:

> Eurasians throughout the East not only show a certain ethnic unity, but speak the same language (English) either as their father tongue or as a commercial advantage, profess the same faith (Christianity) and are conditioned by comparable traditions, prejudices and economic factors which have determined the general uniformity of their dress, food, domestic habits, social outlook and regard for their whiter masters. In fact, in Stalin's definition of a nation as "a historically evolved, stable community of language, territory, economic life and psychological make-up manifested in a community of culture," they could lay more claim to national status than many accepted nations. (Dover, *Know This of Race,* 34)

Coralie Younger cites prominent Anglo-Indian Frank Anthony's assertion that "according to genetic law . . . where people of diverse origins are endogamous, they develop what has been described as homozygosity, that is, common customs, manners, culture and above all the cement of English" (quoted in *Anglo-Indians,* 43). While recognizing the commonalities of group identity, Cedric Dover, a prominent Eurasian Anglo-Indian zoologist and race theorist, rejects the idea of half-castes because "there are no full castes," insisting that "there are only older mongrels and newer mongrels" (*Know This of Race,* 31). Instead of challenging essentialist thinking, the existence of racial hybrids has traditionally reinforced racial boundaries and vigilance against mixture.[4] At the same time, moreover, homozygosity suggests that even hybrid communities police their borders and protect their proprietary lifeways.[5] While we are all older or newer mongrels, we know that even newly hybrid communities monitor their communities and labor to distinguish themselves from others.[6]

In his 1954 novel *Bhowani Junction,* which is set around the partition and independence of India, British army officer and novelist John Masters articulates the predicament of Anglo-Indian identity through the voice of Patrick Taylor. Like other Anglo-Indians of the time, Taylor calls England "Home" (15),[7] even when he knows that "we couldn't go Home. We couldn't become English, because we were half Indian. We couldn't become Indian, because we were half English. We could only stay where we were and be what we were" (27–28). In 1956, the novel was made into a film starring Ava Gardner as Victoria Jones, a beautiful Anglo-Indian serving with the British armed forces, and Stewart Granger as Colonel Rodney Savage, a British army officer. George Cukor's adaptation allowed the British officer to win her hand at the conclusion of the novel, whereas Masters's account of the resolution of the love triangle in the novel describes her returning to Taylor, one of "her people" by virtue of the fact that "she'd tried becoming Indian—but she wasn't an Indian. She'd tried becoming English—but she wasn't English" (*Bhowani Junction,* 390). Although Savage fancifully imagines that "from Bhowani Junction the lines spread out to every Indian horizon for them," the novel leaves the Anglo-Indian characters where it found them at the inception of the novel, at a junction rather than a destination (390).

Anglo-Indian communities challenge us to imagine a diaspora *within* the nation without a movement away from the birthplace, although the Anglo-Indian community is also geographically dispersed internationally in more conventional diasporic forms. Today, as a consequence of the convergence of new media with global diasporic movements, the presence of a virtual nation of Anglo-Indians on the Internet cleaves together otherwise sundered discourses of globalization and nationhood. Where the novel served as the vehicle for articulations of nations as imagined communities with collective addresses and addressees, Anglo-Indian presence on the Web invests digital nativity with the weight of history and proclaims a virtual nation without territorial coordinates.

The technologically enabled virtual Anglo-Indian nation has been convened through the diasporic spread of the population throughout the commonwealth. With about fifteen million crossing borders around the time of the partition, the passage of some half a million or so Anglo-Indian migrants to England and other settler colonies, however, constitutes one of the least remarked diasporas in South Asian history. Moreover, partition for this group could also mean division *within* one family, where some members of the family would go to the mother country or to other settler colonies while others would stay behind, decisions that depended in part on being the right color. One Anglo-Indian interviewee in Blunt's research is reported to have said, "there are six different shades of colour in an Anglo-Indian family. And it often happened that those who could pass off as non-Indian and totally white [did so]." Another spoke of a son who "passes off as a European, blond, blue eyes," refusing to recognize a brother who is dark-skinned (quoted in Blunt, *Domicile and Diaspora,* 44). Many Anglo-Indians who could afford the passage cast their lot overseas in England or in other commonwealth countries.[8] A generation after independence, the narrator of I. Allan Sealy's novel *The Trotter-Nama,* a chronicle of "Anglo" history, offers this elegiac comment: "*not too many of us left and half of those waiting to leave*" (574).[9] There were some who were able to pass in mainstream-white countries, and deliberately disavowed their ties to India.[10] In addition to shedding light on intraregional hybridity and diaspora within the nation without leaving a natal birthplace, Anglo-Indian experiences of passing into the mainstream call into question established notions of overseas diaspora founded in collectivity, family, connectivity, mourning, and memorialization. Given these frequently cited characteristics of diasporic communities, the individual passer who must forego all of the above belongs to an *invisible* diaspora. For all the documented diasporic passages, the most successful of all concern those who, armed with the shibboleth, chose to step across a line, and vanished undetected into an unarchived history.[11] In disavowing nation, community, and the past, what does the *successful* space traveler teach us about other invisible diasporas lost to history in communities that now claim homogeneity and common origins? What were the hazards of border crossing, the labor of passing, and the biobodily toil and toll of mimicry and passing involved in disappearing into the mainstream?

This chapter turns to the picaresque passage of the half-English, half-Indian protagonist of Hari Kunzru's novel *The Impressionist* in order to pursue several lines of inquiry arising from Anglo-Indian experiences in South Asian history. How does the discourse of the nation fare through the lens of the racial hybrid? What did it mean to be racially and culturally hybrid in the heyday of empire? How might we understand the concept of diaspora through populations with a tenuous sense of a territorial homeland? In the arena of race studies, the racial hybrid, destined to blend into one or an(other) mainstream (at "home" or in diaspora), is arguably the living embodiment of identity as that which is what it is, yet is changing; that which is changing, yet is what it is.[12] To think race through Anglo-Indians after the concept has been undone in other academic discussions can be productively regressive, as in working backward from a mathematical solution to show the steps that precede the eventual blending away of difference from the mainstream. The gradual dissolution of the community into the mainstream, one by two by three, observable in the social realm and represented in literature, offers an available living lesson in hybridity as a shared condition in the *longue durée* of history. Given the scale of migrations taking place today, what might the Anglo-Indian experience of passing, hitherto studied poorly in postcolonial theory, teach us about the bioaesthetic dimensions of assimilation? If assimilation is the contemporary iteration of passing in modernity, as I propose, its aesthetic logic demands a reduction in the sensory impact of difference from the mainstream and closer approximation to its preferred forms of comportment, as I have discussed in the introduction.

Žižek notes, "what neighbor means today" is "the one who by definition smells. This is why today deodorants and soaps are crucial; they make neighbors at least minimally tolerable. I am ready to love my neighbors, provided they don't smell too bad ("Tolerance," 680). The substantial literature on mimicry and camouflage in postcolonial theory demands a supplementary understanding of their biomaterial aspects. What kind of global body is under production in the assimilative projects of modernity? Despite the coexistence of various subjectivities, the rule of identity thinking manifests in terms of a demand for material compliance with the logic of modernity, which subtly rewards assimilation and punishes ideological, bodily, formal, and comportmental deviation from dominant eumemic forms. Although Kunzru's novel is concerned with racial passing, the ideological, oral, visual, bodily, muscular, dietary, sanitary, and alimentary training involved in passing, akin to human dressage but all the way down to a bodily core, points to valuable lessons for grasping the relay between racial passing and cultural assimilation in modernity. Pran Nath Razdan, Kunzru's fictional protagonist, with a talent for mimicry and a high success rate in producing convincing impressions of Englishness after fortuitously accidental bouts of requisite training, offers a textbook analysis of the habitations of identity, its mobilization of sensory, aesthetic, and formal impressions upon the world, and a recognition of the muscular deployment of the technology of the body in communicating these impressions.

Ab Ovo: Genesis, Floods, and the Big Bang

In Which the Boy Is Born in a Flood, in a Cave, in Fusion . . .

An elaborate charade mocking the ruse of origins and the imposture of what we think of as identity, the story of Pran (Hindi for "life"), the impressionist in Kunzru's novel, begins in a flood with an exaggerated nod to two conflated genesis myths. Kunzru's hero is conceived when a wandering, disoriented English forester with a "pink, perspiring face" is carried away by a monsoon torrent and lifted up into "the mouth of a cave" at a time when he has been adrift, looking for something, "something to fill a gap," which "more conventional men would have identified . . . as woman-shaped" (*The Impressionist,* 3, 13, 4–5). The gap-shaped woman is Amrita, a wayward opium-addicted young woman who is making her way across the desert with her maid to a chosen husband after the death of her father, a Kashmiri broker. But, as the author notes, "the flood is imminent" (5, 11). Kunzru likens Amrita's survival after the flood to the Hindu creation myth of Manu, the first man, floating above the ocean in a flood, and starting a new race in a story curiously reminiscent of biblical narratives of creation growing out of destruction. The flood, moreover, is also the torrent of history, for "the future is contained in that water. All the world is in the past" (12–13). Kunzru incorporates more secular origin myths in the first few pages for good measure. A version of the big bang theory is suggested in the following passage: "Fire and water. Earth and Air. . . . Collapse them in on themselves, send them spiraling down a tunnel of blackness to re-emerge whole, one with the all, mere aspects of the great unity of things whose name is God" (6). References to black holes and singularity in the unity of things evoke a conception of God as a cosmic, possibly comically inclined, physicist. This narrative is followed by the idea of origin in its more prosaic, earthly guise. Forrester, the forester, crawls out of the flood to confront "the mouth of a cave" (13). Soon "a fire flickers into existence" and the lustful young caveman stands before the "native mother goddess" (13). Before the young colonial officer, the "pearl-skinned man," has had the wit or opportunity to recall "something to do with duty and India Office ordinances" that prohibit interracial mixture, the cave creatures "roll and claw" in sex that is "inexpert and violent," mingling in the flesh until the "sweat and dust has turned their skins to an identical red-brown colour" (15).

After this violent, elemental conjugation, the currents of history wash away the unwitting father on a "tree . . . so freighted with wisdom and routine that it might as well be playing the National Anthem" (16). True to form for all those who returned to England after engaging in the sexual/textual carnivals of empire, the father disappears from the narrative. Amrita stands alone, "mother of the new," as "the old world," a "defunct world [is] swept off into oblivion" (14). In Amrita's womb is the postcolonial subject, Pran, *life*.

Insemination/Dissemination

In Which the Boy Is Cast Out of His Home and Begins Again . . .

Before the hybrid picaro-to-be embarks on a diasporic career so marked by hypermobility as to stand as its very caricature, however, Pran is born into and located spectacularly within a family tradition founded in "the promotion of hygiene, tradition, cultural purity, cow protection and correct religious observance" under the aegis of his cuckolded, surrogate father, the Kashmiri Hindu Pandit, Amar Nath Razdan (23). "Heir to a fortune of many lakhs of rupees," Pran is the only son of a cultural purist who has unwittingly raised a child not his own after his arranged marriage to Amrita ends with the latter's death in childbirth.

In his first appearance in the novel, the fifteen-year-old Pran Nath Razdan is discovered in the act of surveying his domain, including a young servant girl who "has no idea of her peril" (21). Our first impression of Pran is an extended survey of his bodily and facial features: "so beautiful! So pale!," his hair with a "hint of copper," eyes with a "touch of green," and "a covering of skin that is not brown or even wheaten-coloured, but *white,*" with a "perfect milky hue" (20). Pran's light skin is plausible because "Kashmiris come from the mountain and are always fair," but Pran's "colour is exceptional," "proof, cluck the aunties, of the family's superior blood" (20). "Blood is important" to the Razdans, "one of the highest and most exclusive castes in all Hindustan," and the Kashmiri Pandits link it readily with "their intelligence and culture" (20). As the scion of the purist family lustfully eyes the young servant, we are told, "the blood stiffening the bulge in . . . [his] pyjamas is of the highest quality, guaranteed" (20).

The mother of the imperiled servant girl, however, is none other than the maid who found Amrita in the pale man's clothes after the flood and readily grasped the implications. Bribed to hold her tongue, the maid would have guarded the secret had Pran not turned out to be a spoiled monster now threatening her daughter's chastity. Pran's presumed father, a purist insistent on cultural, linguistic, social, dietary, and even sartorial hygiene—intolerant even of "the reckless combination of checks and stripes" in dress—has no armor against the assaults to his cherished notions of purity in the disclosures of the maid (30). Enfeebled by the all-difference-leveling flu pandemic that claimed millions of lives worldwide in 1918, the sick man learns the horrifying truth about having harbored "the bastard child of a casteless, filth-eating, left-and-right-hand-confusing Englishman" (39). The description highlights in particular those differences of culture that are written on the body. The Englishman's beef eating is anathema to the cow protectionist, as abhorrent as the foreigner's habits of excretion and subsequent cleaning, which do not honor the Hindu reservation of the left hand for this particular ablution. Expanding recklessly "on the theme of miscegenation . . . impurities, blendings, pollutions, smearings and muckings-up of all kinds," the maid links the irresponsible spilling of seed to the disastrous plague gripping the entire city. "Finally, she produces her trump card: the battered photograph," extracted from her mistress's borrowed clothes, bearing the legend, "*Ronald Forrester, IFS*" (39).

The sepia image suggests that "but for the skin it could be an Indian face" (39), prompting the reader to recall fables of the shared Aryan heritage of the colonizer and colonized, and a mysterious diaspora whose origins remain disputed, its directional flows lost to antiquity and its remnants coded into links between the Indo-Aryan family of languages. What kind of disaster could have prompted *that* dispersal? Flood, plague, expulsion, violence, economics, or simply the desire to cross boundaries? Does that early scattering count as a diaspora, if it lacks recorded mourning, documented suffering, the availability of technologies of commemoration and links to the homeland, or the prospect of return? Centuries later, the nostalgia of European philologists during the colonial period for a shared racial affinity with a once-great civilization might be understood as a sort of misplaced nostalgia, not for a nation or geographical space but for a chronotopical zone in which past and present, Europe and Asia, could be selectively crimped together to produce both sameness and difference, and to allow Europe a civilizational vintage beyond its own borders and history, while alleging its degradation in its Eastern crucible.

That once (allegedly) shared blood has since mingled with others, developed other genetic, epigenetic, environmentally influenced, culturally shaped body types that bear some resemblance with Northern cousins, but prompt even more horror in the confrontation of differences that have accreted over time. Differences that inhere in bodily uses of the left hand versus the right hand, for instance. The father *malgré lui* sees that "Pran Nath and the photograph are two versions of the same image," that crucially, "*This is not his son*" (40). The very beauties of color and body that had made him beloved of the indulgent father are exposed in an instant as dubiously sourced and responsible for the boy's ugly character. In an exchange the Eurasian Indian community might well recognize for its irony, given its disinheritance by fathers both real and allegorical, European and Indian, the schematic fate of the community reveals itself in the following "exchange" between Amar Nath and Pran: " 'Father?' asks Pran Nath plaintively. There is no response" (40). Amar Nath has died of shock (and ironically of a caste, class, race-leveling influenza epidemic, his face the same blue-black as its other victims). Pran is cast out on the streets before his father's corpse is cool. " 'Please!' he begs. 'Let me in!' " The door opens, but only to drop "a little sepia square in the dust," a memento that will haunt him to the end—a personal amulet of bad luck that will consign him to perpetual wandering as a "nasty little half-baked bread" in the words of a beggar Pran had taunted in better days as heir to the Razdan fortune (43).

"Who are my own people?" asks Pran when told to go to his own by the beggar from whom he is obliged to beg for food after his eviction from his childhood home (44). The clue, of course, is in the beggar's reference to half-baked bread, the metonymic identity bit pointing in the direction of the Anglo-Indian social gathering point and its cultural and commensal regimes. The stripling is sent to the Agra Post and Telegraph Club—an arch reference to the historical Anglo-Indian hockey association, "Agra Telegraph," as well as to the Eurasian community's customary employment in the post and telegraph services, along with the railways. The denizens of the Anglo-Indian Club think of England as home and swap stories about the "disgustingness of natives, the foul Indian-ness of native ways," in "contrast to Home, to the Northern rectitude of English ways and manners" (47).[13] But the club betrays its members' mixed inheritance aromatically upon entrance: "Inside lingers a smell of fried food which cannot be eradicated, no matter how hard the cleaners scrub and polish. . . . There is still the smell of food fried in ghee, the rich unmistakable smell of India" (45). The women are betrayed by the single glass bangle accessorizing cotton, floral-print homemade dresses that look nothing like those real Englishwomen order from the Army and Navy catalogue "that arrives from Home once a season" (45). "Everyone knows none of them has been anywhere near England," the English joke in the "better-smelling and more exclusive Civil Service Club." Their "awful accents" and "chippiness" are mocked, as well as their devotion to hats and the solar *topis* sported, the English ladies joke, "Indoors. *After dark.* . . . What a chee-chee thing to do" (46). The English pronounce the "horrid blackie-whites . . . disgusting. . . . Chewing betel on the sly, their girls chasing after the Other Ranks, *squatting rather than sitting* when they think no one can see" (46; emphasis added). The bodyhood of perceived differences demonstrates itself not only in terms of color, feature, clothing, accent, and sound, but as much in the diet and in bodily postures of peeing, sitting, and shitting in privy situations.

Looking for his own, Pran runs into Harry Begg coming out of the club on his way to a date with fellow Anglo-Indian, Jenny, "who has fine features [and] . . . a complexion the color of parchment," and is susceptible to the attractions of "other, *whiter* men" (48). Harry himself is "the skin colour of a manila envelope. Or a little darker," and considers this "Not a bad hand really, compared to some," alluding to the unpredictable results that the genetic lottery of interracial mixture can produce, referenced in a scurrilous limerick suggesting that a young lady's affair with a "darkie" results in "an eightsome of twins / Two black and two white and four khaki" (47).[14] Among Anglo-Indians, "Harry's type" and Pran's "own people," are exceptional cases such as Skinner (subject of Vikram Chandra's fictional *Red Earth and Pouring Rain*), Lord Roberts, "who commanded during the Boer war," and Lord Liverpool, "yes the Liverpool who was PM" (48). Harry's internal comment, "It is so bloody unfair," as he thinks of those who were able to pass into Englishness successfully "before the advent of biologists and evangelists," is more than a little ironic in its reference both to blood and to fairness and its link to color (48).

On an evening when he is hopeful of success in romance and feeling "noble and white . . . white as a tennis shoe," the "little bastard [Pran] ruins it all" by grabbing Harry's sleeve, "as if it is the most natural thing in the world" (48). "Hello," says Pran "in treacle-thick bazaar English. 'I am blackie-white like you. I am hungry. Do you have some food?' " (48). Harry sees that the boy "has an English face, a face one might even say was fine, in another place, in other circumstances. Its very good-looks and whiteness make Harry furious" (48). They "are probably of the same blood," observes the narrator, "Harry and the street urchin, topped up to more or less the same degree, like two glasses of chai" (49). If anything, Harry is "somewhat luckier than him, knowing proper English and having some semblance of good manners" (49). Pran, spectral reminder of a repressed, tainted history and the effort required to climb "out of the clinging swamp of blackness . . . [through] twenty-three years of chippiness and hat-wearing," is an unwitting agent of anagnorisis. The urchin's dirty but whiter, better-looking face, and the outrageous call to kinship delivered in crude English shock the better-mannered, *proper*

English-speaking Harry. Harry, called out from his reverie by a "ghost-face," knows that he and the gormless, handsomer half-caste are of one mixed blood, the difference of "proper English and good manners" a matter of revisable form, not kind (*The Impressionist,* 49). Unsettled by the specular anomaly, he begins to thrash the boy who eventually flees, his hopes of finding his kin destroyed before he has even crossed the threshold of the Anglo-Indian club. The narrator does not tarry with Harry Begg, for there is other business at hand; the marginal character's belittled hopes of success with the fair Jenny are left behind, although their faint echo may be heard years later in an ironic reversal when Pran's English beloved chooses a black man with "passions, primitive emotions," and the protagonist's plaintive plea, "I am blacker than you think," goes unheard because by then he has learned to pass as English and white (415–16).

Things Fall Apart

In Which the Center Does Not Hold . . .

With his ejection from the threshold of the Anglo-Indian club, the boy's crisis of identity escalates. Who is he? Neither here, nor there, his sort of hybridity offers little cause for "the celebration of cultural difference and fusion," Marwan Kraidy identifies in *Hybridity* (1); nor does it seem to effect a subversion of colonial discourse, as Bhabha's theory of hybridity suggests. Moreover, border crossing has proved dangerous, unpredictable, and violent so far. More violence is in store for Pran, as well as debauchery, emasculation, and lessons in form, formation, and re-formation. Pran's next stop is even more disastrous, for the vengeful beggar he had mocked repeatedly sends him to a brothel, where he is drugged and beaten before he is sold into slavery. During his torture, with his very sense of self violently deconstructed, Pran handles his father's photograph "as if it were a magical item" (64). The IFS (Indian Forest Service) officer's unbearable whiteness looms before him like "an excess of light, a god, impossible to look on directly" (64). Meanwhile, the son is aware that he is losing something, "the pearl faculty, the faculty which secretes selfhood around some initial grain" (65). Against the talismanic wholeness of the "pearl-skinned man," his is but "a spark, an impulse waiting to be reassembled from a primal soup of emotions and memories. Nothing so coherent as a personality. Some kind of Being still happening in there, but nothing you could take hold of" (15, 65). The narrator urges comparisons with cosmic forces exerted over millennia: "You could think of it in cyclical terms. The endlessly repeated day of Brahman—before any act of creation the old world must be destroyed. Pran is now in pieces. A pile of Pran-rubble, ready for the next chance-event to put it back together in a new order" (65). Equally, one might consider Fanon's suggestion that colonialism "makes of the native an object," with the "object man . . . broken in the very depth of his substance" as a precondition of his enslavement and reformation (*A Dying Colonialism,* 35).

In his next incarnation, "Pran-flux" is reassembled as a boy-girl living among eunuchs at the palace of the heirless nawab of Fatehpur (71). Here the hybrid undergoes further deprogramming at the hands of the head eunuch, who taunts him with the phrase "You are *nothing*" until he responds likewise (81). Pran becomes Rukhsana, meaning bright new dawn, a transvestite threatened with a hermaphrodite's identity, "floating between worlds" (101), negotiating a middle passage between the sexes. Unwitting pawn in the drama of empire, Rukhsana observes the Orientalized figure of the nawab in his "silks, the jeweled Jodhpuri slippers, the string of pearls and the egg-sized finger rings [that] seem less true signs of power than elements of a particularly expensive fancy-dress costume" (102). The childless, bejeweled representative of the old order is engaged in a struggle for power with his younger brother Firoz, a new world cultural hybrid favored by the British because he "wears a tie and has promised to let them build factories" (106). The nawab's palace is a hybrid of various Indo-European architectural flourishes, while Firoz's lifestyle is a flamboyant demonstration of privileged cultural hybridity, his thoroughgoing modernity expressed in the installation of a private cinema and a reproduction of the Riviera in the northwest of India. At darkened film screenings, the cultural hybrid watches pornographic interracial fantasy films with titles such as *The Yellow Man and the Girl, Three Little Negro Maids, Country Stud Horse,* and *Jazz Godiva* (146), fingers his foreign lady guests, "and reassures himself that he is no cringing native, ignorant of the ways of the world" (78, 146, 115). The nawab appears before visiting dignitaries in opulent attire, while Firoz is "elegant in his sleekly tailored morning suit," the embodiment of progressive modernity (153). The difference between the nawab and Prince Firoz is also captured in sonic terms: "In the evenings, as gramophone jazz competes with the call of the muezzin, the tension is palpable" (107).[15]

Who will the British representative Major Privett-Clampe choose as a successor? The sonic and aesthetic audit, coupled with Firoz's investment in colonial style development, suggests that the younger brother is far more attuned to colonial interests. The nawab, denizen of an old world incapable of successful reproduction, knows that it is Firoz's world that will succeed his, unless Rukhsana can be deployed for a little blackmail to expose the major's depraved fondness for "beautiful boy-girls" (87). Emasculated, feminized, and chosen to bend over and hold the position as an offering for the British resident, Pran / Rukhsana / *Nothing* is destined to be royally, imperially buggered. The narrator comments: "Some may be tempted to view this as primarily a political situation. It is, after all, Pran's first direct contact with the machinery of imperial government" (98). No less allegorical perhaps is the description of the racial hybrid as both buggered and unmanned, pimped, sold, sold out, used no less by India than by Britain. Beyond allegory, however, the boy's "experience is still painful, like having a fallen log hammered up one's backside with a mallet" (97–98).

Aspiration, Respiration

In Which the Boy's Education Begins . . .

Racked by guilt over his unnatural desires, the major finds himself trying to make amends to his pretty protégé. Recognizing "some English" in the boy, the provenance of which he chooses to remain ignorant of, he rechristens the boy "Clive," dresses him in his school colors, and coaches him to heed the call of his blood: "It's calling to you through all the black, telling you to stiffen your resolve. If you listen to what the white is telling you, you can't go wrong" (109). The major "feels *romantically* towards him"; we learn that "one of the few things which stuck in his head about the Greeks was their admirable tradition of man-boy love. . . . Now he knows for certain that a degree of white blood courses through the young man's veins, this sense of being a mentor, a guide through the perils and pitfalls of life, is getting stronger" (131).

Preparing him for yet another incarnation, the major makes him recite poetry, teaches him to distinguish between *w* and *v* ("It's *whence,* not *vence,* you nincompoop"), and exhorts him to "listen to what the blood is telling you" (110). Language and speech were potent bodily markers of civilization for some early observers of the people of India. In his 1847 study of aboriginals in India, Hodgson established these links:

> The more I see of these primitive races the stronger becomes my conviction that there is no medium of research yielding such copious and accurate data as their languages. Their physical and mental condition is exactly portrayed in their speech and he who can analyse it and separate the foreign elements, has the key to the amount and sources of their civilization. (*On the Aborigines of India,* ii–iii)

Listening to what the blood is telling him entails vocal revisions; to the color and face of English race and blood, Pran must add its sound, learning the subtle differences between /V/ and /W/. He must also add a certain posture, encoded in the angle and stance of his body, correcting the way in which he will hold his very backbone, until "the Major is inspired to shout, 'Tally-ho!'" (*The Impressionist,* 111). Pederasty has given way to an alternative sort of homoeroticism, love of the same now taking the form of making Pran more like himself, in acknowledgment of the boy's ambiguously sourced blood relationship to empire. Pran-Rukhsana-Clive recites "*Gunga Din* or *The Charge of the Light Brigade,* while he [the major] does something pedagogical in his trousers" (132). The martial and sonic poetics of colonial elocution link sound and arousal, emotion and erection, pedagogy and pederasty, until "eventually, in the way of things, Privett-Clampe's noble fiction starts to coincide with reality, and even the trouser-fiddling stops. Clive's accent improves and the Major contents himself with mistily watching his protégé as he stands up straight and declaims" (132).

The major's bid for kinship, founded in the belief that a more historically proximate coupling has produced his "beautiful boy" (131), is more than an allegory for distant Aryan kinship, this homoeroticism more than a queer assault against sociosexual normativity; it is also desire finding root and expression through biobodily means and neuronal reward structures. This is the "carnal stereophony" of which Roland Barthes has spoken: "the pulsional incidents, the language lined with flesh . . . the articulation of the body, of the tongue, not that of meaning, of language" (*The Pleasure of the Text,* 66). As for Clive/Pran, "the poetry baffles him, with its stiffness and violence and thumping horseback rhythms, but he discerns that it is in some way responsible for Privett-Clampe's importance, and the importance, of Englishmen in general, so he pays attention to it, hoping to divine its secret" and "gradually his English accent improves" (*The Impressionist,* 112). Along with the visual effects produced by "short trousers, a white cotton shirt, knee-length woollen stockings with garters to hold them up . . . a tie and a cap . . . decorated with the same pattern of blue and burgundy stripes," Clive is learning to pass in his new *sonic* drag (109).

While Clive is acquiring the embodiments of English cultural identity to complement his racially hybrid inheritance, "the life of the palace continues" (113). Polo, tennis, and hunting events hosted by the eager princes bring together a disparate band of colonials, expats, eunuchs, and assorted freeloaders. The palace drama culminates in the primal site of the forest during a staged tiger hunt. In a carnival of desire and degradation, most of the company have the runs; the nawab is discovered naked with visiting British resident Sir Wyndham's kleptomaniac wife, Minty; Firoz has soiled his underwear; and the major has been shot in a farce of Wodehousian if not Rabelaisian proportions. Sexual desire, shit, and violence are unleashed in the unregulated space of the jungle. Taking advantage of the chaos, tigers drugged for the hunt escape into the night and Clive slips away into the next section, titled "White Boy" (179).

Step across This Line: Border Talk

In Which He Learns to Pass . . .

Discovered next on a buffalo-drawn cart rolling toward Amritsar, a city ravaged by violence in the wake of the Jalianwala Bagh massacre in 1919, is a "sahib [Englishman] who does not speak like a sahib," so thinks its driver, but looks enough like one to pass the scrutiny of anxious "English Tommy guards" (*The Impressionist,* 179, 181). Infuriated by General Dyer's decision to fire on peaceful protestors, the natives have been on a rampage. A white woman missionary foolish enough to "live among her flock" has been raped (so have a bunch of Anglo-Indian nurses, but that triggers no particular outrage), enraging the general, who is now determined to wreak punishment: "If they will behave like animals, they shall be treated as such" (184, 181, 185). A "round of public floggings" is accompanied by the order that natives at the scene of the crime crawl on all fours (185). At the border between different grammars of being and their mutually occult rules, knowledge of the right password can determine life and death. Pran is about to walk into a city that has sprung new, dangerous border points, and it is imperative that he possess the right shibboleth for safe passage. Blundering upon the scene, Pran "realizes with a rush of fear that . . . any moment now they will attack him, arrest him, make him crawl and grovel" (185). Unable to "force his mouth to form words," Pran is spared momentarily by his silence (185). The sergeant on duty mistakes him for a lost English boy.

Pran asks himself, "How can they be so blind? How can they not tell?" (185). Somehow, "despite the sweat, the dirt of five days' travelling in the same clothes, the way he holds his head and hands, the terrified expression on his face, they think he is one of them" (185). But for the fetish of skin color, Pran would have failed the crucial visual test, but he also understands the limits of visual information. "As soon as he speaks they will know," he thinks (185). The regime of looking inaugurates a more complicated identity scan of the multiple texts the body makes available for examination. The sergeant demands confirmation: "Are you all right? Can you tell me your name?" Pran knows that he must confirm that he is not only visually but also audibly all right. Acutely aware that "one move will betray him," the boy wills his body to reproduce the major's lessons (186). The narrator has told us earlier that the boy has inherited or developed a talent for mimicry, albeit employed "in cruel parodies" of the physical disabilities of servants in the Razdan household, from which indulgent paradise he has been forever expelled (28). Having passed the visual color test, he must now play out the rest of the biosensorial mime: "he tries to hold Privett-Clampe's voice inside his mouth," producing the sound, vocabulary, and body stance of whiteness: "I am very well. I am going. Forthwith," he says (186). Pran/Clive has not balked at the fricative of /v/ juxtaposed so dangerously close to the round-lipped sound of /w/ that has betrayed many an Indian English speaker's inadequate instruction in received pronunciation, or indeed from the aspirated voiced plosive of "forthwith" that could easily have exploded his precariously dissembled identity. The choice and arrangement of vowel and consonant sounds is nothing less than daring: "I am *v*ery *w*ell. I am going. For*thwith*" (186; emphasis added). Tongue, teeth, breath, aspiration are the life-and-death determining elements of identity at this crucial moment. Shibboleth or Sibboleth? *Cogito ergo sum* or not, it is clear that Pran's life and future hang on a correctly apprehended sense of *suspiro ergo sum,* in such trivialities as where to let the plosive breath out and how to release the air of the fricative /v/ with audible friction. Toward the end of the novel, the narrator concludes: "People care about outward forms: the width of a cuff, the sound of the labial-dental fricative 'v.' Becoming someone else is just a question of changing tailor and remembering to touch the bottom lip to the ridge of teeth above" (463). The orphic spell of sound and the glamour of grammar carry the day, and Pran turns the corner, beginning to run as soon as he is out of the solicitous sergeant's sight.

The second test will be a contextual one at the station, where he warily approaches a train of white evacuees: "He is a trespasser, a black cuckoo in the nest. . . . The real English boys are all away in boarding schools at Home" (188). Given time to process his presence on the platform, the English women will know that boys of his age who look white in India are likely to be half-caste because they are not permitted to attend schools in England, with official policy specifically prohibiting their travel to England for higher education. As he shuffles along to evade detection, in this most fortuitous of accidental journeys a train puffs into the station. "In the midst of the confusion" that all trains bring in their train, soldiers focus on the transfer of goods by Sikh soldiers (who must be kept away from the watchful women fearful of rape), and Pran climbs aboard the train to Bombay (188).

Missionary Positions

In Which His Education Continues . . .

Pran's third attempt at passing at the "Independent Scottish Mission among the Heathen" on Falkland Road in Bombay is less successful (201). When he arrives at the mission claiming to be an English boy down on his luck, the pastor's wife, Elspeth Macfarlane, sees right through him: "It was plain he was a mongrel, some Tommy's child who had grown up on the streets, but he was fine featured and his manners were good" (203). His subsequent triple-header incarnations as "Robert" to Pastor Andrew Macfarlane, "Pretty Bobby" to the prostitutes on Falkland Road where the pastor has located his mission, and "Chandra" to India-loving Elspeth offer him opportunities for continuing education in "points of morality," Latin, history, English grammar (204), and further accent reduction (or enhancement) until he develops "the prim inflections of an educated lowland Scot" like his mentor (192).

Tongue-in-cheek, Kunzru furnishes in the figure of his next teacher, Pastor Macfarlane, an amateur craniometrist "following in the footsteps of the great [Samuel] Morton," who performed his measurements by filling skulls with "fine lead shot" (196). In that of his wife, Kunzru supplies a cultural hybrid in reverse who is assimilating to native ways in pointed opposition to her husband, who refuses to learn the local "gobble-gobble" adopted by sari-wearing, Marathi-speaking Elspeth. For Andrew, the gospel is clear: "English and Christ, Christ and English. Inseparable" (218). No "gobble-gobble" can adequately convey its sacred import or substitute for its "innately moral character" as "a route to God" (218). On account of his failure to learn the local language, the pastor's message has gone unheeded in his parish; "after almost three years in the country, the Independent Scottish Mission among the Heathen had only two converts, both untouchable men who did odd jobs around the compound in return for food, and on Sunday often had to be dragged out of the paan shop on the corner to attend service" (219). Ambaji Elspeth, on the other hand, has chosen India, despite her initial response to the assault on her senses. We learn of her arrival at Apollo Bunder through the following sensationally charged description: "the hundreds of beggars tugging at her white cotton dress, the furnace heat and the alien smells all hit her like a dirty black hand slapping her face" (216). Following Andrew into "stinking alleys" (216), she had fainted at the delivery of racial difference through an excess of smells, sights, sounds, touch, and heat, leading at first to her blocking out "the nightmarish place in which she lived, holding it at arm's length like a soiled rag" (217). During a difficult confinement and recuperation, she learns to love her adoptive country and its different ways, experiencing "*the wild pleasure at sitting close to the floor and eating with her hands*," as she will come to love her adopted Chandra, who comes to her soon after the death of her sons (222; emphasis added). While Andrew holds himself aloof from the world that surrounds him, on her side of the compound, "men and women, Indians and Europeans, promiscuously mingled together" (226).

Andrew, on the other hand, dabbles in theories of "the superiority of the European mind to that of the Asiatic" (222–23). In a caricature of racial science, the reverend's experiments in phrenology, craniometry, and lamprey grid measurements of facial angles, yield the following insights: "craniometry has revealed the foundation of British imperial domination of the world" on the basis that "differences in brain size correspond exactly to degree of civilization and capacity for rational thought throughout the world" (196).[16] The narrator summarizes the findings of this primitive biobodily measure of racial intelligence and its implications thus:

> The Indostanic group, to which most of the Reverend's dead people once belonged, falls somewhere in the upper middle of this global league. At the top is the European, whose capacious 100-cubic-inch capacity gives him room for brain development far in excess of such benighted fellows as the 91-inched Peruvian or the savage 86-inched Tasman. Hence, Empire. (197)

Pran/Robert makes an intriguing subject for the reverend's experiments: "To the Reverend his fine nose and thin, sharp lips appear strangely pure. For a mongrel, incredibly pure. Really almost too pure. Almost European" (197); "Robert," he declares, "your taint of blood hardly shows at all" (197). The boy in turn looks through pictures "of noble Greek statuary and twisted soot-black nigger faces, and feels, as he often does, a peculiar relief at his resemblance to one and not the other" (197–98), experiencing something of the racial pride of those who are then in power. The reverend makes

> note of the "unusual leucochroicity of the subject's skin," and wonder[s] whether perhaps the very fineness of the features, their uncanny quality, places them under the heading of one of the great Lombroso's criminal types. The tendency to crime of the mulatto has, after all, been well documented in the Americas, and Robert's peculiar disguised form of hybridity might conceal all manner of antisocial tendencies. His excessive care for his personal appearance and his enjoyment of tobacco certainly point in that direction. (198)

Suspicious, but finding him brighter than his own sons, he decides, "Let the boy stay, even if he is a hyphenate" (199). After this parodic nineteenth-century style examination rooted in a now-discredited science, Ambaji jokingly asks the boy, "How was your skull?" "Very good, Amba—I mean, Mrs. Mac—I mean, very good. I am almost English" (199). As she looks up sharply, he amends, "I mean Scottish," in a wry comment on the intricacies of British identity (199).

The reverend's conflicted response to hybridity is informed by textbook ambivalence and desire. In his first mission in Assam, the twenty-four-year-old Andrew "fell, he fell hard," "the tropical climate . . . doing its evil work, dissolving Europe in heat and moisture, turning this man of God into a sensuous thing, a streaming naked body fronted by a bobbing, straining cock," and causing him to give in to the temptation of sex with a mission girl, little Sarah; "It happened once, twice, a third time. No more. By then he was revolted at himself" (227). While his superior, Reverend Gavin, attributes Sarah's swelling belly to "some failing on her part, yet another event in the tribe which had taken place outside or beneath the limits of European understanding," "a pale creature" is in the making who will in time haunt the mission, "always there, playing in the dirt, clapping its chubby hands. Accusing him" (228). She is one of many of her type in the

> villages near to the big tea plantations where whole families of half-breed children lined up to watch the missionaries ride past. Boys and girls of various sizes holding hands in front of their huts, each one bearing the tell-tale crook nose or jug ears of the Plantation Manager, or the Engineer, or the District Medical Officer. (228)[17]

Andrew is advised to find a suitable wife; he assents but adds a test to temptation by deciding to "walk among the harlots, make his home in the most depraved place he knew" (229).

Haunted by his own depravity, Andrew finds in scientific discourse a grid upon which to map and assess his poorly understood desires and fears:

> He wanted to know the exact shape of his sin, and found it in scientific books. Andrew Macfarlane of the Leucodermi, cymotrichous of hair and mesocephalic of head, had coupled with Sarah [whose name is not even her name] of the Xanthodermi, exotically leiotrichous but woefully brachy-cephalic [short wide head]. Their daughter was a collapse. A blur. (230)

With the birth of his legitimate sons, "gradually her [Sarah's] face was obliterated" (231). Forbidden access to the pleasures of his wife's pregnancy-damaged body, however, he remains obsessed with sex, his body a quivering monument to physical desire. His psychocognitive map is crowded by rivalrous texts and images. Among them is this passage from a book on the science of ethnography, Daniel Garrison Brinton's 1902 text, *The Basis of Social Relations: "These are the signs of racial inferiority: simplicity and early union of the cranial sutures. Wide nasal aperture, with synostosis of the nasal bones. Prominence of the jaws. Recession of the chin. Early appearance, size and permanence of 'wisdom' teeth"* (quoted in Kunzru, *The Impressionist,* 231). Equally powerful is the bodily present text of temptation: "These are the parts of women. High foreheads. Eyes rimmed with kohl. Breasts fastened into tight coloured blouses. Bare stomachs. Red sucking mouths, open, waiting" (231). Sexual/textual merging is suggested even in the sound of the word for congress: "Fucking. Make the shape of the word with your red mouth. Lower lip flicking off the teeth, breathy vowel guttering in a strangled click of the throat. Fuck. Fucking" (231). Mixture obviously horrifies the lustful and conflicted reverend. Objecting to natives as monkey people, he perceives his wife's interest in them as reminders of the temptation of physical consort, with animals at that: "It was like watching one's wife debasing herself with a dog or a horse" (233).

Enraged by his desires and haunted by conflicted discursive and bodily texts, the reverend is eventually driven to a violent episode the author describes thus:

> The missionary toils over a splayed girl. Nails dig hard into brown skin. English words. Gibber gibber glub-glub. Screaming. He makes a fist. All the years. Hits hard. Harder. . . . Men came and pulled him off. Brown men who smelled of sweat and garlic and punched his stomach and cut his face. (232)

In due course, tormented by his conflicted desires, his wife's behavior, and the call to violence, he finds a convenient repository for his ugly feelings. It is one that has served many a European racist anxious to project hatred outside the self by finding, locating, and confining it to its most extreme manifestation in the Holocaust, thereby placing the self at some distance from it:

> All sorts of ideas were stewing in his head, Old Testament images of blood and revenge. The Kaiser wiped them out, or rather redirected them, the *Illustrated News* caricature of the bloodthirsty monster in a spiked helmet doing the work the people of Bombay had never managed, rendering the forces of darkness single and visible. He began to hate the Germans with an overwhelming passion. (233)

But with the arrival of Pran / Clive / Bobby at the mission, "It was as if a ghost had come to haunt him. To have to live so close to the thing he feared most:

white yet not white, a diffraction both of his dead sons and his monstrous daughter" (234). The reverend responds by embarking on the boy's education with new missionary zeal, in a move uncannily reminiscent of the boy-girl-loving major: "Soon he was teaching Robert to write and speak proper English, and giving him the rudiments of culture" (234).

Bobby begins to study texts on race, learns to mimic regional British accents, and practices passing on English newcomers at the Bombay port (237). He tries on different names—"Peter Walker. John Johnson. Clive Smith. David Best but call me Bestie"—and colonial occupations: "I work for a petroleum company. A rubber company. The school board. A department store" (245). He sees how racial typing and categorization work: "The thing is, they believe him. They hear an accent and see a face and a set of clothes, and put them together into a person" (245). But "he soon learns that looks and accent are not enough" (249). There is more:

> There is, for example, the question of smell. Like everyone, Bobby has always wondered about the grim English war against cookery, their inexplicable liking for tasteless slabs of meat, unspiced vegetables and sweetened concoctions of flour and fat. A conversation with a naval rating reveals the side-effects of a diet devoid of garlic and onions. Bobby is pretending to be a man of influence, heir to an Edinburgh import-export business. The sailor snorts with laughter and tells him frankly that, money or no money, he stinks like a wog. Unless you sort yourself out, lad, you'll die a bleeding bachelor. Bobby is too intrigued to be offended. What do wogs smell like? Is there a typical English smell? (249)

Determined to follow the olfactory trail, Bobby bribes a servant at Watson's hotel to let him sniff white laundry: "Face buried in burra mems' smalls and burra sahibs' dirty shirts, he finally puts a name to it. Rancid butter. With perhaps a hint of raw beef. The underlying smell of empire" (249–50). The body's habitual traces not only look and sound out their difference; they also leak out through its pores. In his earlier incarnation as Clive, Pran had stumbled on the smell of Englishness at the Amritsar railway station:

> The place is packed with people waiting to be evacuated. A stench of sweat hits him like a fist. . . . The stink of their bodies, suddenly isolated from all the other stinks of India, is shocking. One attar note smelt raw on a perfumer's glass rod, nasty and unblended. Pran has been taught the rhyme. Fee-fi-fo-fum. Be he alive or be he dead. This is the smell of Englishmen, an incitement to the mob, the ogre, to attack. (187)

Along with bodily lessons in biochemistry, Bobby is learning about the socio-cultural mannerisms and phrases—what I have referred to earlier as identity bits and metonymic aesthetics—with which to stitch together the impression of English personality:

> Calico arms. Wooden head. A hat and a set of overheard opinions. How perfectly impossible it is to grow a good lawn in India. The positive moral effects of team sports. The unspeakable vileness of Mr Gandhi, and the lack of hygiene of just about everything. Lay them out one by one, like playing patience. It does not matter if you believe them. Belief is nothing but a trivial sensation in the stomach. (250)

Belief is a gut feeling; identity is biology, chemistry, culture, genes, but also engineering and architecture, "built according to blueprints of class and membership" (251). Finally invited into the colonial Majestic club by an unsuspecting new arrival from England, Bobby joins "a sea of pink faces," and by way of further dress rehearsal, experiences the thrill of whiteness: "tersely ordering a gin and tonic and taking a white man's pleasure in the brown man's deep salaam" (252). When he sets his sights on the reigning English beauty, Lily Parry, he suffers his first rebuff. At the first opportunity they have to be alone, she confronts him: "Right, you. What the hell do you think you are doing?" (263). A stunned Bobby learns that Lily has not only seen through him, but is, moreover, the far superior passer. "You poor little half-and-half. You don't have a clue, do you?" she asks (265). Outside the orbit of detection, she slips into a more familiar argot: "What are you after, yaar? Go on, you can tell me." "As she talks," the narrator observes, "her voice, her clipped English accent that is so very like his own, has changed, slipped, thickening, warming. All the Northern ice and suet falling away" (265). She leaves him with a useful tip: "Don't do that with your head. It's a dead giveaway. The two cardinal rules are never to waggle your head, and never let them see you squatting on your heels. All right?" (265).

The drama of biological re-formation is played out on the corporeal bearings of Kunzru's fictional hero. Armed with his genetically accidental looks, newfound sensitivity to diet and the smell test, accent training and other education provided by the pedophilic major and the missionary lover/hater of native women, and coached in the fundaments of desirable body stances furnished by his fellow passer, Pran/Bobby is ready to embark on his next adventure.

The Truest I/Eye: Bridge-Man

In Which the Orphan Goes Home . . .

The next opportunity for passing is presently made available to the aspiring impressionist when he runs into country-bred, England-bound Jonathan Bridgeman in a tense moment of anticolonial and labor unrest. Mrs. Macfarlane is arrested for Bolshevist sympathies, and Bobby fears he may soon be homeless. At this point, "it is not a good time to look English in Bombay," and Bobby has to explain "who he is," presumably in a native tongue or in Indian-accented English, when belligerent men "try to block his way" (275). The city is deserted, except for a "second-generation drunkard," the intoxicated Englishman Jonathan Bridgeman, discovered in conversation with a cow: "Steak, you idiot! Jerky! Stew! . . . I don't give a fig for your bloody Cow Protection Societies . . . I'm going to eat you, you pig of a cow" (276). Jonathan has never been sent Home for schooling because of an irresponsible alcoholic parent whose belated discovery of temperance is finally accompanied by a late-breaking desire that his son attend one of England's great universities, pending remedial schooling in "Blighty" (280). Jonathan is on the razzle, looking for one last fling before he embarks on the dying-man's errand. "I don't mind telling you," he confides to Bobby,

> my balls are like two ripe melons. Tried to get my leg over with a little half-caste nurse on the train, but she wasn't having any of it. Told me she would pull the emergency handle, frigid bitch. One would have thought she'd be grateful, but there really is no pleasing some of them. (280–81)

Bobby obliges him with a visit to Madam Maria Francesca's Goa House, where he is duly supplied with more liquor and a more accommodating half-caste. Before the evening is over, they are set upon by intoxicated rioters on the rampage who are enraged at the sight of ironically described "Sisterfucking feringhis" (283). Bobby flees as the Indian-bred Englishman is beaten, returning later to collect Jonathan's wallet, passport, and hip flask. As he turns the corner onto Falkland Road, he sees that the mission is on fire. Turning his back on it, Bobby decides to embark on the voyage and education intended for Jonathan.

The next scene places Bobby/Jonathan at the "stern rail of the *SS Loch Lomond*" on its way to England. During the passage, he has the pleasure and anxiety of being mistaken for an available "spare man" by all the disappointed Englishwomen who have failed to find a husband while in India (290). His experience with Amanda, one of these "Returning Empties," supplies further confidence in his project of passing: "Her smell, her colours, even the texture of her hair, are all tiny victories to him, and, as he stands at the rail with her scent in his nostrils, each time he lifts his cigarette he feels like an explorer" (291). She, too, is emblematic of the incarnate text of England that he must study and master.

Once in England, he is introduced to further ingredients of Englishness: "Everywhere Jonathan finds the originals of copies he has grown up with, all the absurdities of British India restored to sense by their natural environment." Mirroring Martin's observations about climate and culture, Bobby offers his own theories about the English character and way of life. He sees "the need their climate instills in them to pad their blue-veined bodies with layers of horsehair and mahogany, aspidistras and antimacassars, history, tradition and share certificates. Being British, he decides, is primarily a matter of insulation" (299). Kant had argued that races were differentiated in our original ancestors by four germs or seeds *(Keime)* containing *in potentia* a range of racial characteristics. The actualization of these characteristics would be determined by geographical and climatic conditions *(Anthropology)*. Hippocrates, Aristotle, and others also posited theories of physical difference caused by temperature, geography, and climate. The narrator's comments about climate considerations in the formation of Englishness reveal a fluid notion of their significance in the development of biocultural dimensions of identity, reflected in cultural practices that may have developed largely to warm the body struggling against "the fug of . . . dampness" (*The Impressionist,* 298). Plants (aspidistras) and protective covers from the East (antimacassars) also seem to be attempts to cozy the English room with imported elements of warmth that have nonetheless been domesticated to convey an aggregate English surround.

The boy's next stop on his way to Oxford finds him in another quintessential English location as he "walks into the oak-panelled entrance hall and for the first time smells the combination of carbolic soap, mud and boiled cabbage that is the unique aroma of the English boarding school" (306). The shoe is on the other cultural foot, the nose in another place with other smells, what Bhabha calls the "truest eye" of the migrant—and other sensory and cognitive faculties—eagerly taking in the new environment (*The Location of Culture,* 5). In a joke that seems to go on for too long, Dr. Noble, orchidist and headmaster of said school, "is discovered in the act of hybridization" (307–8). An arch disquisition on hybridization follows, with further allusions to early theories of race and the development of the concept of species based on herbarium material in the Linnaean schematic. Dr. Noble explains:

> Though the bees in our gardens transfer pollen indiscriminately from flower to flower, still we do not find crosses between dahlia and delphinium, or between geranium and gentian. Why? Because their essential natures are different. Just as it is with flowers, so it is with boys. Each boy has his essential nature, and yours, Mr. Bridgeman, is historical. Surely, as observers of creation, we must look upon these boundaries as a good thing? Were there none, the flowers would lose their identities in a hybrid swarm and nature would be in a desperate mess. (309–10)

One recalls Kant's similar advice against mixture on the grounds that it "gradually extinguishes [race's] characters" and "is not beneficial to the human race," even though "nature aims at assimilation" (*Anthropology,* 182).

At school, the changeling passes successfully as Jonathan, secure in his adopted identity until a sudden visit by a hitherto unknown great-aunt Berthilda. The threat of family "instantly drains this pretence of all reality and, with it, drains him of personality, anima, of the power of speech and action" (319). But the lady turns out to be no lady, and poses no credible challenge to Jonathan's identity, which she cannily intuits to be false. She herself neither smells nor sounds right, insufficiently processed into acceptable, educated Englishness. Dr. Noble registers several objections to her: "Apart from the smell, there are her undisciplined vowels, which slide around her palate entirely uncurbed, and her weird habit of making her crusty skirts rustle and crack beneath her haunches by shifting around on her chair" (320). The original English native is clearly not the best specimen of Englishness and a poor match for its better-crafted copy in Pran/Bobby/Jonathan. For a certain kind of pretender, "to be Anglicized is *emphatically* not to be English" (Bhabha, *The Location of Culture,* 86), but the racial hybrid with the right perceptible affordances may pass for English more effectively than the alleged original. However implausibly, our hero not only passes, but in doing so exposes the class-tethered and aesthetically contrived construction of Englishness.

The aunt's uncouth behavior convinces Dr. Noble and the Bridgeman family lawyer to have no further contact with her, and the boy's secret is secure. Noble adopts the boy eagerly, becoming yet another useful mentor. To help him fit in better, he recommends that Jonathan develop an interest in sport: "I suggest cricket" (332). But the boy is hit by hay fever, "as if the English countryside is taking revenge, making some point about people who belong, and people who may pretend but whose bodies betray them" (334). On Founders Day, the foundling wanders the school halls alone, looking at photos of old school teams, one from 1893 featuring F. M. V. Bridgeman, "Father of" (336). He hurries away from the disturbing reminder of his imposture and "so does not see, standing slight and school-uniformed beside eleven white-clad figures, a pale boy with a large leather-bound book. According to the legend he is R.A. *Forrester, scorer*. [Like Bobby/Jonathan.] If you were to look closely, you would see that his eyes are misty with hayfever" (336–37). It is the English body of his father that has lent him this genetic legacy of unbelonging to the countryside. Unathletic, but "a good enough historian," "Jonathan Bridgeman" makes it to that bastion of elite educational opportunity: Oxford.

Ahmad has written that "the figure of the migrant, especially the migrant (postcolonial) intellectual residing in the metropolis, comes to signify a universal condition of hybridity and is said to be the Subject of a Truth that individuals living within their national cultures do not possess" ("Postcolonial Theory," 371). Pointing to Bhabha's assertion, *pace* Rushdie, that "the truest eye may now belong to the migrant's double vision" (*The Location of Culture*, 5), Ahmad complains that

> most individuals are really not free to fashion themselves anew with each passing day, nor do communities arise out of and fade into the thin air of the infinitely contingent. Among the migrants themselves, only the privileged can live a life of constant mobility and surplus pleasure, between Whitman and Warhol as it were. Most migrants tend to be poor and experience displacement not as cultural plenitude but as torment. ("Postcolonial Theory," 373)

Although Ahmad's observations are valid in broad terms, Rushdie and Kunzru both emphasize the price of border crossing in *The Satanic Verses* and *The Impressionist.* Bobby as "Bridgeman" between two cultures and races is poised to make trenchant comparisons from the privileged perch of migrancy, but only after he has stolen an identity and colluded in a murder by abandoning the original to a riotous mob. A string of outrageously advantageous accidents combined with daring opportunism have permitted this unusual stance. Bobby/Bridgeman's truest I/eye is hard won: it has involved murder, deaths, theft, abandonment of his adoptive family, lies, secrets, deceit, and ruthless exploitation of unbelievably fortuitous opportunities. The violence through which this double vision has been gained requires a reassessment of those tenets of hybridity and diaspora that unwittingly glamorize border crossing and minimize its challenges and suffering, alongside its capacity to deform and alienate the self from itself until it begins to release its repressions in destructive forms.

At Oxford, Jonathan slides into outright racism in a rejection of his past. His peers speculate about him at Barabbas, "he has some odd ideas about civilization . . . racial ideas" (*The Impressionist,* 342). We learn that he is into theatrics and, ironically, is cast in the role of traitorous Iago in the college production of *Othello,* with an English boy playing the Moor in blackface. Jonathan's self-fashioning continues:

> In this latest version of himself he has been sure to emphasize everything that is honest, true and English. He is seen to frown upon novelty, and to deplore the current decline in social standards. In literature he is a Georgian, and in politics a Tory. He speaks little of his family, but lets it be known that he comes of old Gloucestershire farming stock. He is, in every possible way, the average undergraduate. (345)

To disarm residual suspicions, the changeling's approximation of whiteness requires its corollary, taking its distance from his "hidden layer" by embracing the empire that has produced him, in the psyche and in the flesh (346). In a debate on the motion, "this House believes Americans are Humans," he is recorded as making "a long and otiose statement of the White Man's mission to 'farm the world,'" and advised to "avoid appearing hysterical in the future . . . to remain relevant" (346–47). His views garner disapproval from many of his peers but also result in an invitation to tea by the duce of the Oxford Fascisti. A caricature of the anxiously assimilated migrant, Bridgeman identifies with positions that target the very vulnerability and lack of power that generate his anxiety in the first place.

Bridgeman's unrelenting desire for whiteness finds its human object in a blond beauty in due course of time. She is "Elgar and tea roses . . . rolling fields with drystone boundary walls . . . willow trees, fruit cup, sunset over"—fragments of landscape, martial imperial music, and classic summer drinks agglomerated in a multisensorial symphony of Englishness that links beauty and metonymic aesthetics with civilizational and political power. "Brimming with the aestheticism of it all," he decides that Astarte Chapel is "the pattern, the type, the very essence of the English girl"; in this, she is something like Chamcha's upper-class wife, Pamela, "Bloody Britannia. Warm beer, mince pies [and] common sense" (*The Satanic Verses,* 175). The "quintessentially English" girl, he finds out, has been named Astarte after the Phoenician goddess of love and fertility by her father, an anthropology professor. Jonathan, soon to be Johnny to "Star," reads that "the sacrificial death and resurrection" of her male lover "is taken to symbolize the regenerative cycle of the earth," an unrecognized clue to his impending fate (*The Impressionist,* 353).

Under the influence of the bright and volatile Star, Pran-flux is about to be buffeted by the vagaries of this capricious representative of Englishness. Star straddles the antipodes of the classic liberal English position, romanticizing those who are in "contact with the earth," echoing Fanon's phrase in *Black Skin White Masks,* while disdaining those who are in contact with the earth but savages because "they've never even seen a bath," for example (*The Impressionist,* 358, 363). Civilization, according to her, "is the problem" because it has stifled the Western natural self, but Star can only sustain this position until it comes to lavatory and toilette facilities (358). Invited to join Star's father on an expedition to Fotseland, a location that had made his reputation as a professor, Johnny observes that anthropology "is the very highest mark of civilization." Professor Chapel's lectures represent to him "the end of a long journey, a hard climb up to a giddy elevation from which it is finally possible to survey the world and the people in it. All the earth is available. Everything and everyone has a place" (375). Confronting his own repressions, Jonathan/Johnny is reminded of his racially and culturally mixed body as a site of betrayal: "As the Professor speaks about taboos or marriage customs, Jonathan looks around the hall, afraid of catching an eye or seeing a smirk on the face of someone who *knows*—who understands that he is called to blackness and savagery by his tainted blood" (382). Knowing that his "only connection to [Star] is through her father," "Johnny" abandons his designs of joining the civil service and exerting the empire's "civilizing influence on other races" (358), choosing instead the classificatory impulse of anthropology without understanding the connection between the two, or the psychological sources of the impulse in the professor's obsessive compulsive disorder, or the judgmental voyeurism that has replaced natural and repressed curiosity about the body and its range of expressions.

As Johnny will learn from the English cartographer George Marchant once he reaches West Africa, "it is all more or less a question of latrines" (432). The logic of the latrine is a substantial force in separating the British from their imperial subjects. At the nawab's tiger hunt, we recall that Imelda, a European woman "works out how many hours she is away from the nearest flush toilet, and begins to cry" (171). In unusual moments of "gastric awareness" following a mass intestinal outbreak, the European visitors are reduced to undeniable bodily states. Sir Wyndham observes the hapless Imelda in something he has never seen: "a woman in the act of excretion." As he watches her "with mingled horror and fascination," he thinks, "Minty [his wife] must do that. God" (170–71). Linking perversions and zoomorphic degradation, Freud speculates that "as long as smell (or taste) is dominant, urine, feces, and the whole surface of the body, also blood, have a sexually exciting effect" (*The Complete Letters,* 279). In the "sensational" scene of the hunt when Pran/Rukhsana first confronts formal representatives of empire and the native ruling class, Kunzru comically conjoins blood, sex, and dysentery as various characters are discovered in "varying states of undress," and nervously discharged bullets bloody more than one participant, yoking coprology and copulation together. Anus, nose, sexuality, and the organic sources of repression feature prominently in Freud's celebrated exchanges with Fliess. In one letter, he writes of "the changed part played by sensations of smell: upright walking, nose raised from the ground, at the same time a number of formerly interesting sensations attached to the earth becoming repulsive—by a process still unknown to me." Freud speaks without pretensions to politesse in explaining the links between civilization, psychology, and organic repression: "To put it crudely, the memory actually stinks just as in the present the object stinks; and in the same manner as we turn away our sense organ (the head and nose in disgust), the preconscious and a sense of consciousness turn away from the memory. This is repression" (*The Complete Letters,* 279–80). The basic functions of the body and its eliminative practices, postures of squatting reminiscent of these functions, the smell of other places linked to what is taken in and put out by the body, constitute the fundamentals of classification and repression of what is alienated from the self in the process of becoming civilized. Bodily practices, toilet facilities, and smells become grist for the classificatory mill in sociocultural versions of theories of evolution.

Prior to his departure with Professor Chapel's expedition, when he comes across the Fotse Village exhibit at the Empire exhibition in Wembley, Jonathan confronts blackness in "all its horror." The embodiments of blackness and associated savageness on display prompt Pran/Jonathan's fear of being thought *not quite / not black,* a fear that finds its expression in a scatological metaphor as he recalls a repressed past in which he and those with the "dull sooty skin" would both have been far from the giddy elevations of anthropological study, consigned instead to the cesspits of civilizational hierarchy: "It was like staring into the toilet bowl, looking at what he had expelled from himself" (*The Impressionist,* 381). On their way to Fotseland, the party stops in Paris to visit Star, who has a further shock in store for the young man who has begun to fancy himself as explorer "Beau Bridgeman" (399). The merry young girl takes him to a nightclub, "a mongrel place" where he sees "Negroes cutting through the crowds like they own the pavement" (410). "The black men, with their canes and silk shirts, seem like a bad omen" to Johnny, who is waiting to propose to Star with an engagement ring in his pocket (410). He feels that "it is as if Africa is already reaching out towards him, before he has made sure of his foothold in Europe" (411). Star is busy romanticizing the blacks. Listening to "black" music, Star comments, "So sad. You can tell how much they've suffered," locating them in a past no longer available to the West. "They have something, don't they? Something we've lost" (412).

In his essay "On Jazz," Adorno observes that this sound "is supposed to subject the over-stimulated Western nerves to the vitality of blacks [*Negervitalitat*]" (471). Explaining that what the Führer banned as *Negermusik,* the occasion of the essay, was in fact not even jazz as produced by African Americans but rather a sort of European production trading on its novelty value, Adorno, writing in 1936 as Hektor Rotweiler, uncovers its blatantly commercial appeal to repressed primitivism. Although the music featured at the club is part of African American cultural contributions to the entertainment scene in Paris between the wars, Adorno's perceptions are borne out in Star's muddled relationship to otherness.

As Johnny is preparing to propose, a black man appears and begins to kiss his beloved "full on the lips":

> He is kissing her. This man. Kissing. Her. Kissing Star. And he is (this cannot be, this absolutely is not happening)—*black*. Black as night, as tar, coal, pitch, liquorice and the suits of funeral directors. Black as a Bible, his skin shining in the candle-light like something made of polished wood. The palms of his black hands contrastingly pink, his thick lips pressed on hers, kissing her, kissing Star. Kissing. Star. Black man. Star. (*The Impressionist,* 413)

In prose redolent of the rhythms of the ambient music, the narrator communicates the thrusting, rebarbative implications of Star's (and colonialism's) capricious logic. Flustered at being caught out in what is evidently a concealed relationship, Star struggles to explain, "Sweets is different. He plays the piano. You should hear him play. He's wonderful. And he's different. Exotic. Strong. I've never met anyone like him" (414). Mouthing words that Fanon would mimic in *Black Skin, White Masks*—"meet my black friend . . . when people like me, they tell me it is in spite of my color" (116), Star is rehearsing the position familiar to this day and captured in the exceptionalism accorded to some despite their color, but in this case also because of it. "Different? To whom?" asks Johnny, "To me?" (*The Impressionist,* 414). Star's response leaves Pran-flux in a familiar rubble: "Yes, Johnny, to you. Come on. I know you, Johnny. I feel I know all there is about you. Gloucestershire, Chopham Hall,

Oxford, blah blah blah. You're very sweet, but you're exactly like everybody else" (414–15). Against this textbook caricature of upper-class Englishness, Star demands primitivism: "I want passion, primitive emotions. I want to be in contact with the origin of things. . . . He knows about things. He actually shot someone once. And his family were terribly terribly poor. Things like that happen to Negroes. That's why they have soul" (415). When Johnny complains that he has soul, Star explains: "English people have a soul, which is why we go to church on Sunday, but we haven't got *soul.* Sweets explained it to me. It's about music and suffering. And it's something to do with food as well, but that's slightly different. Anyway, you don't have it and Sweets does" (415). Johnny pleads with her, "I love you and though I may not be as black as him, I'm blacker than you think. Honestly. I've got soul, Star. I have" (416).

The narrator has warned us earlier in the text about the capricious Star: "Later, when he is wiser to the ways of Miss Astarte Chapel," he will learn that "relations with her are composed of a series of dyads, positive and negative held together by a strong bond" (357). In this capsule-form introduction to ambivalence, Kunzru locates the contrary drives of fear and desire, loathing and longing characteristic of the colonial impulse. When Star eventually consummates her desire for otherness, it will be with the forgotten Prince Firoz—a figure that accords with what Bhabha describes as "a *reformed,* recognizable other" (*The Location of Culture,* 86)—as much as his "asset liquidity and breeding," qualities that Star, "like any well brought-up English girl . . . has been taught to rate" more highly than "mere attractiveness" (357). In the meanwhile, our itinerant protagonist has had a rude awakening. Everything he has built his identity upon—the idea of the Great Chain of Being, a stepladder to climb upon—has been shattered: "When you have organized your whole life as a ladder (with, for example, something shining and white at the top, and sticky blackness at the bottom) there are consequences when someone kicks it away" (417). In a "state of collapse," Jonathan realizes: "This is what happens. This terrible blurring is what happens when boundaries are breached. Pigment leaks through skin like ink through blotting paper. It becomes impossible to tell what is valuable and what is not" (417).

Hominidae: In and Out of Africa

In Which He Will Travel On . . .

The last segment, titled "The Impressionist," finds the shape-shifter in West Africa. On this journey, Beau Bridgeman, the romantically imagined adventurer, is in for further adult education. Colonialism and the civilizational structures associated with it are about to be exposed to him as motivated by an undisguised economic bottom line:

> All his preparations for Africa, from his studies in the university library to his conversations with Professor Chapel (and further back, through history lessons, head-measuring, poetry reciting . . .), have shown him the same edifying picture: a lone adventurer, heroically inscribing the English character on a blank land. Instead he is to be some kind of tax inspector. (433)

Born in the rough middle of the cultural color spectrum, having traveled to its aspirational polar end in whiteness, the impressionist is now bound for a reckoning with the opposite pole on the spectrum of racial identity. He is about to discover his truest eye/I somewhat belatedly, not in the assimilative move to the humanity encapsulated in whiteness as the top of the civilizational chain but rather in a journey toward the most urgent objects of its civilizing mission, those who stand at the nadir of its classificatory regimes, the "sticky blackness at the bottom" (417).

The abstract recipients of colonial attention and its epistemological exertions, it turns out, are no "mere possessors of beliefs or participants in social organizations. Instead they seem irreducibly, disquietingly physical. These abstractions breathe, eat, talk and laugh—laughter that he can kill by walking into the room" (433). Occupying the vestments of colonial authority in a persona that Star has described as "so English" (324), Jonathan recognizes the deception and pretense of authority at the same time that he understands the bodyhood of the natives and his impact on their bodily expressions in his presence. He also comes to understand the mechanics of prejudice as he observes it among the West Africans who are no abstract clump but riven by their own aesthetic preferences and standards; the porters, for instance, dislike the Fotse because "they are heathens and eat forbidden food" (451). If anything, their humanity and sameness with the visitors inhere not least in their internal differences and plural ways of bodying forth their beliefs and anxieties. Like the colonizers, the sample population is internally diverse, invested in boundary tests of religion and diet, prone to prejudice, apt to engage in displays for visitors, and able to revise their codes and structures in dynamic engagement with the course of history.

Indeed, the Fotse appear to have changed substantially since Professor Chapel's last visit. To the annoyance of Professor Chapel's colleagues, the Fotse are no longer available as specimens of insulated primitivism. Lacking in necklaces, combs, and status marks, Fotse laborers brought in by Europeans to build a road look nothing like their erstwhile counterparts who "were supposed to be *pristine*" (448). Chapel and the visiting expedition are not greeted with "the customary party of women singing lilting traditional songs of welcome" (447). Farms are deserted. The Fotse have retreated to the caves, a practice Chapel insists is completely unprecedented. Instead of "a docile, joyous people, almost untouched by the ills of modernity," this is a suspicious group that wants the professor whose work "has made them world famous" to go away (448). Chapel ascribes the change to those who are too keen on "getting the natives working." They "haven't a thought for science. . . . All you can ever get them to talk about is their blasted tax base" (449). Jonathan's naive question, "If they want us to go . . . shouldn't we go?," is answered with stares that suggest he is quite mad. In the ensuing silence, the Fotse begin to emerge from their caves. The team will have its anthropological opportunity after all.

After a ritual exchange, however, "the Fotse avoid the white men completely" (452). Frustrated at the native's performative noncompliance with Professor Chapel's pedagogic descriptions of their practices, some members of the party take issue with the professor: "Is there actually anything they did before that they still do now?" sneers Marchant. Marchant's expectations of synchronic stasis in Africa, Professor Chapel's pedagogic understanding, their collective blindness to their own practices, and the administration's repurposing of science for profit are of a piece with Edward Said's descriptions of professional Orientalism. Kunzru's exposure of the colonial mission, its knowledge structures, and its dissembling the motivations of economic greed answers tragedy with the tools of comedy.

In a comic reversal, the tragedies of history returning as fabulous farce, the Africans are engaged in their own representational practices. "Jonathan stares at Africa with uneasy recognition" (417). Here hawkers vend dolls: "Jonathan looks down at the carvings. They are Englishmen, little painted *colons* in white uniforms, with bulbous topis on their heads. Their features stand away from their faces, eyes and mouths and noses sharp and oversized. Their stiff poses give them a formal, hieratic quality" (425). Hieratic is a cursive writing system used in the provenance of the pharaohs in Egypt and Nubia that developed alongside the hieroglyphic system. The author's reference to hieratic representation invites consideration of the stiffness of the body rigidified to represent a fixed identity. In the reversed gaze of Africa, it is the visitors and their ways that seem exotic, and by turns absurd and threatening. Following the rift between different members of the expedition, the anthropological gaze is turned on the anthropologists in a farcical description of a "feud conducted in the traditional British manner" (453).

When the visitors fall victim to diarrhea—like the hunting party of another crew in the jungles of India where Pran was Rukhsana—the members of the expedition use their thunderboxes, fighting over the right to use them. The Fotse observers report to their chief, "curiously enough, even at the height of their affliction, none of the white men think of doing their business in the bushes. The spiritual significance of the boxes is, they suggest, penitential" (465). Speculation, judgment, evaluation, and oversignification, it would seem, are not the exclusive preserve of one group. Moreover, the visitors' irrational adherence to the propriety of the onomatopoeically named thunderbox designed for what the English describe euphemistically as the urgent call of nature, is a product of their investment in repressing behavior they are ingrained to associate with animality, despite serious illness in a life-and-death situation. Peristalsis must be resisted and the bowels must not move, while control overtakes urgency until the right receptacle and confined structure allow for a response to bodily demand. The rigid, repressed response to the urgent call of nature underscores the extent to which "the truth about life in its immediacy must scrutinize its estranged forms," as Adorno notes in *Minima Moralia* (15).

Stumbling upon a Fotse performance, Jonathan and Gittens, another member of the visiting expedition, find, along with a ritual dance in which the spirit of the ancestors ostensibly inhabits the dancers, another tableau that gives them pause:

> The women they are inhabiting move with a rigid, pompous gait, swinging their arms swiftly to the side, or holding them behind their backs. One clutches something square in its hand, slapping it and waving at the audience. Others hold sticks, jamming them against their shoulders and aiming them like rifles.
>
> "My God," breathes Gittens. "I think that's us." (*The Impressionist,* 455)

"At once resemblance and menace," the performance reveals not just the ruse of authority but its real bodily threat and force for a people whose way of life is about to change as never before in the face of its armed colonizers (*The Location of Culture,* 123). In the glare of the Fotse gaze, the visitors confront not what they have come to find—the other—but how they are perceived as threatening others, one with the technologies of conquest and destruction. The new predatory animal in the jungles of Africa, the colonizer is provided a mirror in which hunger for profit disguised in the language of development, humanity, and globalization is exposed. In making us privy to some of the spectacles uncovered in the bidirectional gaze, Kunzru unsettles our perspective. Descriptions of the Fotse's speculative and leveraging practices, for instance, invite comparison with the FTSE index, a point hammered home by further references to Lifi "winning the hand of the sky princess Neshdaqa" (*The Impressionist,* 367). Studying the Fotse is not only "like visiting our own distant past," as Gittens puts it, without having fully understood the lesson on offer, but also akin to the visitors' present and their future indicated in speculative practices that can destroy whole economies and ways of life overnight (467).

Jonathan, the only traveler with an eye for the complexities of the situation, is accused of lacking "team spirit" when he reiterates the obvious: "Don't you think they'd rather be left alone?" (468–69). Failing to hear the right response from his team, he retreats, struggling for awareness in a narrative that never permits him the coherence of a character with a past and present united by consciousness. In a surreal state between dream and imagination, "he becomes aware that cables and wires are strung between every object and person in the darkness around him, forming a single interconnected mechanism," a vision that suggests the world wide web of virtual and real globalization where none are free of history at the end of history. At the same time, "he imagines the Fotse as their huts are bulldozed and they are marched toward their new settlements by the side of their new roads" (469). Asking himself if he got lost a long time ago, he abandons camp the following day on an ostensible census survey, and embarks on his final avatar: having begun as a nomad after his unhappy expulsion from the Razdan household, he ends as one.

By the end of the novel, no longer named, the protagonist, "he," leaves camp, falls sick, and is tended by a Fotse healer who covers him in mud, "which dries, caking him like a new kaolin skin" in an image reminiscent of another itinerant traveler, "three years after the beginning of the new century," who is lifted into a cave and after congress with Amrita, "the mother of the world," finds that "sweat and dust has turned their skins to an identical red-brown colour. The colour of the earth" (473, 3, 15). These references, reminiscent of those associated with funeral services, "earth to earth, ashes to ashes, dust to dust," are drafted here for a sense of new times and new beginnings, as new worlds await their inception from what we could construe as a gesture toward humanity's common ground. The desert and dust of Rajasthan and the sand dunes of Western Africa are crimped together, as are time and space in an alternative history and alternative temporality to suggest a saga that has been unfolding beyond our limited perspective.

Before the protagonist's destiny is revealed and the narrative is concluded, Kunzru makes arch gestures to a utopian society evocative of Hardt and

Negri's multitudes on the one hand, and on the other to key tropes in the work of Deleuze and Guattari: the war machine as a grassroots affair, and rhizomatic, nomadic, and intermezzo states of being. Kunzru's joke is to ascribe these visions of a "new society"—"how men have imagined this beauty"—to Fotse conceptions of a premodern rather than a postmodern utopia (474–75). Despite the temporary victory of the multitudes who have "no head, no centre," and who rise up in a bid to "destroy sorcery forever," however, (475), the new times are upon the Fotse and they promise to be "bitter" (456). As the "grid of roads creeps closer, spawning villages of roofless concrete houses which as yet have no inhabitants" (479–80), Africa, and the Fotse with it, are about to become a "historical part of the World"; their "Unhistorical, Undeveloped Spirit" as yet only "on the threshold of the World's History," due for an appointment with a future they did not imagine or invite (Hegel, *Philosophy of History,* 99). As the Fotse healer draws out the traveler's evil spirit, Kunzru leaves us to ponder what it might be like to have the European spirit, arguably *der Geist seiner Zeit* (Hegel's conception of the spirit of one's time) exorcised? What possibilities might emerge if the journey rather than the destination, itinerant being rather than teleologically driven becoming, were to determine our meaning of identity?

Pran / Rukhsana / Clive / Bobby / Robert / Chandra / Bridgeman / Jonathan / and the nameless "he" has been reduced to a shambles, along with any idea of a progressive history enacted through the body and person of the suggestively named "Pran." In refusing priority to postmodern conceptions of a nonhierarchical imagined beauty, Kunzru seems to demand from us a double vision of space and time outside the dominant narratives of history and commandeered space. At the beginning of the end of history for this part of Africa, what might it look like to step outside of history and imagine not the future but the past? Trade, nomadism, hybridity—Hausa being a prime example of a language produced by these supposedly postmodern, postcolonial developments—are phenomena that can be imagined *avant la lettre—la lettre européenne* to be precise. The Fotse appear to have knowledge not only of water-borne diseases but also a sense of the future through speculation, betting, leveraging, and hedging the odds. They have conceived of a new society through an appealingly egalitarian, liberal aesthetic. What else could this dying world have known that we will never know because we could not perceive them as a historical part of the world? Kunzru entertains us with the notion that non-Western others have conceptions of beauty and order as well as a sense of the un-beautiful. He nudges us to remember that primitivism had to be invented to validate the superiority of Western forms, that the world has gone about its business for a long time before Europe's entry into global trade, and that the "discovered" world is also internally riven and diachronic.

A similar drama of perceptions is performed by and through the personae of Pran-flux. If he is an aslant, unexpected symptom of the changing, unsettled body of culture, he also comes to rest in freeze-frames of being before he takes new shape, urging upon us a consideration of identity as process as well as product. The aesthetic logic of Kunzru's narrative traffics in deliberately short strokes. In distinct segments that will never add up to a whole, each identity bit performs the narrative teleology of a short story in a series that cannot be sustained over time to allow for the coherence we expect from the novel and its treatment of character. Episodic, akin to the characteristic short brush strokes of the impressionist movement, the narrative places Pran-flux in situations that permit dramatic rehearsals of various subject positions: heir to a purist nation; half-caste hybrid flotsam; transvestite object of pederasty; ward to a mission divided; opportunistic pimp, procurer, pretender to Englishness; country-born expatriate finished at public school and ushered into Oxbridge circles; anthropologist invited to be tax collector; subject stripped of dominant ideology; nameless nomad. Each of these short-lived identities is bristling with sensory appeal, full of sensory receptivity, making and receiving impressions and judgments, discovering new boundaries and new passwords. What is this art of fragments intended to communicate? Although the narrative exposes the hollow fictions of race and the notion of identity itself as compositionally fragmented, the thoroughgoing deconstruction of Pran portrays more than the deflated postmodern soufflé of identity. It asks us to engage in a serious consideration of the world of forms and appearances—a phenomenal world, to indulge an easy pun—in which the effects produced by what has materialized in, on, and through the body are what create the impression of a boundary with other collective bodies. Pran-life has become a dead thing subject to the rigor mortis of empty form, or what I have referred to in the introduction as the sclerosed form of life that once lived more freely. At the terminus of this sketchy treatment of identity, where journeys are not at an end, the author also leaves us to ponder who might we be, or who might we be like, outside the guiding spirit of imperial modernity and its teleological narrative. At history's alleged end, this appears to be a futile exercise. We are already consumed in a globalized world by anxiety about what *looks right* on the world stage, and what is the correct passe-partout in the new times.

In considering the question of identity beyond the anxieties of the moment, the culmination of Pran-flux's picaresque passage in Africa prompts a final, outrageous question: Does the purported origin of hominids in Africa and their subsequent scattering and evolution into different races count as diaspora on a breathtaking, spatio-temporally telescopic scale? Does nomadism articulate a different vision of migrancy than diaspora? Pran/Bridgeman has been reduced to a shambles in Africa, where he had hoped to locate himself at a "giddy elevation from which it is finally possible to survey the world and the people in it" in a possessive, classificatory, imperial gaze (*The Impressionist,* 375). Instead, his truest I/eye reveals not only the advent of new times but a recollection of *other* new times through a fugue on the theme of beginnings and ends. This fugue joins his deconstruction and the narrative of return to Africa, long thought to be the origin of animal/human life, and later the first hominid. Whether or not Africa is the birthplace of humankind, in a paleoanthropological view, the nomads of yesteryear, to be confused neither with the Orientalized productions of colonial anthropology nor the hopeful metaphors of postmodern theory, have been afoot long before the break in time, long before the global migrants of modern times. The novel's bewildering conclusion attempts to stir us into recollection of a possibility that existed once upon a time. That may have been the first of all diasporas so lost to antiquity that it lacks the capacity even to haunt the present into anamnesis of a shared past as the imagined prospect of a shared future. In historical time, sooner or later, however, the nomad who "has no thoughts of arriving anywhere" will come to a border somewhere in the future when only the right shibboleth will permit safe passage (481). Shibboleth or Sibboleth? Pran-life hangs in the balance between them.

3 DOYLE PLAYS SHERLOCK

Julian Barnes's Unofficial Englishmen, Arthur and George

> The history of civilization is the history of the introversion of sacrifice.
> —**MAX HORKHEIMER AND THEODOR ADORNO,** *DIALECTIC OF ENLIGHTENMENT*

> Will you try to imagine how sacrifice originated? . . . he must have died in the animal, for only thus could the animal die for him. . . . everything rests on the fact that he, too, died in the animal, for one moment.
> —**HUGO VON HOFMANNSTHAL, QUOTED IN THEODOR ADORNO,** *PRISMS*

The Sherlock Holmes Way

The charms of detective fiction arguably lie in our hunger for truth, the need to know who is good and who is evil, what really happened, and not only whodunit, but also how and *why* he or she "dunit." In a genre that tolerates ambiguity poorly, mysteries must be solved. In effect, however, Slavoj Žižek explains in *Looking Awry* that the narrative usually dupes us with a successful fiction that evades an encounter with the truth of the real:

> The detective "proves by facts" what would otherwise remain a hallucinatory projection of guilt onto a scapegoat, i.e., he proves that the scapegoat is effectively guilty. The immense pleasure brought about by the detective's solution results from this libidinal gain, from a kind of surplus profit obtained from it: our desire is realized and we do not even have to pay the price for it. (59)

Detective narratives leave the mystery of our desire and guilt draped under the cloak of rationality and facts. The solution is a ruse, a narrative contrivance that allows the reader to go scot-free while the *sujet supposé savoir,* whose "business is to know things," absolves the reader by indicting the fictional suspect held responsible for the crime in question.[1]

Neither solution nor absolution is easily available when fact and fiction are forced into a mutual confrontation with their limits, as in Julian Barnes's novelization of a real-life criminal case in *Arthur and George*. The titular Arthur of the novel is Sir Arthur Conan Doyle, creator of the best-known detective in the history of the popular genre, while the relatively obscure George Edalji, an Anglo-Indian—or rather *Scottish* English-*Parsi* Indian, as we are frequently reminded in the novel—is the son of Charlotte and Shapurji Edalji, a converted Parsi from India who is appointed vicar in rural Staffordshire. After a hostile campaign of anonymous letters and pranks against the Edalji family, George becomes the chief suspect in the Great Wyrley Outrages, the name given to a series of episodes involving nighttime mutilation of farm animals near the Edaljis' vicarage. George is subsequently arrested, convicted, and imprisoned for maiming a horse, and disqualified as a solicitor. After his release, George pleads his innocence in a letter to Doyle. Accustomed to rejecting requests for playing detective "ever since Sherlock Holmes solved his first case," Doyle agrees at a time when he is distraught after his consumptive wife's death, but also in love with another woman (257).[2] In a curious subversion of the discrepancy between their stature in the public eye, the novel presents Arthur and George on a spurious equivalence, two "Englishmen" occupying the marquee space of the cover on a Christian first name basis. Their lives are presented in alternate chapters, interspersed with segments involving law enforcement figures.

The novelization of a real-life crime, rendered the more intriguing by Barnes's own turn at detective fiction under the pseudonym Dan Kavanagh, and Doyle's turn as a detective in real life, ironically exposes the hoax of detective fiction as well as the unacknowledged mysteries of prejudice. Playing detective in real life, Doyle—the surrogate *sujet supposé savoir*—repeatedly confronts projectional fantasies and scapegoating techniques in lieu of rational investigation, devices unfortunately reminiscent of more than one Holmes story featuring grotesquely Orientalized figures in Doyle's own literary corpus. George is turned into a scapegoat for the heinous mutilation of farm animals through a formal investigative process that bears uncanny similarity with implausible expedients in Doyle's stories. In many ways, the novelization of the George Edalji case by Barnes puts the writer of sensational, sometimes racist, fictions to the test in his real-life reckoning with colonial prejudice. It also forces a confrontation with the idea of fair play and good form associated with Englishness and the civilizing mission. The contradictions and deceptions of the progressive, meliorative logic of the enlightenment project and civilizing mission are hardly news, but the novel goes a long way toward disclosing the reasons for their persistent appeal. In what might be described as a tragicomedy of manners, the novel draws us into turn-of-the-century England as if into a biosocial laboratory. Real-life people Arthur and George are recast in the fashioned character of unofficial Englishmen, performing creatures shaped and haunted by the sacrificial, renunciative logic of civilization and good form.

Barnes's fictional retelling of the case shows us a world in which everyone—suspect, detective, inspector, savior, and victim of the miscarriage of justice alike—is trapped in a world seduced by questions of breeding and aesthetic form, as if in a carnivalesque house of mirrors. In a drama that foregrounds animal mutilation as the central crime bedeviling the socius, the novel offers readers an opportunity to review the results of a long experiment in biosocial engineering in which the nature/culture dichotomy relies on a complicated relationship with the animal. The management of the animal body, its urges, appetites, emissions, biological functions, and indeed, its capacity for violence, provide the basis for the civilizing process. What Horkheimer and Adorno describe as Europe's "underground history," which is arguably also applicable to other societies, entails "the fate of the human instincts and passions which are displaced and distorted by civilization" in a philosophical tradition that expresses "the idea of the human being . . . in contradistinction to the animal" (*Dialectic of Enlightenment,* 192, 203). What is called culture must be understood, they insist, as that which "defines the body as thing which can be possessed . . . as the object, the dead thing, the '*corpus*'" (193). The feats of civilization should be recognized as "the product of sublimation" and as the "transformation [of the body] into dead matter" (194). In fossilized forms of civility, we recognize its secret mandate, "nothing shall be allowed to live" (195). In *Metaphysics,* Adorno shares his sense that "the most important thing of all . . . what really mattered [was] the zone of the carcass and the knacker," the latter being the person in charge of rendering farm animals no longer suitable for human consumption (117). The capacity for bodily feeling—"the true basis of morality" for Adorno—is redirected into objectification, reification, and estrangement from nature and all that lives (116). Schooled in this regimen, those who learn "to measure the other with the eye of the coffin maker" turn human beings into specimens, scan incarnate forms for signs of restraint and reform or appropriate redirection of animal urges, and condemn sensory excess or deviance from the prevailing norm (*Dialectic of Enlightenment,* 195). Elsewhere, Adorno refers to the production of a deadened, bourgeois subject who is allowed to survive because he has restrained and renounced the impulses that betray him as biotic being. In the introduction, I refer to this indoctrination into civility as the inculcation of a postanimal aesthetics aimed at the reform of sensory expression into rigid modes of comportment. The monuments of civilization are raised upon a charnel house as its foundation. Ritual sacrifice and modern forms of scapegoating are on a continuum with this war on life and nature, turned upon the self as upon the weak. Without belaboring the use of the particular animal metaphor of the sacrificial "scapegoat" used in the novel, the targeting of George for crimes that have never been solved—the Great Wyrley Outrages involving horrifying mutilation of horses, cows, and sheep—might be better understood if we placed it within a larger biosocial project characterized by a conflicted relationship with the animal displaced onto an exaggerated investment in the manipulation of human plasticity into rigid forms. Enchanted by symbol and its logic of substitution and displacement, modern man "seeks to save himself by throwing himself away and making himself a mouthpiece of things" (Adorno, *Prisms,* 207).

The Beginning and the Foregone Conclusion

"The Mystery of Uncle Jeremy's Household," an early story by Doyle, furnishes an intriguing backdrop for Barnes's *Arthur and George.*[3] Uncle Jeremy's household includes the quixotic lord of the manor, his nephew John Thurston, who hopes to inherit his estate; an Anglo-Indian governess, "a stylish-looking brunette with Indian blood in her veins"; two children (a third having died mysteriously soon after the governess's arrival); and the proprietor's "imperturbable secretary," Copperthorne, who "is somewhat gone in [the] direction" of the attractive Anglo-Indian (44, 42). The story is hardly alone in inviting charges of "improbable and illogical developments in the narrative" (Cuningham, "Sherlock Holmes and the Case of Race," 113), but is of particular archival interest as a precursor to the Holmes franchise and in featuring an Anglo-Indian racial hybrid. Published in seven episodes in *Boy's Own Paper,* a popular vehicle for miscellany and stories on subjects including adventures with empire, in it Holmes and Watson "made their first bow in prototype" as Hugh Lawrence and John Thurston, several months before the publication of *A Study in Scarlet,* which featured the sleuth who would become a household name throughout the world (Haining, *The Final Adventures of Sherlock Holmes,* 34).[4] It is also one of several stories in the Holmes canon in which an Oriental figure arrives in England to commit bizarre ritual murder (Lycett, *The Man Who Created Sherlock Holmes,* 115). The half-Oriental governess in this story alongside a full-fledged Oriental straight out of an illustration from colonial ethnological texts are part and parcel of a discourse that views racial hybrids with suspicion because of persistent Orientalist prejudices, a problem that the composer of this story and others trafficking in this stereotype would confront in real life in Doyle's defense of George. Although the storied governess is quite unlike the straitlaced barrister George Edalji, both have British mothers and are Anglo-Indian by virtue of racial mixture, even if they are not so by the letter of the Indian Constitution, which does not include European maternity as an admissible factor in defining the group. Both, however, are reduced to the status of specimens in the sociobiological laboratory of the British Empire.

Miss Warrender is "the child of an Indian chieftain, whose wife was an Englishwoman" ("Uncle Jeremy's Household," 43). The chieftain "was killed in the mutiny fighting against us" (the "us" clarifies the implied community of readers), whereupon the fifteen-year-old destitute orphan is adopted by a German merchant and eventually makes her way to Dunkelthwaite in response to an advertisement for the position of governess. Thurston's invitation to his Holmesian friend, Lawrence, throws out "the brunettish governess" as "bait to you if you retain your taste for ethnological studies" (43). Even though his nebulous suspicions involve both Copperthorne and the governess, it is "the beautiful Anglo-Indian" that the incipient Holmesian detective decides "to study . . . as an entomologist might a specimen, critically, but without bias" (55, 53). She is to him "an interesting psychological problem, nothing more" (56). He plans to study her, in other words, with what Horkheimer and Adorno describe as the measuring gaze of "the coffin maker" that has already fixed her as one might an insect (*Dialectic of Enlightenment,* 195). It is not the criminal but the crime that remains to be discovered in the course of the narrative. The unprompted, uninvited investigation pursued without any reported crime is designed to confirm the apprehension that the half-caste governess's beauties of face and figure will not be matched by concomitant beauties of mind—that bad blood will tell, as it obligingly does. Lawrence, the narrator of the tale, hints "there were other things in [Thurston's] second letter which prevent me from quoting it in full" (43). Whether these are extraneous, trivial, or of a salacious nature to sweeten the bait we shall not know, but the omissions hint at the suggestive alliance of sex and race, and heighten the mystery of "a princess for governess," who turns out to be heir designate to the cult of Thuggee associated with ritual strangulation. Although Lawrence "solemnly aver[s] that up to the last moment I had not the smallest suspicion of the truth," the story's conclusion suggests that this sensational inheritance biologically predisposes the half-blood not only to poor form in artistic performance and daily habits but toward senseless, ambiguously motivated acts of homicide of innocent white children, and casual violence toward small animals (67).

More doctor than detective, in this early piece Doyle invests in physiognomic and sensational information as diagnostic data, eager to find signs "that transform the body into text" (Sollors, *Neither Black nor White Yet Both,* 151).[5]

Gentlemanly comportment put aside at will, the would-be detective claims, "John Thurston made me peep into her private sitting-room one day when she was out," allowing him to observe her questionable aesthetic choices in producing an effect "ludicrously tawdry and glaring" in the decorations ("Uncle Jeremy's Household," 54–55). Lawrence notes that her "Oriental love for bright colours had exhibited itself in an amusing fashion" (55). Using stock colonial verbiage and animal imagery, Doyle tells us that despite Lawrence's Holmesian immunity from feminine lure, he "could not help admiring the beautiful litheness of her figure . . . [and her] feline grace," thus explaining her appeal to the dour secretary, Copperthorne (48). She appears to him as a "pythoness" (59). Claiming to have gained "a deeper insight into her character" over time, Thurston offers a series of observations on the "great dash of savage in her nature" underneath "the veneer of culture" (54). Readers are asked to believe that despite being "fairly well read," acquainted "with several languages," and having "a great natural taste for music," "in the course of her conversation she would every now and again drop some remark which would almost startle me by its primitive reasoning, and by its disregard for the conventionalities of civilization" (54). Miss Warrender's compromised aesthetics are symptomatic both of "savage" blood and insufficient cultivation. In due course of time, evidence of deficient aesthetic form is followed by that of poor moral form. During one of their walks, "her wild original habits suddenly asserted themselves," as she stops to strike and maim a rabbit in "an outbreak of the old predatory instinct of the savage, though with a somewhat incongruous effect in the case of a fashionably dressed young lady on an English high road" (54). That Lawrence and his friend, despite their obligations to their studies, hope to "have time for a crack at the rabbits for all that" goes unremarked (44).

With Thurston's disclosure that the governess's youngest charge, Ethel, was found dead in the shrubbery within a week or two of her arrival, the reader's suspicions are aroused (47). Intrigued by Copperthorne's power over the governess, Lawrence provokes an outburst during which the governess claims that if she had a lover, she would ask him to "Kill Copperthorne" (59). Observing his disapproval, she sheepishly confesses, "it is the Indian training breaking out again" (59). Happening upon her strangulation of Ethel, Copperthorne, we learn later, has been blackmailing her into killing Uncle Jeremy, who has witlessly made a will in his secretary's favor. In the inconsistent logic of the story, only the governess's behavior and oddities need explanation in racial terms, whereas the superstitions of the local staff, the odd, clownish appearance of the proprietor and his risible attempts at versification, and

Copperthorne's clear motive and criminality need no explanation as to their sources in deficient aesthetics, inferior civilization, or primitive religion. We learn of Copperthorne's dubious antecedents, and his being sent down from university "under a cloud," but we get no sense that the coincidence of bad blood, poor form, and irrational criminality are to be allied in any figure but that of "the beautiful Anglo-Indian" (55–58).

Miss Warrender, rediscovered as Princess Achmet Genghis Khan, is not only part Indian, but born of a father who represents an amalgam of the empire's worst nightmares: he is simultaneously mutinous, devoted to savage rituals, married to but unreformed by a gentle, Christian representative of the empire, and leader of a band of professional thieves and assassins who perform ritual sacrifice to propitiate an alien, wild, über-female goddess. To arrive at the conclusion that she is the "daughter of a fierce fanatical warrior rather than of her gentle mother," Lawrence performs a sociocultural version of nineteenth-century racial science's calculation of genetic ratios (66). In this calculation, the aesthetics of comportment furnishes part of the required but usually concealed *qualitative* data set. Corroboration and embedding within the larger text of Orientalism confirms that the savage spirit manifests in savage beliefs, and primitive cultural forms.[6] Although he has perished in the worst excesses of the mutiny, the fanatical warrior's spirit apparently lives not only in his daughter but also in an incongruous, intertextual apparition who duly materializes on the bleak Yorkshire landscape and prostrates himself at the feet of the combination governess-princess-high priestess.

Doyle mentions several ethnological texts and sources in the story in a bid to establish historical heft for introducing elements of an alien deus ex machina into a narrative in search of a crime after it has already committed to unmasking a criminal with bad blood. The last-minute introduction into the desolate dales of Yorkshire of an obliging acolyte of Miss Warrender's father serves to dispatch Copperthorne in a ritual strangulation using the customary "roomal," a long kerchief, as weapon, a crime Lawrence is privileged enough to witness in person. Providentially, he has also overheard a conversation between the governess and the secretary in which we learn of not only the murder of Ethel but also that of her adoptive father's daughter in Germany. Miss Warrender has murdered (or sacrificed) two young children, presumably because she can't help it, not because she is seriously disturbed but because she is half (textbook) Oriental and therefore inclined to meaningless murder.[7] Motivated neither by money nor social prestige, love, or revenge, unless the murder of innocent children can be seen to avenge the violence of massacres against the 1857 mutineers and her father, the princess admits that she has "grieved much over" Ethel's death, "for what had the poor child done that she should be sacrificed!" (68). Should the reader balk at this uncharacteristic duality, the narrator explains that as a descendant of thugs—an occupation rather than an identity, but that need not detain us—she has succumbed to "the terrible power the homicidal craze has over every other mental or moral faculty" (71). Since she was "already a woman when she had left them," the narrator explains, "it was no wonder that the varnish of civilization had not eradicated all her early impressions or prevented the breaking out of occasional fits of fanaticism" (71). Heedless of the poor logic of the next assertion, Lawrence continues thus: "In one of these apparently she had put an end to poor Ethel, *having carefully prepared an alibi to conceal her crime*" (71; emphasis added). Lawrence will have it both ways; the crime is uncontrollable as well as premeditated. Mindful, perhaps, of the injustice of casting her as a criminal without any hope of profit or gain, the narrator not only describes her as an "unfortunate woman," but permits her to escape the gallows and the narrative unscathed, although her guilt and the fearful figure of foreignness have been firmly stamped on the avid reader of these fictions. Lawrence decides that Copperthorne, who is willing to use an "unfortunate woman's horrible conceptions of religion to remove Uncle Jeremy in a way that no suspicion could possibly fall upon the real culprit," also "should not escape the punishment due his crimes" (72). Instead of the due process of legal indictment, however, Copperthorne is eliminated by the Oriental wanderer in a bizarre outsourcing of the murder, the motive, *and* justice.

The introduction of an exotic princess-priestess with unfathomable motivations and an equally outlandish dispenser of rough justice seem oddly excessive to the story of a nefarious plot hatched by a malevolent secretary who seeks to dispossess Thurston of his legitimate inheritance. Thurston's unexamined stakes in the narrative surely involve the protection of his inheritance, which may just as plausibly be threatened by an attractive governess as they might by an unscrupulous secretary who has gained his employer's trust. In other words, we have here the makings of a plausible crime with recognizable, rational, mercenary motives and a real villain with a suspicious history and poor antecedents, who is ready to achieve his ends by any means at his disposal. Copperthorne's motives—money and profit—are plausible in a rational world, even if they are not seemly. The profiling of *irrational* motives belongs to later technologies of investigation and detection in the genre of shows such as *CSI, Criminal Minds, Dexter,* and so forth. In these narratives, the detective attempts to explain motive through the discourse of psychology (rejection by a lover or higher authority, slight at work, stalled career, inferiority or a lack of being taken seriously, abuse as a child, trauma, etc.), aiming to domesticate if not to rationalize that which seems irrational: the evil of taking another (usually innocent) life. Denied this satisfaction, we are given in the governess's crime, guilt, and unaccountably chivalrous evacuation from the scene of retribution and justice a foregone conclusion about race and racial mixture as the prima facie crime awaiting punishment.

Displacing the weight of crime, guilt, and ungovernable urges on the "governess" and that of the dispensation of justice on a mysterious emissary Oriental other who then disappears permit the story to end without confronting the evil that may lurk in homeland, Christian breasts. The story concludes with a letter from "Dr. B. C. Haller, a man of encyclopedic knowledge," who corroborates Lawrence's understanding of Thuggee, and ends with a justification for proselytization: "Truly 'the dark places of the earth are full of cruelty,' and nothing but the Gospel will ever effectually dispel the darkness" (79). The Christian farewell, drawing from Psalms 74:20, invokes and then outsources evil to "the mysteries of Thuggee" and unspecified but legion others awaiting enlightenment (78).

The English Way

Barnes's *Arthur and George* exhumes two themes that have appeared in "The Mystery of Uncle Jeremy's Household": (1) the displacement of original sin onto Empire's other, or significantly *half*-other and (2) the peculiar situation of those others who have seen the light, in the divine as well as the secular sense, and attempt to follow the English way. The problems of residual evil and an incorrigible primitive core continue to beset the latter, despite their religious as well as cultural conversion. Both themes are animated, moreover, by the idea of the "extimate," which Adorno describes as "the non-I, *l'autrui,*" and Miller as the alterity within the subject (*Negative Dialectics,* 23). With enlightenment, Christianity entered into a complex engagement with its premodern core, conceptualizing tragic sacrifice within a narrative of redemption. Motifs of ritual sacrifice and the redemption of humankind through one scapegoat exist in the continuity between the "pagan" figure of the Corn King and in the person of Christ the redeemer. In Doyle's short story, the relocation of collective guilt for the bloodlust that accompanies the scapegoating of the melded figures of the Corn King growing into the redeemer onto a bizarre, irrationally motivated crime and an insufficiently converted foreign body emerges as a symptom of the lack of rapprochement with a primitive core that resists management. It is also possible that Doyle's interest in spiritism and the supernatural world—which cost him credibility and stature later in life—make an early appearance in these exaggerated and displaced forms. Finally, in the casual alliance of savagery and lack of good form in the novel and the story, we see intimations of a civilizational project that evaluates its success by the extent to which it has been able to disguise and displace biological and animal being into rigid forms of comportment and control. Instinctively aware that he is a suspect "for some reason [he] does not understand," George is the selected sacrificial figure who must pay for the sins of a world driven by the need to exercise technical mastery over nature and bare life. Barnes's novel presents a modern-day scapegoat who is chosen to carry the collective sins of a repressive, violent civilization, while disclosing the secret trump card of aesthetic form as the alternative bio-logic informing its repressive classificatory impulses. The novel discloses both texts simultaneously, allowing us to understand the continued incentive to mimic recognizable codes of civility despite the lack of immunity granted by this conversion to the English way.

By the conflicted rubric of the civilizing mission, George Edalji is an exemplary specimen. A Christian education cautioning against "the sins of the flesh" and unquestioned subscription to the aesthetic forms of English civility make George a designer convert to the epic intentions of the civilizing and the Christian mission (*Arthur and George,* 82).[8] Lacking in imagination, George is prone to "following the inventions of others," including the biblical injunction heard "many times on his father's lips": "I am the way, the truth and the life," from John 14:6 (4–5). Another familiar homily in the Edalji household presents England through a biological allegory as "the beating heart of the Empire," with "The Church of England" as the blood that reaches "even its farthest shore" (21). Growing up, George's world is the church, the churchyard, and the Great Wyrley Vicarage inherited by his father from his Uncle Compson (7). Of a nervous disposition, George prefers this world to that beyond the vicarage wall. At the local school, where "other boys are not so neat," George wears a bow tie, waistcoat, and jacket, and responds politely when told, "you're not the right sort," with a rote and civil greeting: "How d'you do, my name's George" (11). By the time he is sixteen, George "knows our Saviour's birth to be a solemn truth," begins to study law, and imagines himself "with a desk, a set of bound law books and a suit with a fob chain slung between his waistcoat pockets like golden rope. He imagines himself respected. He imagines himself with a hat" (30). These, in sum, are articles of faith for the postulant Englishman. England's version of the *mission civilisatrice* (civilizing mission) was founded in part in a mandate to "[administer] . . . an impartial justice, based on a belief in a fundamental English decency," as Robert Young argues in *The Idea of English Ethnicity*. Simon Gikandi, too, points to this conjunction: "Within the symbolic economy of English identity, the idea of the law bestows the authority of nature and totality to the nation and its imperial ideology" (*Maps*, 66). Indeed, in the Hegelian schematic, it is in the law that the spirit of a people finds its ideal manifestation. In his own estimation, founded in this amalgam of beliefs about Englishness, George is a "full Englishman . . . by birth, by citizenship, by education, by religion, by profession" (*Arthur and George*, 268).

Very soon, however, it is precisely through an encounter with the law that good form and genteel upbringing count in George's disfavor because they come to be read as smug and arrogant, inappropriate to someone who remains alien despite "birth . . . citizenship . . . education . . . religion . . . profession" (268). Sergeant Upton describes him as an "uppish little fellow" despite or perhaps because of his pretensions to these attributes, reminding us that Miss Warrender was also disliked by Uncle Jeremy's retainer for "her 'uppish ways'" ("Uncle Jeremy's Household," 31, 74). Inspector Campbell's report to Anson, "The odd thing was, listening to his voice—it was an educated voice, a lawyer's voice—I found myself thinking at one point, if you shut your eyes, you'd think him an Englishman" (*Arthur and George*, 112), is met with a direct reference to what is unassimilable, as Anson responds, "Whereas if you left them open, you wouldn't exactly mistake him for a member of the Brigade of Guards?" [historical elite of the British army] (112). Anson goes on to elaborate: "It sounds as if—eyes open or eyes shut—your impression was of someone who feels himself superior. How might I put it? Someone who thinks he belongs to a higher caste?" (112).

The impossibility of being sufficiently English is coded in a history that George cannot shed, announced both in his person and his last name as vital code for these disjunctive elements of identity. At sixteen, George is accosted by a policeman who interrogates him after he has found on the vicarage doorstep a key that turns out to be stolen:

> "Name?"
> "You know my name."
> "Name, I said." . . .
> "George."
> "Yes. Go on."
> "Ernest."
> "Go on."

"Thompson."

"Go on."

"You know my surname. It's the same as my father's. And my mother's."

"Go on, I say, you uppish little fellow."

"Edalji."

"Ah yes," says the Sergeant. "Now I think you'd better spell that out for me." (32)

Much of the narrative that follows on this sneak preview of the workings of racial prejudice is an attempt to spell out the significance of the last name, unshaken residue of a history that cannot be erased by conversion or sufficiently outweighed by the three Christian names that precede it. Doyle's attempts to bring Anson to reason flounder on the problem of this foreign history. Conceding that it was unwise to introduce "a coloured clergyman into such a rude and unrefined parish" in what he believes is a mistaken bid "to demonstrate the universality of the Anglican Church," Doyle attempts to establish common ground with the truculent officer. Anson follows this agreeable trail in a conversation that unfolds to reveal the insurmountable double bind in narratives of conversion:

"And then to introduce three half-caste children into the neighbourhood."

"George, Horace and Maud."

"Three half-caste children," repeated Anson.

"George, Horace and Maud," repeated Doyle.

"George, Horace and Maud Ee-dal-jee." (328)

Anson closes this thread of the conversation by drawing attention to what follows those Christian names, and will forever follow, the whiff of foreignness, which sits poorly on the English tongue.

Edalji is a name that spells out the incarnate sound of difference, pronouncing its incommensurability with Englishness. Moreover, as George explains to a sympathetic Doyle, "It's *Aydlji,* actually, if you don't mind. . . . I am used to it. But since it is my name . . . all Parsee names are stressed on the first syllable" (260). Aware of its potential impact on the English ear, George's lawyer resists his client's tutelage in the correct Parsi pronunciation. Tone deaf to the implications, George suggests that the lawyer make "an announcement at the beginning of the case as to how to pronounce my name." Mr. Meek, the lawyer, reassures him, "Of course it's your name, and of course Mr. Vachell and I shall endeavour to pronounce it correctly. When we are here with you." "But in court . . . ," he continues, "I think the argument would be: when in Rome" (148). In a maneuver assimilated immigrants will recognize readily, Mr. Meek explains, "What you call mispronouncing, I would call . . . making you more English. . . . Less Oriental" (148). The domestication of its foreign sonics in court notwithstanding, George Edalji's is a name unlikely to overcome its threatening and unsympathetic aspect in spelling and sound. The Parsi last name remains a persistent reminder of George's half-ness, and that of religious conversion as unconvincing in the colonial theater. Understandably then, in due course, George's brother Horace changes his last name in a final bid to leave its freighted history behind. Reviewing his life in later years, George writes that Horace "was now lost to the family: he had married, moved to Ireland and changed his name" (418).[9]

The inadequacy of three Christian names against the last word of the last name is matched by suspicions about the quality of conversion by the others of empire. Gauri Viswanathan observes: "Even when Hindus or Muslims were converting to Christianity, the decisions made by the [colonial] civil courts denied that such conscious change occurred, and the Christian convert was treated as essentially someone who had *not* converted. . . . Their religious identity was subsequently recast in the form of the religion they had renounced" (*Outside the Fold,* 14). Anson's assessment of George's uppishness is associated metonymically with "higher caste" supremacism, even though the latter is a convert to Christianity, and even though Zoroastrianism, his father's religion before conversion, contains nothing analogous to caste. Father, son, and family all find their religious status under question. Relying on available records, Barnes tells us that Reverend Edalji's parish endured significant "ill feeling when the Vicar was first given the living. People saying they didn't want a black man in the pulpit telling them what sinner they were, that sort of thing" (*Arthur and George,* 101). Moreover, suspicious of the conversion, the parish also exchanged rumors about "new moon, pagan rites and such like" (101). In the short story discussed earlier, one of Lawrence's first questions about the governess broaches the issue head-on: "What view of religion does she take? Does she side with her father or mother?" ("Uncle Jeremy's Household," 47). Thurston's confused response, "We never press the question. . . . Between ourselves don't think she's very orthodox," is intended as a clue to horrifying disclosures planned for a dramatically propitious narrative moment, emanating supposedly from the insufficiently converted Christian half-caste's "horrible conceptions of religion" (47). Anson is baldly vocal in his doubts about the conversion as credible. In response to Doyle's assertion that he "cannot picture a priest of the Church of England placing his hand on the Bible and knowingly committing perjury," Anson parries with, "Try to imagine this instead. Imagine a Parsee father putting loyalty to his Parsee family above loyalty to a land not his own" (*Arthur and George,* 330). Despite George's detailed account of Shapurji's conversion by Scottish missionaries in his conversations with the famous author, Doyle himself would write in his memoirs, "'How the Vicar came to be a Parsee, or how a Parsee came to be the Vicar, I have no idea'" (quoted in Barnes, *Arthur and George,* 414).[10]

Barnes's novel uncovers the anatomy of racial thinking in a creative reconstruction of the case indicting George against all odds, and indeed, contrary to obvious evidence. Inquiring into irrepressible and untrustworthy instinctual impulses, Freud chooses the *Mischling* as his master analogy for the traffic between the unconscious and the preconscious: "Their mixed and split origin is what decides their fate. We may compare them with individuals of mixed race [*Mischlingen Menschlischer Rassen*] who taken all round resemble white men but who betray their coloured descent by some striking feature or other and on that account are excluded from society and enjoy none of the privileges" ("The Unconscious," 191). Freud's interest in exposing the inconvenient irrepressibility of instinctual impulses, akin to the "striking feature" that betrays a body, even the bodies of those "who taken all round resemble white men," braids sex, race, instinct, repression, and civilization into an inextricable weave. George, the convicted criminal, is "a goggling half-caste," "a poor, bookish, solitary boy with bulging eyes," afflicted both by myopia and exophthalmos (*Arthur and George,* 341). While George's myopia offers Doyle, a trained ophthalmologist as well as writer of detective fiction, confirmation of innocence because the alleged criminal is too nearsighted to have committed the nocturnal mutilations, exophthalmos suggests "an unhealthy degree of sexual desire" and atavistic barbarism to Anson, the chief constable in charge at the time of the investigation (341). Doyle believes that the moral certainty of George Edalji's innocence lay in "that singular optical defect," but he also understands that "therein lay . . . the reason why he should have become a scapegoat" (289). Anson is able to spin a fantastic narrative of biological peculiarity, racial mixture, and inadequately channeled urges into a motive for violence against animals in blatant disregard of facts.

George's conversion to Englishness and subscription to Christian principles not only do not bring him the redemption promised by both, but his singular optical defect overturns all the other signs of normative subjectivity: "Self-control presents itself as secretiveness, intelligence as cunning. And so a respectable lawyer, bat-blind and of slight physique, becomes a degenerate who flits across fields at dead of night, evading the watch of twenty special constables, in order to wade through the blood of mutilated animals" (*Arthur and George,* 289). In an aesthetic order that defines the human by upright stature, the hierarchy of the senses typically places smell, touch, and taste far below the privilege of sight, "the noblest, since, among all the senses, it is farthest removed from the sense of touch, which is the most limited condition of perception" (Kant, *Anthropology,* 43). German naturalist, botanist, biologist, and ornithologist Lorenz Oken identified the European as "eye-man" in a racial hierarchy of the senses (quoted in Classen, *Color of Angels,* 67). In light of an arbitrary hierarchy of the senses founded in distance from the ground and from the more animal senses reliant on touch and smell, George's optical deficiency is not just a "striking feature" betraying his "coloured descent," but a symptom of his inadequacy within an elaborate postanimalist aesthetic system in which sight and vision have been uniquely privileged: "Therein lay . . . the reason why he should have become a scapegoat" (*Arthur and George,* 289).[11]

In blatant disregard of the exculpatory fact of George's myopia, Anson considers racial mixture reason enough for a predisposition to crime in its unfortunate by-product, selectively adducing a facial feature that allegedly explains the redirection of frustrated sexual desire into the instinct to torture animals. Anson repeatedly betrays his unthinking prejudice in statements often drawn directly from Barnes's extensive research into the case, while remaining clueless about the extent to which he is a product of a regime of false reason that has distorted his sensorium and his ability to use the evidence of the senses. In Doyle's assessment of the inception of a process culminating in the miscarriage of justice, Anson has made George "a target from the beginning" (329). Anson's inheritance presumably includes a fund of stories similar to "Uncle Jeremy's Household," creative fictions he unwittingly draws on in establishing George's guilt, even as he smugly brags about having taught Doyle "a thing or two about the real world" during their conversations (345). The consensual projectional fantasies that serve as the "solution" to "The Mystery of Uncle Jeremy's Household" would not have seemed aberrant or illogical to the implied reader. In a definitive history of *Boy's Own Paper,* Jack Cox notes that the story "was a great success with house parties" (*Story of the Boy's Own Paper,* 56). The farce of detection and deduction, first enacted in Doyle's creative fiction, is replicated by Anson in real life, resulting in a tragedy that will destroy an insufficiently English lawyer's life. The structural similarity between the irrelevance of logical motive in "The Mystery of Uncle Jeremy's Household" and in Anson's construction of the Edalji case emerge forcefully in an intertextual reading of the novel. In his confrontation with the official responsible for investigating the mutilations, Doyle repeats the most urgent demand a mystery makes after it has identified the person responsible for the crime: "I ask you simply, Why?" (*Arthur and George,* 336). In an earlier conversation with Inspector Campbell, Anson has already admitted to Campbell, "the why interests me less than the how and the when and the what" (112). Questioned by Campbell with regard to motive, Anson attempts to supply a series of possible motives: "There might be some deep hatred of animals. . . . Or . . . there is some pattern in the timing of the attacks . . . there might be some sacrificial principle involved. Perhaps the mysterious instrument we are seeking is a ritual knife of Indian origin. A kukri or something. Edalji's father is a Parsee, I understand. Do they not worship fire?" (112). Even his fellow officer Campbell notes the "loose speculation" (113). The fetish object as instrument of crime, like the roomal used by thugs in Doyle's short story, unites a perception of religious practices in dark places with dire potential for violence. The illogical and delusional nature of these projections about racial others, and of miscegenation as original sin and manifest guilt, become starkly visible in the mirror the investigating officer Captain Anson holds up to Doyle in *Arthur and George.*

To Doyle's question regarding motive, Anson returns a response uncannily reminiscent of Lawrence's explanations of the unpredictable consequences of mixed blood: "When the blood is mixed, that is where the trouble starts. . . . Why does human society everywhere abhor the half-caste? Because his soul is torn between the impulse to civilization and the pull of barbarism" (339). The Irish-Scottish Doyle's piqued response, "is it the Scottish or the Parsee blood you hold responsible for barbarism?" is met with a trenchant rejoinder: "You yourself believe in blood. You believe in race. You told me over dinner how your mother had proudly traced her ancestry back five centuries" (339). Apart from boasting of his second wife's family ancestry, Doyle had once responded very coolly to his sister Connie's interest in Ernest Hornung, a suitor whom he describes as "Half Mongol, half Slav" by the sound of his name, asking his sibling, "Could you not find someone wholly British?" (*Arthur and George,* 74). "There's something odd about him," he allegedly said, proceeding to employ sensorial justification, "I can sniff it" (75). Attention to the body is part of the influence of Doyle's teacher Joseph Bell on Holmes's diagnostic organon:

> It was Bell's dictum that a doctor had to be not only learned but also immensely interpretive of all relevant features of a patient. Diagnosis, he taught, was not made just by visual observation but also by the employment of all the senses: do not just look at a patient, he advised, but feel him, probe him, listen to him,

smell him. Only then could a diagnosis be attempted. (Quoted in Booth, *The Doctor and the Detective,* 50)

Like Miss Warrender for Doyle's Lawrence and Hornung for Doyle, George is a suspicious character ab ovo for Anson and the Yorkshire constabulary.

Doyle's belief in blood and race manifest in conflicted ways. Like Anson, Doyle locates George within his Parsi ancestry regardless of his father's conversion, with the difference that it is not to him a sign of deficient morality. In fact, he refers repeatedly to the superiority of the Parsis, their penchant for charity, and their distinction as "the most highly educated and commercially successful of Indian sects," in a response analogous to that of George's Uncle Stoneham, who has previously testified in a letter in defense of George, "Our friends at that time too felt as we did that Parsees are a very old and cultivated race, and have many good qualities" (*Arthur and George,* 338, 191; underlining in original). The hierarchical evaluation of different "Indian sects" couples with Anson's troubling response to Doyle's commendation of the race: "They are not called the Jews of Bombay for nothing" (338). Moreover, Anson's blatant prejudice, which extends beyond Indians, Jews, and Parsis to the Irish, is made clear at several points in the novel. Also emphasized, however, is Doyle's preoccupation not only with race, blood, and ancestry, but also with class and evidence of cultivation and good form. He extols the virtues of the Parsis for the same reasons that he enjoys his race pride. In his description of Parsis to his second wife, Jean, Doyle speaks of their "historical origin . . . characteristic appearance, their headgear, their liberal attitude to women," but "he passes over the ceremony of purification, since this involves ablution with cow urine" (318). Doyle wisely suppresses information about the Parsi belief in the healing and spiritual power of the bodily discard of an animal because he is acutely aware of how such a detail might be perceived in a culture founded in unease with animals and the animal body.

Inspector Campbell tells Captain Anson that the man who performed the mutilations would be someone who was "accustomed to handling animals" (84); this assumption would clearly rule out George. Yet George is pursued as the single suspect. On the night a horse is mutilated, Anson already has his force on guard, focusing on George because the chief constable is convinced that "he will do something" (113). George's earlier suggestion, that the next time there is an incident they employ bloodhounds, for "they have . . . an excellent sense of smell," is met with a rejoinder indicting Doyle's sensational, racist fictions: "It sounds like something out of a shilling shocker. 'Mr. Holmes, they were the footprints of a gigantic hound!'" (106–7). The logical uses of the sense of smell are disregarded in the mockery, although the inspector duly reports the suggestion to Anson, who in turn responds with the following: "You're sure he didn't say native trackers?" (111). Creative license and the demands of the ludic drive notwithstanding, Doyle's imaginative extensions stand revealed as part of that nexus between culture and imperialism that permitted race to acquire its power not only through pseudoscience but through the equally persuasive medium of *a good story.* As a creative fiction accountable to no particular standard of logic or verifiability, the storied other thus made available to a populace hungry for information and entertainment, and struggling tacitly or otherwise with its own psychoses, becomes a suspicious character in advance of an actual crime, and readily available for scapegoating when evildoing occurs. In Barnes's narrative, Doyle is forced to confront the sensory triggers of prejudice and understands why George might seem a misfit among the "unenlightened":

> [Arthur] tried to imagine George Edalji in the village of Great Wyrley, walking the lanes, going to the bootmaker, doing business with Brookes. The young solicitor—well spoken and well-dressed though he was—would cut a queer figure even in Hindhead, and no doubt a queerer one in the wilds of Staffordshire. He was evidently an admirable fellow, with a lucid brain and resilient character. But if you merely looked at him—looked at him, moreover, with the eye of an ill-educated farmhand, a dimwit village policeman, a narrow-minded juror, or a suspicious chairman of Quarter Sessions—you might not get beyond a brown skin and an ocular peculiarity. He would seem queer. And then, if some queer things started happening, what passed for logic in an unenlightened village would glibly ascribe the events to the person. (288)

The trope of always already inadequate conversion is familiar to us from accounts of "flawed colonial mimesis, in which to be Anglicized is *emphatically* not to be English," as Bhabha explains (*The Location of Culture,* 87). In fact, the postcolonial mimic was often targeted especially for mockery. The partial infusion of English blood in racial hybrids similarly exaggerates their difference from the English, even though it is understood that the structure of English ethnicity betrays its own contradictions and conflicted inheritance. So far, so unremarkable. One *other* mystery, however, abides to command our attention. Positioned as detective and champion of truth and justice in real life, Doyle asks the chief investigating officer—in what we would like to think of as the rationalist Sherlock Holmesian way—why Horace, George's brother and equally "mongrel" half-caste, is not under suspicion. Why does Horace pass muster and George fail? Who is chosen as scapegoat, and who escapes unharmed? Who invites projectional fantasies, mockery, and disdain, and why? Who, moreover, does not? By juxtaposing two hybrids within one family as potential scapegoats, Doyle's question and the selection of firstborn George imply that racial prejudice is not always a foregone conclusion. In asking and exploring "why not Horace?" the novel exposes the final mystery of racial and cultural prejudice: its unpredictable plot, inconsistent logic, creative fictions, and hysterical obsession with good form (*Arthur and George,* 340). It betrays, moreover, the exceptionalist logic that continues to fuel the engines of colonial mimicry and hybridity in new forms in a globalized world.

Strait Is the Gate

In a narrative that repeatedly refers to Doyle's belief that "life was a chivalric quest," Barnes suggests that it is a recollection of this missionary belief that stimulates the author into action in defense of George at a time when he is confused after his first wife's death (*Arthur and George,* 69). Doyle gives this account in his memoir: "What aroused my indignation and gave me the driving force to carry the thing through was the utter helplessness of this forlorn little group of people, the coloured clergyman in his strange position, the brave, blue-eyed, gray-haired mother, the young daughter, baited by brutal boors" (quoted in Barnes, *Arthur and George,* 414–15). Wlad Godzich proposes the following structure for the Arthurian code, one that Arthur, named after the legendary knight, has learned at his mother's knee:

> The paradigmatic conception here is that of the quest in romances of chivalry, in which the adventurous knight leaves Arthur's court—the realm of the known—to encounter some form of otherness, a domain in which the courtly values of the Arthurian world do not prevail. The quest is brought to an end when this alien world is brought within the hegemonic sway of the Arthurian world: the other has been reduced to (more of) the same. The quest has shown that the other is amenable to being reduced to the status of the same. (*The Culture of Literacy,* 263)

The judicial system's unfair treatment of George, the vulnerability of his helpless mother, and Doyle's lifelong quest to right the wrongs done to his "Mam" by his alcoholic, indigent father, collude to set the celebrated creator of detective fictions on his romantic rescue mission. Doyle conjugates George's attributes in terms that Godzich describes above, recognizing in the half-caste lawyer a "professional Englishman," whereas Anson, who believes that "police work is not just punitive but also prophylactic," targets them as signs of incorrigible and inferior difference, forms of contagion identified for containment (*Arthur and George,* 330, 329). Described in the novel as "a Staffordshire man through and through" (95), Anson might be of the camp that finds it "ideologically inconceivable that there should exist an otherness of the same ontological status as the same, without there being immediately mounted an effort at its appropriation" (Godzich, *The Culture of Literacy,* 264). Anson responds with prejudice rather than chivalry.

Doyle's chivalrous defense of the Parsis clearly did not extend to all of empire's others. Writing about his voyage to West Africa in "On the Slave Coast with a Camera," Doyle states, "I had a great desire to 'astonish the natives' by representations of their own hideous faces" (16). Ruminating further, he observes: "A great deal has been said about the regeneration of our black brothers and the latent virtues of the swarthy races. My own experience is that you abhor them on first meeting them, and gradually learn to dislike them a very great deal more as you become better acquainted with them" (19). On the same voyage, the young Doyle had a "momentous encounter," as his biographer described it (Edwards, *Biographical Study,* 255). Doyle recalls it in these words:

> The most intelligent and well-read man whom I met on the Coast was a negro, the American Consul at Monrovia. . . . This negro gentleman did me good, for a man's brain is an organ for the formation of his own thoughts and also for the digestion of other people's, and it needs fresh fodder. (*Memories and Adventures,* 55–56)

The "negro" in question was a famous black abolitionist and former slave, Henry Highland Garnet. Doyle confessed himself open to the intelligent, well-read gentleman's views, acknowledging the black man's superior form in contrast to others of his racial group. In the adjacence of two conflicted responses to "our black brothers" lies the classic ambivalence of colonial discourse. At the same time, however, in Doyle's negative response to the faces identified with a generalized black social body and in his positive one to the particular encounter with an intelligent, educated, *well-formed* "negro gentleman," we might see beyond ambivalence a more erratic, case-by-case situation that reveals another portion of the catechism additional to what George learned so well at his father's knee ("I am the way, the truth and the life"). This portion reveals, "*Strait is the gate* and narrow is the way that leadeth to life, and few there be that find it" (Matthew 7:14).

Freudian theories of ambivalence in the interaction between the races have been productive in revealing the mechanics of colonial interaction: the importance of fetishized stereotypes of the other, the piecemeal nature of Englishness, and the fissures inherent in colonial commands to mimicry. What remains insufficiently understood is the working of structures of exceptionalism in invitations to mimicry of privileged forms. Those who pass muster racially or culturally do so through their ability to approximate most closely forms that are riven by inconsistency but are nonetheless privileged within the particular social laboratory in which mimicry and conversion take place. Without a built-in reward structure, no cultural system can sustain its hold as a desirable ideal, particularly in light of its inconsistency. I have suggested that attention to the aesthetic dimensions of mimicry can help us understand how and why some cultural forms exert their power and invite modes of passing, not as white, but as recognizably reformed or different from those who do not or cannot attempt this mimicry. It is also worth considering that those who "fit" within a privileged norm of Englishness do not thereby necessarily fit in every "English" situation.[12] Doyle's anxieties about his own identity are expressed in a curious self-description: "You and I, George, you and I, we are . . . unofficial Englishmen" (268). George, understandably,

> is taken aback by this remark. He regards Sir Arthur as a very official Englishman indeed: his name, his manner, his fame, his air of being absolutely at ease in this grand London hotel, even down to the time he kept George waiting. If Sir Arthur had not appeared to be part of official England, George would probably not have written to him in the first place. But it seems impolite to question a man's categorization of himself. (268)

A fuller exploration of Doyle's simultaneous and rivalrous positioning within the national and imperial text is beyond the scope of this chapter, although it is important to note the odd junction between his chivalric code, attachment to justice, and advocacy of empire in verse and prose.[13] Anson's sly references to Doyle's ancestry suggest that the extension of English identity to the Celt was still under way, a process Young describes as part of a larger global development, that of "Englishness . . . defined as a transportable set of values" (*The Idea of English Ethnicity*, 232). Instead of a stable set of attributes, Englishness seems to function as a social yardstick that adapts to various situations, but most commonly in alliance with hierarchical thinking. Doyle's formal evaluation of George includes setting him apart from his social inferiors as he reminds Anson that they "are talking . . . not of some butcher's boy, but of a professional Englishman, a solicitor in his late twenties, already known as the author of a book on railway law" (*Arthur and George,* 330). In this estimation, while the lower classes may enjoy the wages of whiteness, George enjoys the wages of education and superior class in those circles where these attributes are valuable. Arguably, Doyle is not indicting racial prejudice as much as the withdrawal of protection to a near exemplary subscriber to the English way in its upper-class, professional mode, one that he himself valued highly.

Instead of a generalized notion of the border, then, the process of passing or mimicry might be better understood through that of a turnstile or gate that only permits passage to one person at a time. The passer confronts the baffle gate repeatedly and cannot be assured of passage at every turnstile. Those who have just the ticket, acquired through a rigorous aesthetic and liberal education, might pass some gates and not others, preserving the promise of a reward structure with just enough exceptionalism to inspire a long line of empire's others at the baffle gate.

Attempting to inspire George to similar feats, the vicar holds out the example of successful Parsis who have breached the color line. "Dr. Dadabhoy Naoroji," he recounts, "was elected to Parliament for the Finsbury Central district of London" in 1892 . . . even though the PM, Lord Salisbury "said that black men should not and would not be elected to Parliament" (51). Ignoring George's protest, "But I am not a Parsee, Father. That is what you and Mother have taught me," the vicar insists that the boy "remember the date," which is to say remember the exception, and to remember it *especially when* "unfair things happen, even if wicked things happen" (52). In the face of growing harassment, Barnes confides, the vicar has "chosen to respond to the crisis in what seems to George a peculiar fashion: by giving him short lectures on how the Parsees have always been much favoured by the British." Through his father's hagiographic history, George learns that the first traveler to Britain, the first student to study Christian theology in a British university, the first student at Oxford, the first woman student, and the first Indian to enter the Indian Civil Service were all Parsi. "As a second Parsee, Muncherji Bhownagree is elected to [the British] parliament," the vicar's bedroom catechism expands to include not only the tenets of religious scripture but the text of English values and the advocacy of cultural mimicry of certain privileged forms of Englishness on the grounds of demonstrable success (55). The vicar also seems to understand the price and cost of admission. When he finds "twenty pennies and halfpennies laid at intervals across the lawn," "the Vicar decides to regard them as a donation to the church" even though there are "also dead birds, mostly strangled; and once excrement has been laid where it will be most visible" (44). The vicar's belief in exceptionalism rather than justice, perhaps based no less in his own experience in being selected as a vicar of color in a rural parish, suggest that he may have a more realistic grasp of the English way.

In hopes of a similar reward for adherence to this path, the vicar trains his older son to assimilate to beliefs and lifeways that optimize the possibility of success.[14] Like his father, George is apt to minimize the role of race in the behavior of others. Despite harassment by coworkers who question his Englishness, George persists in thinking that he is not the subject of racial prejudice. Doyle, on the other hand, recognizes a pattern he has himself used creatively in his fictions. George does not *look* right despite sporting the correct accessories and facial hair growth. Although Inspector Campbell admits, "if you shut your eyes, you'd think him an Englishman" with "an educated voice, a lawyer's voice" (112), in visual descriptions by the Staffordshire constabulary and the press, George is depicted as a "little fellow. A bit odd-looking" (101), as someone with "little of the typical solicitor in his swarthy face, with its full, dark eyes, prominent mouth, and small round chin" (140). The vicar, on the other hand, is described by Inspector Campbell as a "short, powerful, light-skinned fellow with none of the oddities of his son. White-haired, but good-looking in a Hindoo sort of a way" (118). George himself "is aware that some consider him odd-looking" (116), and Doyle describes him as a man "small and slight, of Oriental origin, with hair parted on the left and cropped close" (259–60). It is nonetheless possible to construe what seems to be George's willful blindness to racial prejudice as a form of alternative insight. Indeed, between father and son, there are glimpses of a more complicated understanding of prejudice than in its glib reduction to racism or skin color. While the Edalji family undergoes various forms of harassment, another family, the Brookes, is also receiving letters, a fact that the vicar takes as proof "it is not merely race prejudice." George astutely asks, "Is that a good thing, Father? To be hated for more than one reason?" (51). George points to the multiple sources of prejudice, while the vicar's own experience and that of other successful Parsis confirm his faith in the possibility of selective redemption. Their subscriptions also imply that racial prejudice exists among other forms of discriminatory thinking; indeed, the vicar and his son both display their own brand of prejudice against those they consider ill formed and undereducated. When George registers his concern about early experiences of prejudice, he is urged to "pity and cherish the feeble of mind" because "the centre of England is still a little primitive" (39, 52).

The language of evolutionary development is used both by a prejudiced police force and those who are subject to this prejudice. The antagonisms of racial difference emanate from the same belief systems that find their roots more pervasively in the disdain of nature and ways of living that are close to nature and animal life. George expresses his distaste for boys who come from farms; he "thinks they smell of cows," resists his father's fair-minded explanation of the association between smell, poverty, and farm life, and is glad to escape a school with "stupid farm boys and odd-talking miners' sons" (11, 16, 23). When George is seven years old, George's great-aunt asks him who his friends are. George names Harry Charlesworth and explains, "the rest of them are just smelly farm boys" (15). When the vicar asks him why he calls them smelly, George responds, "Because they are, father," and when asked, "Why are they?" he answers, "Because they do not wash" (16). The vicar explains, "if they are smelly, it is because they are poor. We are fortunate enough to be able to afford soap, and fresh linen, and to have a bathroom, and not to live in close proximity with beasts," adding that it is the humble who will inherit the earth, but George does not believe him (16).[15] On his daily walks, George "ignores the landscape, which does not interest him; nor do the bulky, bellowing animals it contains" (83).

Although he is myopic in more than one sense, George seems to recognize the aesthetic logistics of class delineations, mirroring in his own prejudices those that lie at the heart of a civilizational process devoted to a suppression of overt reminders of animal nature and bodily being. The violence of this dominative relationship to the self targets the animal within and without in a civilizational context that justifies hunting and routine carnivory alongside the need to care for animals as a particularly human value. To Inspector Campbell's eye, Captain Anson's study offers an unremarkable mis-en-scène of the colonial British drawing room: "two high leather chairs on either side of the fireplace, and above it the looming head of a dead elk, or moose. Something antlered anyway" (95). Early in his career, Doyle had sailed to "the Arctic ice field, off after seal and anything else they could chase and kill . . . like any healthy Briton, he enjoyed a good hunt," feeling "little but male competitiveness when they were out on the endless ice battering seals to death" (32). Displaying his familiarity with railway law, George regales his siblings with the story of "a hunting man" in Belgium, "who took his retriever on a train and sued when it was ejected from the seat beside him in favour of a human being." The court finds for the plaintiff because "in Belgium a dog may have the status of a passenger so long as it has a ticket," presumably because it shares his master's propensity for hunting and supplements this desire with its enhanced nasal competence (66).

In light of the glorification of hunting, it is more than a little ironic that the indictment and incarceration of George on unsubstantiated grounds of animal mutilation marks him as a racial and moral degenerate who betrays "excessive urges" channeled into violence toward defenseless animals (343). Along with hunting, the routine violence of the consumption of "prison beef and mutton" (195), the place of the butcher in everyday life, or the delivery of a "baron of beef" and "dead birds, mostly strangled" to George's father's vicarage as part of a harassment campaign against the interracial household elicit no outrage or comment. Casual, habitual violence toward animals in daily life points to the inherent contradictions of a project that defines civil behavior mostly by what kind of barbarism or violence it will tolerate and toward whom (44–45). In Barnes's narrative, Doyle experiences a challenge to his "way of thinking," however, when he sees a whale's eyes "slowly dim over in death," leading him to muse on "the mystery of the victim" (33). As "he continued to shoot ducks from the snowy sky, and felt pride in his marksmanship," an uncontainable feeling assails him: "Every bird you downed bore pebbles in its gizzard from a land the maps ignored" (33). It is interesting to note that gizzard stones are technological aids to mastication and digestion for the birds who use them as teeth, a sign of intelligence disregarded by the hunter who takes pride in his status as *homo faber,* the exclusive maker, user, and manipulator of tools and technology. Later, when he examines the corpse of a young man, Doyle notes its "post-mortem muscular relaxation . . . as if the strain and tension of living had given way to a greater peacefulness" (33). "The human dead," he concludes, "also bore in their gizzard pebbles from a land the maps ignored" (34). Doyle's apprehension of "the mystery of the victim" enfolding the world of the animal and that of "the rough developing animal" human present an alternative vision of the shared sanctity of breathing, sensate life (90). At the same time, his observations point to the violence done to life not only to the nonhuman animal but also to the human on whose dead face he has observed a release from "the strain and tensions of living" in a mapped, chartered world given to the cultivation of sclerosed forms of comportment.

Rigor mortis does not await death but begins in sclerosed life. The redirection of the idea of civility into rigid forms of comportment, dress codes, accents, and bodily dilations constitute acts of enormous creativity on the one hand and self-delusion and constraint on the other. George's mimicry of Englishness—ostensibly the making of a living subject whose notions of the good life, the *right* life, is lived in the English and Christian way—involves an attachment to dead forms displaced onto commodities, extensions, and dilations: "He has a respectable mustache, a briefcase, a modest fob chain, and his bowler has been augmented by a straw hat for summer use. He also has an umbrella. He is rather proud of this last possession, often taking it with him in defiance of the barometer" (92). He has fashioned himself as the "mouthpiece of things" (Adorno, *Prisms,* 270). These bodily dilations earn him the acknowledgment and salute of ticket collectors and stationmasters as the better sort of gentleman. But what does this elaborate disguise *disguise?* Not merely a half-English body, but also everything that must be refused to the animal. As Derrida observes:

> In principle, with the exception of man, no animal has ever thought to dress itself. Clothing would be proper to man, one of the "properties" of man. Dressing oneself would be inseparable from all the other forms of what is proper to man, even if one talks about it less than speech or reason. (*The Animal That Therefore I Am,* 5)

Derrida reminds us that "the most powerful philosophical tradition in which we live has refused the animal" a range of the properties of man: "culture, institutions, technics, clothing, lying, pretense of pretense" (135).[16] In the listing of cold commodities, we see the sources of George's confidence and oblivion about his subscription to an elaborate confidence game. The prejudice directed toward other races and cultures is on a continuum with the violence inherent in the making of the human through a series of repressions, disguises, and a violent regulation of the state of nature in the dominator and in all that is subject to domination, including the animal within.

Captain Anson himself draws attention to "urges and appetites" and their necessary redirection in a conversation with Doyle because, as he says, "We are men, Doyle, who understand this side of things" (*Arthur and George,* 342). Anson's comments on sexual urges unwittingly illuminate the reason for his animus against miscegenation. If, as Horkheimer and Adorno remind us, "sex represents the body in its pure state," miscegenation is a reminder of animal urges insufficiently restrained, leading to the transgression of the lines that must be maintained between the races (*Dialectic of Enlightenment,* 235). The segregation of colonial quarters from native ones in colonial urban planning marks the possession of the idea of superior civilization in the coded language of "Civil Lines," a reference to white neighborhoods with housing allotted to members of the English civil service. If these lines represented a moral cordon sanitaire from the lesser races, they also implied the governance and regulation of the lesser self prone to surrender to animal urges. Such urges may be natural, Anson concedes, but they must find appropriate channels of expression. George, he notes, is unmarried and has no friends, "neither male comrades nor, for that matter, friends of the fairer sex. He has never been seen with a girl on his arm. Not even a parlourmaid" (*Arthur and George,* 341).[17] Worse yet, "He does not engage in sporting activities either. . . . The great manly English games—cricket, football, golf, tennis, boxing—are all quite foreign to him," as are "Archery [and] Gymnastics," which are less conventional but acceptable options (341). As he explains to Doyle, "the choice often lies between carnal self-indulgence which leads to moral and physical enfeeblement, even to criminal behavior, and a healthy diversion from base urges into manly sporting activities" (343). Prevented by his circumstances of isolation and a peculiar appearance from indulging his sexual urges, George should have but "chose not to divert himself with the latter," according to Anson (343). Herbert Sussman describes the Victorian preoccupation with "the management of energy, and partly of sexual desire" (*Victorian Masculinities,* 3). Bourgeois masculinity in Victorian colonial discourse is associated with the confinement of "affectionate and sexual life within marriage" on the one hand, and on the other with self-discipline expressed as "the ability to control male energy," whose power is to be deployed "not for sexual but for productive purposes" (11).

Anson admits that although "boxing would not have been his forte," George could have pursued "gymnastics, and physical culture, and the new American science of bodybuilding" (*Arthur and George,* 343). Doyle is horrified at the suggestion that "on the night of the outrage there was . . . some sexual purpose or manifestation." Anson concedes the lack of a direct connection but insists that sexual deprivation can "turn a man's mind" (343–44). On a visit to Inspector Campbell, an officer of the law he had hoped to enlist in his aid, George himself recites the reasons he stands out in his father's parish: "I do not play in the Great Wyrley cricket team," "nor for that matter do I patronize public houses," "nor for that matter do I smoke tobacco" (106). George's odd looks aside, he is also insufficiently English in ways that might have compensated for the deviance in his features from the acceptable visual norm. He does not do with his body what English men are ostensibly *supposed* to do: imbibe intoxicating drink, inhale smoke, display muscular force, or have sex with girls, "not *even* a parlourmaid," whose subservient position might have permitted her to overlook his odd appearance or upon whom a more muscular man would have imposed himself in order to release animal urges (341; emphasis added). At a time when Victorian technologies of the self required manly sport and imperial ambitions, both of which "tall, broad-shouldered" Doyle excelled at (67), George is myopic, bookish, friendless, and ill at ease with women. George is measured both by a racist scale that preconceives relative worth and by a new set of criteria that gauges the subject's attempts to overcome the initial deficit of race by adhering to aesthetic norms and bodily technics that have evolved in the process of civilization, including accepted forms of discharging animal urges, even if they are not only arbitrary but also sexist, or even violent.

At age fifty-four, George ponders that "he has never done most of the things that afford his compatriots pleasure: drinking beer, dancing, playing football and cricket; not to mention things that might have come if marriage had come" (426). His brother Horace has done all of these. At a comparable age, Horace was a "sturdy and straightforward sixteen-year-old" (61). Never quite the scholar, he nonetheless fulfills some of the vicar's belief in Parsi exceptionalism later when he acquires a position in the civil service, albeit at the "clerical level" and "with help from a cousin of mother's" (82). Later, George notes enviously, he is "a happy-go-lucky penpusher with the Income Tax in Manchester." We are told that Horace seems "to glide through life unscathed; he goes from day to day, his ambition amounting to no more than a slow climb of the ladder, his contentment deriving from female companionship, about which he drops unsubtle hints" (115). Horace, too, is exercising a brand of Englishness, with less exertion and greater success, and if not reward, then exemption from punishment and scapegoating. He will make a passable unofficial Englishman—or at least a less other Irishman—when he sheds his family history and changes his last name, disappearing into Ireland through marriage. In George's view, "quite in which order he had done these three things George was not sure, but they were all clearly linked, and the undesirability of each action bled into the others" (418). Horace's selective assemblage and disassembly of partial bits of identity, unsavory to George, serves as sufficient expedient in his escape from Wyrley and survival in the world beyond.

Horace's passage is a less glorious analog, of course, to that of Doyle's: "Irish by ancestry, Scottish by birth, instructed in the faith of Rome by Dutch Jesuits, Arthur became English. English history inspired him; English freedoms made him proud; English cricket made him patriotic" (28). Unofficial or otherwise, both Horace and Doyle conform more closely to masculine models of cultural Englishness, unlike the unfortunate George. With his myopia, exophthalmos, and Oriental features, coupled with inadequate sexual and athletic exercise, George can never hope to reduce sufficiently the sensory load of difference from accepted modes of masculinity in English society, however riven it might be by reasons of class, occupation, speech patterns, vocabulary, or otherwise, and however diversified by location in the countryside as opposed to the city. Indeed, firstborn but the runt of the litter, George, the "little fellow," enjoys the great writer's favor largely because he is weak and Doyle's preferred version of Englishness locates its "root" in the "invented world of chivalry," which requires that "the strong aided the weak" as "chivalry was the prerogative of the powerful" (101, 28). By this logic, Doyle's advocacy of George as a "professional Englishman" makes the writer powerful, and so more English, while diminishing the Englishness of his protégé. Doyle's chivalric code finds its expression and its sources in a world in which the strong have learned to prey on the weak, and the logic of dominative rationality has justified necessary sacrifices in the name of progress and civility. Moreover, Doyle's chivalrous mission, coupled with his lifelong preoccupation with "money, breeding, taste, history, power" betrays its sources in the very logic that creates the structural possibilities for its exercise (322).

As Barnes's narrative draws to a close, the mystery of the Great Wyrley Outrages remains, while Horace, the *other* other, has stepped out of the book and broken out of history, with its spatial hold on identity and its temporal narrative of becoming, leaving the mysteries of race and hybridity unsolved while reiterating their exceptionalist logic. The scandalous kernel of developmental modernity is revealed in its random dispensation of reward and punishment, disguised by the authoritative quality of a discourse that had promised redemption. This version of biological warfare redirects its own repressions and suffering into the domination of others, choosing survivors and scapegoats. Horace's move to Ireland is not without some irony given Doyle's anxious evolution as an unofficial Englishman, but he has managed to glide through the narrative without harm. Having passed through the baffle gate, Horace, whom Anson describes as "the epitome of an English country gentleman but with a clever incisive brain," vanishes from a history that will not remember his passing (Oldfield, *Outrage,* 130). George, on the other hand, has failed to measure up to the standards of passable Englishness. George's failure is tantamount to a modern-day sin against the articles of faith that allow individuals to survive in the new jungles of civility. Here, civilization has introduced the velvet-gloved menace of those who find and prey on the weak with a measuring gaze that should be reserved for corpses rather than living beings.

Doyle's campaign on his behalf makes George "the only man to be granted a free pardon for a crime he never committed," at once both "guilty *and* innocent" (*Arthur and George,* 382). George considers his situation:

> Innocent yet guilty. Innocent, yet wrong-headed and malicious. Innocent yet indulging in impish mischief. Innocent yet deliberately seeking to interfere with the proper investigations of the police. Innocent yet bringing his troubles upon

> himself. Innocent yet undeserving of compensation. Innocent yet undeserving of an apology. Innocent yet fully deserving of three years' penal servitude. (388–89)

George, we may recall, has been raised by a father who, despite glimpses of realistic understanding of the way of the world, is also a past master at utopian illusions that include the belief that "the world's future depended upon the harmonious commingling of the races," a prospect that has failed to materialize more than a century later (414). In a demonstration of his unshaken faith in the systems that have failed his son, the vicar attempts to ascribe a grand purpose to George's suffering, encouraging him to occupy the space of martyr: "George's father had hinted to him on various occasions that his sufferings had a higher purpose to them" (389). But George, we are told, "had never wanted to be a martyr, and still saw no Christian explanation of his travails" (389). At the conclusion of Barnes's narrative, George has lost faith in the Christian way, although he knows "that he would doubtless go on living as he had done, observing like the rest of the country—and mainly because of Maud—the general rituals of the Church of England, observing them in a kind of half-hearted, imprecise hopeful way until such time as he died, when he would discover what the truth of the matter was, or, more likely, not discover anything at all" (420–21). The other redemptive narrative, the tenets and rationale of the civilizing mission, however, seem to survive this loss of faith. Locked into the logic of enlightenment modernity, George believes that he may be "a kind of martyr after all, if of a simpler, more practical kind—a legal martyr whose sufferings brought about progress in the administration of justice" (389). His unassuming accession to a sentence he serves for three years without complaint and subsequent meditation on martyrdom take shape within a prosaic, modern sensibility that leave his belief in English law as a redemptive narrative unaltered. "Might it not be some consolation," he asks himself, "if this terrible fracture in his life led to some ultimate good for his profession?" (390). As it turns out, the George Edalji case would become a factor in the 1907 creation of the Court of Criminal Appeal for England (426). George's assumption of an overarching purpose and justification for necessary suffering within the arc of imperial enlightenment obscures the stochastic and violent character of the enlightenment project from its victim's sight. George's internalization of the instrumental logic that turns the scapegoat into *necessary* sacrifice is the unannounced tragedy of the triumph of false reason, that the sacrificial animal who suffers justifies its own suffering.

EPILOGUE

The Good Life

The culture of the enslaved people is sclerosed, dying. No life any longer circulates in it.

—**FRANTZ FANON**, *TOWARD THE AFRICAN REVOLUTION*

There is life no longer.

—**THEODOR ADORNO**, *MINIMA MORALIA*

Life after Empire

A gateway to exploring the drama of form and flesh, the figure of the hybrid invites us to begin a sustained dialogue on hybridity—the darling word of globalization—as a physiological, bioformal, somatic, and inter- and intramental process in the making of the human in imperial modernity. In the strange light of literature and art, the last "refuge of mimetic comportment," we are called to see ourselves as plastic creatures, open to the world, and susceptible to mimicking forms and ways of living associated with privilege (Adorno, *Aesthetic Theory,* 53). Inhabiting particular moments in a history that precedes and succeeds it, colonial hybridity is suggestive for an understanding of current processes within a story that neither began nor ended with it. What I have dubbed "postcolonial biology" is a phenomenon cast within multiple historical coordinates. Together, these histories bring us to a shared global moment in which several elements are interconnected: the politics of neoracism, in which culture functions much as race did;[1] the global rule of capital and corporation, with its fixation on "thingified" aesthetic form and meliorism; and a state of crisis in the ability to imagine frameworks for a good life alternative to it. These intertwined contexts set the stage for exploring the ongoing formation of the postcolonial subject in the currents of history. Fanon and Adorno, seemingly so differently employed and motivated, direct us to explore the future of the modern subject, distorted by instrumental reason and imperial modernity, now revealed in full harness to the exploitative regime of capital since their prescient warnings first came to light.

At a moment of imaginative foreclosure in the pursuit of utopia, colonial and capitalist-style, this book can only hint at alternatives to dominant models of global subjectivity. Without imbuing it glibly with a capacity for agency, we can speculate that if the *leibhafte* incarnate moment is involved both in the production and recognition of suffering, attention to it in our own lives and that of others could also be a catalyst for reinvestment in the consequential question of the content of a good life. The will to freedom, Adorno reminds us, is born of an "impulse intramental and somatic in one" (*Negative Dialectics,* 228–29). A crucial preliminary to the formation and expression of this impulse, however, is an honest encounter with the self as a heteronomously determined historical and biological being. How are we living out the sentence of history in psyche and flesh? In *Minima Moralia,* Adorno bemoans philosophical neglect of the field's true purpose, "the teaching of the good life." Anyone who wishes to understand "the truth about life," he suggests, "must scrutinize its estranged form, the objective powers that determine individual existence even in its most hidden recesses" (15). Even if right life has become impossible (*Minima Moralia,* 39), the desire for it exists in a recognition of manifest "bodily feeling, in identification with unbearable pain," which constitutes for Adorno the "true basis for morality": "the demand for right living [*richtiges leben*], lives on in openly materialist motifs . . . not . . . the pure idea" for Adorno; this transition of "metaphysics itself to the stratum of the material is what is repressed by the conniving consciousness" (*Metaphysics,* 116–17). A corporeal turn does not reinstate the body-mind divide; it merely asks for recognition of the exaltation of thought as an obfuscation of the problem of the suffering, repressed body struggling with the power of capital and corporation. The heteronomously determined body-minded organism under pressure of *ad simulare* in global capitalism is a living, breathing combat zone. Almost infinitely plastic, the body-mind is capable of beginning again and again, rendering its psychic and material inputs a matter of urgent inquiry and meditation.

In the globalized world, the market's aggressive turn to the body yokes the experience of the biological body-mind securely to historical forces. Its investment in the emotive and affective dimensions of consumer behavior, manipulation of affects through advertising, exaggeration of perceived lacks, and affective inducements to expenditure on products for grooming, depilation, deodorization, and myriad forms of self-modification recall some of the technologies of the better body from the colonial civilizing mission.[2] Jameson's discussion of "Utopian corporeality" identifies an ideological project that "invests even the most subordinate and shamefaced products of everyday life, such as aspirins, laxatives and deodorants, organ transplants and plastic surgery [with] muted promises of a transfigured body" (*Archaeologies,* 6).[3] Forfeited to capitalist personhood and its suasive advertorial governance, the plastic body is an open invitation to ideological and material product placement. Adorno reminds us that "what the philosophers once knew as life has become the sphere of private existence and now of mere consumption" (*Minima Moralia,* 15). Living the so-called good life exposes the body to reformation all the way down to its "hidden recesses," at the level of muscle memory, neuronal circuits of reward and pleasure, cellular composition, and digestive flora seriatim (15). In a globalized world, moreover, the hybrid body-text now includes chemical, environmental, technological, and corporate inputs on an unprecedented scale, inviting us to develop a program for an object-oriented postcolonial studies that explores the role of race, class, and geography in relation to the ontology of "things things things" (*Midnight's Children,* 526).

How should we imagine a *techne tou biou*—Plato's code for the aesthetics of existence—lived in accordance with principles that have not been prefabricated by the market or political ideologies in hock to the new empire of capital and corporation? At this juncture, when racial and cultural prejudice masquerade in the guise of developmental aesthetics in a cozy alliance with capital and corporation, it would be well to recall Fanon's admonition regarding one of the fundamental tasks for the once colonized: the need for "a continual struggle against colonialism in its new forms" (*The Wretched of the Earth,* 235). Fanon's turn to flesh and psyche in thinking through the impact of colonialism warned us that "cultural mummification" under colonialism leads to "a mummification of individual thinking" (*Toward the African Revolution,* 34). A turn to native forms of existence as an alternative offers a compromised vista. Colonial devaluation of native forms of existence produces a distorted relationship to the culture that has "vegetated," been "abandoned, sloughed off, rejected, despised . . . put into capsules . . . since the foreign domination," only to be selectively, guiltily overvalued later without being "grasped anew" (41, 44). No longer organic but dissimulated, native culture surfaces disjunctively. Trendy forms of global citizenship allow for a selective return to native ways once they have been sanitized, usually through repackaging for purposes of commodification.[4] In a telling instance, Kraidy explains the nexus between market mentality and hybridity understood as the "cultural logic" of globalization. In this dispensation, hybridity "entails that traces of other cultures exist in every culture, thus offering foreign media and marketers transcultural wedges for forging affective links between their commodities and local communities" (*Hybridity,* 148). Yoga studios, patented breathing techniques, "art of living" courses, slow food movements, and the hypercapitalization of farm-to-table culture are but a few examples of the retail reclamation of ways of living that are otherwise disappearing from mainstream experience. Assimilation to the new world order, therefore, goes well beyond mimicry of "Western" forms. As during colonialism, but perhaps now even more so, recombinant hybridity reconciles both native and global forms of elite existence; cultural, national, religious, and/or class fundamentalisms coexist and meld with cultural and technological memes associated with capitalist modernity.

In the high noon of globalization, the privileged postcolonial subject binds his or her native prejudices, hierarchies, and ways of living with norms evolving in the new world order. The pressure to assimilate to these norms grows in the nation and without, not least for immigrants in developed nations. Characteristics of assimilated global citizenship include the suppression or privatization of modes of enjoyment likely to be derided by those in power, self-conscious mockery in the indulgence of de-privileged forms of bodily expression, and tacit or overt prejudice against those seen as aesthetically disabled by the norms of the new world order. Preoccupation with the atomic individual self and its artful construction and melioration dominates global culture, supplanting the need to conceive of a postcolonial aesthetic of the *bios* responsive to the challenges of conceptualizing the problem of living a good life in the aftermath of empire on a *collective* rather than individual basis.

Love of the Same

What has gone under the name of modernity, Jameson argues in *A Singular Modernity,* is a "concept of otherness," an "optical illusion nourished by envy and hope, by inferiority feelings and the need for emulation" (211). Founded in hierarchy and class division, the imperial civilizing mission now travels under new forms that offer the illusion of parity in an amorphous model of global citizenship that promotes individualism and scarcely pays even lip service to growing divides. In the name of the new world order and the seductive rhetoric of global citizenship, racial thinking goes undercover.

Fanon's dream, "once the colonial status is irreversibly excluded," offered a utopian vision of reciprocity conceived in terms that are tantamount to release of muscular tension: "The occupant's spasmed and rigid culture, now liberated, opens at last to the culture of people who have really become brothers. The two cultures can affront each other, enrich each other" (*Toward the African Revolution,* 44). In this view of humanism, "universality resides in this decision to recognize and accept the reciprocal relativism of different cultures" (44). Rather than insist on the sameness of all humans, a vision that failed to redeem the black man as indistinguishable from any other in histology, morphology, and philosophical humanism, Fanon pleads for recognition of differences without hierarchy, a sentiment echoed by Adorno. Adorno warns us that "to assure the black that he is exactly like the white man, while he obviously is not, is secretly to wrong him still further. He is benevolently humiliated by the application of a standard by which, under the pressure of the system, he must necessarily be found wanting, and to satisfy which would in any case be a doubtful achievement" (*Minima Moralia,* 103). Adorno derides formulaic versions of mélange and tolerance on the grounds of equality in response to human differences:

> The familiar argument of tolerance, that all people and all races are equal, is a boomerang. It lays itself open to the simple refutation of the senses. . . . Abstract utopia is all too compatible with the most insidious tendencies of society. That all men are alike is exactly what society would like to hear. It considers actual or imagined differences as stigmas indicating that not enough has yet been done, that something has still been left outside its machinery, not quite determined by its totality . . . nothing that is different survives. An emancipated society, on the other hand, would not be a unitary state, but the realization of universality in the reconciliation of differences. (*Minima Moralia,* 102–3)

Indeed, it is in the tyranny of sameness that Horkheimer and Adorno locate the common core of dominative rationality. In *Dialectic of Enlightenment,* they establish continuity between elements of anti-Semitism, the treatment of blacks, the subjugation of workers, and the violent expression of responses rooted in biological prehistory in a class society: "Race . . . is a regression to nature as mere violence, to the hidebound particularism which, in the existing order [class society], constitutes precisely the universal. Race today is the self-assertion of the bourgeois individual, integrated into the barbaric collective" (138). They rage against an order that responds to difference with a hysterical project: "to make everyone the same" (139). The attempt to bind the diversity of the particular into the conceptual can never offer a successful model for utopia. Nor indeed should it be a goal to strive for a concept adequate to identity with the idea of equality. The ineluctable challenge and elusive goal of a desirable society demands diversity without hierarchy. And yet, the more or less unisonant narrative of progress in global discourse—with pockets of resistance that are arguably constituted by it—suggests that leveled sameness is the answer to the prayers of an almost seamlessly global corporate culture industry.

The sociobiological body rendered as similarly as possible to others in as many ways as it can be in its plasticity is the fantasy of the global marketplace. Its composite developmental goal includes the duplication of a Baconian subject of reason that pays lip service to difference while becoming increasingly intolerant of it. In this vision, contempt reigns for the body requiring and consuming less, costing the planet as little as possible, living close to the ground, and resisting "development." The body that is "raw" in Gandhi's description and "rude" in James Mill's is a routinely dispensable casualty in the name of progress throughout much of the postcolonial world, as it had been in the colonial one.[5] In crudely postural terms that are cryptic but suggestive, differences between "sitting mankind and squatting mankind" with "profound biological echoes" surface as an unacknowledged dividing line nationally and internationally (Mauss, "Techniques of the Body," 81).

"Pure races do not exist, but humans differ," observes Albert Memmi (*Racism,* 7). Yet to insist on our differences—chromosomal, genetic, phenotypic, cultural, behavioral, postural, visceral, ingestive, evacuative, or comportmental— constitutes a barely adequate response to the current global moment defined by the rule of identity. Resistance at the site of the body to counter the pressure for participation in *ad simulare* through a reversion to frozen precolonial cultural moments, or newly assembled ones that smack of cultural, national, or religious fundamentalisms or holistic forms of living ratified by a market that continuously seeks to repackage and renew traditional products, all carry their own dangers. Cutting across the longitudinally and latitudinally conceived divides that have long dominated our thinking about race and relations of domination, there is another line that skirts the fourth world or the alter globe with subaltern populations that resist incorporation into globalization either by failing to adopt, or simply by lacking the social and other capital required to adopt, the norms and forms that make the impact of global capitalism recognizable in daily life. Nonconformity with

global memes of consumption and comportment can signal resistance or meaningful difference, but it can also be another name for a naked lack of resources and opportunities.

Although the term "Global South" is used to refer to economically disadvantaged nation-states, locations within the developed world deprived of its economic and other privileges, or to transnational resistance to structures of disenfranchisement and marginality, I argue that an additional conceptual border be recognized in thinking about the Global South: a civilizational border between human and the human as animal being that constitutes a distinctive global fault line. In the contact zone between peoples across and within nations, the triumph of certain ways of living directed by the intimacies of capital and global culture over indigenous ones constitutes a potent borderland. Those who live closer to a state of nature, in huts or the jungle, eat with their hands, and do not want or cannot afford the aesthetic prosthetics of modernity are the internally colonized, disdained by their own "superiors" who sport signs of primacy associated with the Global North: cars, computers, cosmopolitan cuisine, fashion, vacations, and other forms of spectacular overconsumption. This internal borderland commands but rarely receives attention. Its inclusion in thinking about the Global South will do much to expose the material conditions and phenomenological manifestations of global divides.

"A respect for cultural difference, while a *sine qua non* of any just society," Eagleton reminds us, "cannot be the *telos* of it. . . . Differences cannot fully flourish while men and women languish under forms of exploitation" (*Illusions,* 120).[6] This is a tall order. I have suggested a beginning here through a conscious engagement with the regulation of plastic body-minds and their biological processes to bring the politics of imperial capitalism home to the body in which we live. This is a point of departure, not arrival.

Ecce Animot

Plastic by nature, capable of perceiving and generating forms, responsive to authority, labile and open to the world in psyche and flesh, marked by civilizational repressions, simultaneously cerebral and sensory, what should we do with our body-minded body?[7] What should we do with our capacity for sensation and perception, for experiencing, discerning, and inflicting suffering, our pretensions to individuality coupled with our submission to authority, and our need to be the same as our superiors and better than a host of those we tacitly consign to domination? Adorno claims that it is "the physical moment [that] tells our knowledge that suffering ought not to be, that things should be different" (*Negative Dialectics,* 203). But this is the very response that has been vitiated in the course of modernity, generating a "weakened sensorium" and an anaesthetic "bourgeois coldness that is only too willing to underwrite the inevitable" (*Minima Moralia,* 237, 74). Adorno claims: "Whoever imagines that as a product of this society he is free of the bourgeois coldness harbors illusions about himself as much as about the world; without such coldness one could not live. The ability of anyone, without exception, to identify with another's suffering is slight" ("Marginalia to Theory and Praxis," 274). Horkheimer and Adorno's is a chilling vision of the *novum organum,* the subject dreamt of in Bacon's vision now come to cold life in a world where "personality is a caricature of freedom" (Adorno, *Negative Dialectics,* 299). Modern society has produced a mechanized subject whose very biology it sought to modify, dissolving the border between the social and biological, leaving no separable ontic interior or substratum beneath the deformity. Sclerosed, hard of heart, ill-equipped to deal with reminders of a shared animal prehistory, this is a creature often indifferent to the suffering of others, unable to recognize even its own, or apt to justify it in the name of historical inevitability. The rational *novum organum* is poorly equipped to imagine happiness independent of the definitions circulating in the marketplace. Transformed down to the level of reflexes, instincts, and entrails, this is a creature driven by the logic of rationalization, hollow civility, and retail therapy. Led and fed by the market and corporation, its hybrid inputs include dominant global cultural memes as much as what it breathes and ingests, knowingly or otherwise.[8] Adept in the language of instrumental rationality, more in touch with the life cycle of a market brand than the workings of their own psychophysiology, numbed by exposure to suffering instead of being animated by it, these are subjects seduced into believing that life is good when they have put as much distance as possible from what they conceive as the animal state of existence. In an extreme version of anti-biotic warfare, life turns on itself as an intruder on the scene of human existence.

Summarizing Adorno's position on the impossibility in Kantian ethics of a conception of life in which one might live with the objective of believing oneself to have been "a good animal [*gutes tier*]" (*Negative Dialectics,* 299), Derrida explains that "nothing is more abhorrent, more hateful, more odious to Kantian man than a memory of a resemblance or affinity between human and animality. . . . The Kantian feels only hate for human animality" (*Paper Machine,* 180). Adorno argues that in "socialized society, no individual is capable of the morality that is a social demand but would be a reality only in a free society." In effect, "the individual is left with no more than the morality for which Kantian ethics—which accords affection, not respect, to animals—can muster only disdain: to try to live so that one may believe himself to have been a good animal" (*Negative Dialectics,* 299). "Fascism begins," Derrida goes on to say, echoing Adorno, "when you insult an animal, including the animal in man" (*Paper Machine,* 181). Underlining the dialogue between conceptual reason and the repression of biological functions in civilizational development, he explains, "authentic idealism (*echter Idealismus*) consists in insulting the animal in man or in treating a man like an animal" (*Paper Machine,* 181). Adorno traces the etiology of this pathological process thus:

> The constantly encountered assertion that savages, blacks, Japanese are like animals, monkeys for example, is the key to the pogrom. The possibility of pogroms is decided in the moment when the gaze of a fatally-wounded animal falls on a human being. The defiance with which he repels this gaze—"after all, it's only an animal"—reappears irresistibly in cruelties done to human beings, the perpetrators having again and again to reassure themselves that it is "only an animal." (*Minima Moralia,* 105)

In the Western philosophical tradition, something that merely has life, Heidegger's *Nur-lebenden,* which Derrida translates as "living but no more, life in its pure and simple state" has not been considered a good enough life (*Animal,* 22). Mere life has been voided of a meaningful existence as an end in itself. With deliberate exaggeration, Adorno issues an aphoristic proclamation in a dialogue with Horkheimer: "Animals could teach us what happiness is" ("Towards a New Manifesto?," 35). "Philosophy exists," he states, "in order to redeem what you see in the look of an animal" (51). In the end, in failing to challenge the propensity to think about animals as mere life, tools, meat, or experimental life forms in distinction from humans, we may have failed to recognize the logic of instrumental rationality that also defines us.[9] One of the lessons of thinking through a long history of love-hate with the body as mere life is that the animals we oppress are us. We, too, die in the animal that dies in us.

The oracle for the future reveals but this: know thyself. With our *sarx* (flesh), soma, and psyche administered from within and without, our bodies are the site of product placement and environmental inputs with and without our knowledge or permission. Our very guts are available today for a largely unregulated variety of pharmaceutical, pesticidal, and alimentary experiments. These elements of our unwitting hybridity and reverberating echoes of biological repression and redirection in our daily comportmental aesthetics rooted in disdain for mere life point to a corporeographic front line in the continuing politics of difference. Given the fraught history of the role of the biological sciences in histories of racism, it was with a mix of trepidation and compulsion that I staked a claim to biology, conceiving of it as life lived in mind and body in the broadest sense with manifestations in specific, special effects produced by the interaction of form and flesh. An interest in the biological now leads urgently to the questions, What is the postcolonial way of life long after formal colonialism has supposedly ended? Is it a good life? For whom is it good? The privatization of the idea of the good life answers poorly to the realities of the global moment and our hybrid, interdependent existence. The world is writ large within us even as we write upon it the plot of a history that hurts. We are victims and agents of our plasticity, poorly equipped to, but nonetheless charged with, the need to imagine a future for the future.

ACKNOWLEDGMENTS

Books are rarely born out of solitary endeavors. Fellow travelers in the academy and in my life offered inspiration, guidance, encouragement, and the gift of productive criticism to coax its passage into the world. To name them all would tax the constraints of this genre, but I am thankful that they are many. I am particularly grateful to Parama Roy and an anonymous reader for the University of Minnesota Press for their incisive comments and helpful suggestions. Parama Roy's work on intercultural traffic and the somatic body has been enormously generative for my thinking, and her rigorous but generous criticism has made this book both richer and clearer.

Among the scholars who offered critical stimulus or inspiration are Bill Ashcroft, Simona Bertacco, Munia Bhaumik, Elleke Boehmer, Renate Brosch, Carol Colatrella, Rick Denton, Laura Doyle, Joyce Flueckiger, Carla Freeman, Ralph Gilbert, Walter Goebel, Angie Heo, Geraldine Higgins, Abdul JanMohamed, Birgit Kaiser, Ivan Karp, Corinne Kratz, Scott Kugle, Ruby Lal, Vinay Lal, Valérie Loichot, Vijay Mishra, Judith Misrahi-Barak, Mary Odem, Gyan Pandey, Mitali Pati, Laurie Patton, Sandra Ponzanesi, José Quiroga, Velcheru Narayan Rao, Sangeeta Ray, Saskia Schabio, Henry Schwarz, Nathan Suhr-Sytsma, Harish Trivedi, George Yancy, and Robert Young.

For their unsurpassed collegiality, I thank Angelika Bammer, Geoffrey Bennington, Pat Cahill, Mikhail Epstein, Rosemarie Garland-Thompson, Elena Glazov-Corrigan, Elizabeth Goodstein, Larry Jackson, John Johnston, Walter Kalaidjian, Barbara Ladd, Elissa Marder, Jim Morey, Laura Otis, Walt Reed, Benjamin Reiss, Jill Robbins, Joseph Skibell, Natasha Tretheway, Deborah White, and Kevin Young, my colleagues in English and in comparative literature.

A vibrant group of students—Namita Goswami, Stephanie Iasiello, Rebecca Kumar, Roopika Risam, Caroline Schwenz, Molly Slavin, and Jennifer Yusin, among others—lent their vivid intelligence in classes and in conversations. I would like them to know how formative for my thinking their participation in the teaching process has been.

I am extremely grateful for the institutional support I received while writing this book. A semester's teaching leave from the University Research Commission allowed me to begin my explorations through intensive reading. Lectures at the Emory Center for Mind, Brain, and Culture convened by Professor Robert McCauley and participation in the Gustafson Seminar on Race (2009–2010) stimulated my thinking. Dean Robin Forman generously supported the completion of this project, while Dean Elliott consistently provided intellectual engagement and support. My year at the Fox Center for Humanistic Inquiry as a senior fellow, with Martine Brownley as benevolent director (and rigorous taskmaster), granted me the structure, space, and intellectual fellowship without which this project could not have grown or come to fruition.

Special thanks are due to Danielle Kasprzak, the best of editors, and to Anne Carter at the University of Minnesota Press.

Versions of several chapters were tested on generous and helpful colleagues at Appalachian State University, Claflin University (National Endowment for the Humanities Lecture Series), Delhi University, the University of Louisville, Oxford University, the University of Stuttgart, the University of Tampa, the University of Utrecht, the University of Wisconsin–Madison, and the Melbern G. Glasscock Center for Humanities Research, Texas A&M University. Closer to home, a vibrant group of colleagues and students in the Program for Global and Postcolonial Studies and in the South Asia Seminar Series at Emory engaged wholeheartedly with my work and helped to refine my ideas.

Finally, thanks to my late parents, Kushal and Sudarshan Bahri, whose love of literature bred mine.

NOTES

Introduction

1 In *The Moor's Last Sigh,* Rushdie quotes at length from Macaulay's minute, interspersing the original text with editorial comments emphasizing the parliamentarian's dismissal of India's dialects as "poor and rude," and its literature, history, and science as risible (376). Some three hundred years before Macaulay's 1835 articulation of the goals of English education in India, the spirit of the 1537 Act of Henry VIII, designed to promote "a conformity, concordance and familiarity in language, tongue, in manners, order and apparel" among the Irish, Britain's *white* neighbors, offers a comparable example of the modus operandi of the civilizing mission. There are echoes of the same spirit in the words of Lord Justice of Ireland Sir William Parsons a century later: "We must change their course of government, clothing, customs, manner of holding land, language and habit of life" (quoted in Kiberd, *Inventing Ireland,* 10).

2 Forms of Westernization and Englishness may well have been reduced to triviality and farce as they were translated and domesticated in the Indian context. Moreover, the models for mimicry may not always have been Englishmen, but could have been Anglicized Indians or Anglo-Indian racial hybrids. The colonized also mimic each other, particularly those of a better class and position in society, producing copies of copies of an elusive but nonetheless identifiable range of displaced effects associated with Westernization and its coding as modern.

3 In *Quantum Anthropologies,* Vicky Kirby contends that "culture" is the name given to an otherwise "articulate enclosure without limits," producing "Nature as Culture's creature . . . to mark its denaturalization," in a move that betrays an incorrigible commitment to "the logic of origins and causal determination, simply replacing one domain or one notion of initiating efficacy with another—not Nature but 'nature,' that is, Culture" (12–13). Kirby goes on to explain that "everything is *always/already* a cultural construction" as "an elaborated form of Cartesianism . . . [that] foregrounds ideation and the human mind's now enlarged and collective success" (14). Having argued earlier in her book that grammatology and deconstruction do not furnish a predictable set of methodological rules, Kirby suggests that the divide between the sciences and the humanities is linked to "the fear of opening *the concept* 'text' to an outside whose determinations

do not begin and end with the human subject. . . . Instead of opening the question of the object *again* . . . science is read as the bad boy to the humanities' denigrated yet superior sensitivities" (15). Kirby's argument rests on the extension of textuality to nature in order to "[appreciate] that our corporeal realities and their productive iterations are material reinventions" such that life "reads and rewrites itself" and marks on the page appear as "effective transubstantiations" (xi). Kirby's work offers exciting possibilities for a simultaneous mobilization of materialist and deconstructive methodology.

4 In his reading of the "physiology of style" in Proust, Walter Benjamin reminds us, "his sentences are the entire muscular activity of the intelligible body" (*Illuminations,* 214).

5 Although Sneja Gunew argues that "learning to speak English structured, or at least choreo-graphed, bodies in certain ways," she is more interested in its emotional impact than its physiological one ("Technologies of the Self," 736). Elsewhere she writes, "femaleness acquires different forms in the new [second] language" ("Feminism," 12).

6 What Elaine Scarry, in *The Body in Pain,* calls "the extreme fact of the body" intrudes on consciousness with undeniable insistence (126).

7 Similarly dissatisfied with some parts of Ashton's translation, Dennis Redmond translates the phrase as "the corporeal moment" and knowledge as "cognition" (http://members.efn.org/~dredmond/ndtrans.html).

8 See Barkan, *The Retreat.*

9 Critics of hybridity and its poststructuralist coordinates abound. Some postcolonial critics complain that "the postmodern preoccupation with the crisis of meaning is not everyone's crisis" (Sangari, "The Politics of the Possible," 243). Even those sympathetic to postmodern frameworks have asked for a more meaningful historicization of the concept of hybridity. Abdul JanMohamed accuses Bhabha of repressing "the political history of colonialism, which is inevitably sedimented in its discourse," and of ignoring "Fanon's definition of the colonizer/colonized relation as a 'Manichean struggle'—a definition that is not a fanciful metaphoric caricature but an accurate representation of a profound conflict" ("The Economy," 60). Materialist critics question Bhabha's overreliance on the discursive and enunciative dimensions of postcolonial resistance. In "Signs," Benita Parry writes, "The construct of binary oppositions, if epistemologically faulty, retains power as a political category" (15). Ella Shohat finds the idea of culture as in-between unsatisfactory, complaining that "post-colonial theory's celebration of hybridity risks an anti-essentialist condescension toward those communities obliged by circumstances to assert, for their very survival, a lost and even irretrievable past" ("Notes on the 'Post-Colonial,' " 110). Ahmad's summary of Bhabha's notion of hybridity "as a critique of essentialism" and "a carnivalesque collapse and play of identities" denounces its production of a subject "remarkably free of class, gender, historical time, geographical location, indeed any historicisation or individuation whatever" ("Postcolonial Theory," 370–71). Young recognizes that Bhabha's elaboration of hybridity (as well as mimicry) as a threat to colonial authority produces a complicated, and for some critics an ultimately dissatisfying sort of "agency without a subject" that is "not a form of resistance as such" (*White Mythologies,* 148). Anthony Easthope argues that

Bhabha's reliance on a Derridean notion of the presence/difference binary offers no account of the identity that is undermined by hybridity ("Bhabha, Identity, and Hybridity," 344). Wary of the potential for misunderstanding, Daniel Boyarin warns that while Bhabha's hybrids represent "a difference 'within'" the subject, "the literal ascription of hybridity on the part of hegemonic discourses to one group of people, one set of practices, disavows the very difference within by externalizing it" ("Hybridity and Heresy," 343). Žižek (*The Ticklish Subject,* 220) and Friedman ("Global Crises") find that the concept of hybridity is valuable only for a cosmopolitan elite. From the perspective of political economy, Michael Hardt and Antonio Negri, however, endorse Bhabha's "critique of the dialectic," while insisting that postmodern forms of power operate not in binarist modes but in hybrid and heterogenous ones (*Empire,* 143–45).

10 In one of the pedagogic master texts in the field, Ashcroft, Griffiths, and Tiffin claim that "hybridity and the power it releases" stand out as "the characteristic feature and contribution of the postcolonial" (*The Post-Colonial Studies Reader,* 183). As I explain in "Hybridity, Redux," the concept of hybridity is closely associated with Bhabha even when it is deployed without the careful provisos and contexts that inform the critic's work. Moreover, its circulatory force relies in part on key developments in critical theory. Bhabha's theorization of colonial hybridity and mimicry is informed by a compendium of the most influential theoretical contributions of the twentieth century by a diverse range of thinkers, including Bakhtin, Lacan, Foucault, Benjamin, and Derrida. Bhabha's ideas arrive upon a reading public seasoned by decades-long engagement with ideas generated by the linguistic turn (Edward Sapir and Benjamin Lee Whorf in anthropology; Ludwig Wittgenstein, Alfred North Whitehead, and John Dewey in philosophy; Ferdinand Saussure and J. L. Austin in linguistics; and George Herbert Mead in sociology), supplemented by the poststructuralist theories of Derrida, Lacan, and Jean-Francois Lyotard. Twentieth-century developments in critical theory have also influenced discussions of race and identity. African-American Studies scholar Robert M. Young suggests that in 1985 during the highpoint of poststructuralist theory, Gates's edited volume *Race, Writing, and Difference* aims "to deconstruct, if you will, the ideas of difference inscribed in the trope of race" ("The Linguistic Turn," 336). In the volume referred to by Young, Bhabha's essay, "Signs Taken for Wonders," launched a powerful assault on the colonizer/colonized binary using a deconstructive modality in combination with a postcolonial thrust. Structuralism, poststructuralism, postmodernism, and deconstruction are terms with specific genealogies and coordinates. See the introduction to *Poststructuralism and the Question of History,* edited by Derek Attridge, Geoff Bennington, and Young, and Robert J. C. Young's *White Mythologies,* chapter 1, for detailed and nuanced discussions of this terminology.

11 Marwan Kraidy establishes a relationship of synonymity between the two in the title of his book *Hybridity, or the Cultural Logic of Globalization.* The widespread use of the term "hybridity" in connection with globalization has occasioned concern among some critics. Paul Gilroy is one of many critics impatient with "banal invocations of hybridity in which everything becomes equally and continuously intermixed" (*Against Race,* 275). Gayatri Spivak points out, moreover, that the extrapolation of hybridity as a

generalized problematic nonetheless does not indemnify the term against the need to explore its political ramifications: "If you were to say that hybridity is everywhere, irreducible, then all of the old problems apply" (quoted in Hutnyk, *Critique of Exotica,* 35).

12 "Don't separate word and history!" Derrida enjoins in his comments on apartheid in an open letter clarifying his position on text, language, and history. Derrida asks, "Has the word apartheid effaced its 'sinister renown' because the South Africans wanted to retire it from circulation and precisely because of its 'sinister renown'?" He notes that "in spite of their efforts to 'retire' this 'sufficiently stigmatized' term, the renown has not been effaced: it has gotten more and more sinister. This is history, this is the relation between words and history" ("But, beyond . . . ," 161). If we pursued the deconstructive project of locating a history for hybridity by following the paleonymic burden of the sign so that "the history will not be forgotten," hybridity emerges not only in mimicry as repetition with a difference but also as repetition in biological reproduction, despite the colonial interdiction against racial crossing (159). Significantly, Bhabha tethers his formulation of hybridity to a historically charged context by referencing James Baldwin's meditations on the "American color line" in "Black and White and Read All Over." Bhabha insists that "hybridity . . . is no jejune post-Modern lark, nor is it simply my invention." Baldwin's meditations on the "Negro" as hybrid strike Bhabha as profoundly generative for his own investment in the production of difference in the crucible of contact. Bhabha points out that "hybridity is not . . . about new 'alloys' conceived in an amoral state of historical amnesia" but "a form of social and psychic recognition; it is an awareness of the graftings, transitions, and translations through which we define our present" (114–16). Instead of assuming a disabling incompatibility between historical and poststructuralist approaches, this stance on hybridity suggests a joint maneuver, even if Bhabha nonetheless avoids any discussion of the sinister conjugation of racist notions of biology in historical discussions of hybridity.

13 Surveying its development in the *Cambridge Companion to Postcolonial Literary Studies,* Andrew Smith notes that "in everyday usage," the term implies "the mingling of once separate and discrete ways of living." Although the term still carries traces of "essentialist assumptions" and "structural inequality" at "the theoretical level," "the language of blood and racial descent," Smith observes, "has been precluded" (251). Shu-Mei Shih observes "the strongly ambivalent relation" of "South Asia-based postcolonial theory" to race studies and a more general "ascendancy of . . . neoliberal color-blind racism" ("Comparative Racialization," 1347, 1354). In *Hybridity,* Anjali Prabhu notes the "tendency . . . to move away from . . . the notion of race" toward ideas of "multiplicity, plurality, and difference in a less specifiable way," except for texts that are "closer to a 'social ground' " (xiii). Discussions of *métissage* and *créolité* are more apt to acknowledge the historical origins of the terms in the Caribbean context, even if their current usage has also moved in the direction of celebrating "synergistic cultural forms" (122). In *Autobiographical Voices,* Françoise Lionnet preserves the term *métissage* in reference to Glissant to honor "the racial context," even though, as Anjali Prabhu has observed, the term "more generally in her writing refers to an enabling 'reading practice' " (8). Valérie Loichot's valiant attempt to distinguish biological *métissage* and *créolité*

in "Creolizing Barack Obama" acknowledges the distinction while pointing to its inadequacy for grasping the complexities of identity.

14 See Malabou, *The Future of Hegel,* 9, and *What Should We Do with Our Brain?,* 13.

15 William James, widely considered the father of embodied cognition, points to Nicolas Malebranch as the mouthpiece of the intellectualist creed that rejects the body and the senses as a source of knowledge: "Impose silence on your senses, your imagination, and your passions, and you will then hear the pure voice of interior truth, the clear and evident replies of our common mistress [reason]" (quoted in James, *Some Problems of Philosophy,* 76). In writings straddling psychology and philosophy, James labors to challenge this legacy and rehabilitate the unity of the mind-body, thought-feeling, and precept-concept. In the same volume that identified and deplored the long-dominant "traditional intellectualist creed" (76), he writes of the mutuality of sensation, perception, and knowing: "'Things' are known to us by our senses, and are called 'presentation' by some authors, to distinguish them from the ideas or 'representations' which we may have when our senses are closed. I myself have grown accustomed to the words 'precept' and 'concept' in treating of the contrast, but concepts flow out of precepts and into them again" (45). "Sensation and thought in man," he concludes, "are mingled" (45). In the groundbreaking "What Is an Emotion?," he observes that physiologists had limited their exploration of the brain's functions to "its cognitive and volitional performances," a consequence of "dividing the brain into sensorial and motor centres" (188). Thomas Dewey's subsequent development of the idea of the "body-mind" makes a similar move, choosing a term that bespeaks the history of their bifurcation along with his rejection of this history. For Dewey, employing the hyphenated phrase "simply designates what actually takes place when a living body is implicated in situations of discourse, communication and participation" (*Experience,* 217). In "Sociology of the Senses," Georg Simmel points out that "we perceive our fellow-men . . . through the medium of the senses" (356).

More recently, neurologist Gallese and linguist Lakoff argue that "conceptual knowledge is embodied, that is, it is mapped within our sensory-motor system. . . . The sensory-motor system not only provides structure to conceptual content, but also characterises the semantic content of concepts in terms of the way that we function with our bodies in the world" ("The Brain's Concepts," 456). In neurocognitive terms, Damasio explains, "The ensemble of sensory detectors are located throughout our bodies and help construct neural patterns that map the comprehensive *interaction* of the organism with the object along its many dimensions" (*Looking for Spinoza,* 199). What architectural theorist Juhani Pallasmaa calls "the eyes of the skin" are the organs of sensation and perception distributed throughout our organismic selves (*The Eyes of the Skin*). In net terms, we take in the world through the senses. To tarry with this proposition is not to posit a new duality between the mind/body or the brain and the senses, but to reengage them in the complex theater of aesthetic cognition with the understanding that in a whole-body conception of cognition, the senses matter as much as the brain. Popular science can sometimes veer in the direction of reinstating a binaristic model, as in the statement that "the brain isn't always in charge of the senses. In fact, there is reason to argue the opposite: the senses run the brain" (Brynie, *Brain Sense,* 113).

16 In his foreword to Andrew Clark's *Supersizing the Mind,* philosopher of mind David Chalmers summarizes the extended mind thesis thus: "When parts of the environment are coupled to the brain in the right way, they become parts of the mind" (ix). In his earlier book, Clark suggests in a similar vein that it would be "wise to consider the intelligent system as a spatio-temporally extended process not limited by the tenuous envelope of skin and skull" (*Being There,* 221). Clark perceives cultural tools such as iPhones not merely as tools but as extensions of the cognitive system. In insisting on the "mutually modulatory influences linking brain, body, and world," Clark's work is suggestive for exploring the impact of the use of products and a range of things on cognition (163).

17 As a mutable archive, the body overflows with information about the histories working through it; everything that "touches it," Foucault explains, "diet, climate, soil," is part of the body's emergence (*Herkunft*) into history; its complex encounter with history is inscribed, moreover, on its "nervous system . . . temperament . . . digestive apparatus . . . diet," and so on ("Nietzsche, Genealogy, History," 82–83). Arguably, as Slavoj Žižek notes, "there is nothing 'inner' in this true ideological identity of mine—my innermost beliefs are all 'out there,' embodied in practices which reach up to the immediate materiality of my body" ("Tolerance as an Ideological Category," 680). In her reading of hybridity and passing, Sara Ahmed acknowledges this materiality through the "work and labour" involved in the "act of theft" of the desired identity. Ahmed identifies passing as a "technique of the self," and submits that "bodies become reconstructed through techniques which serve to approximate an image" ("She'll Wake Up One of These Days," 98, 101).

18 In "Foucault and the Paradox of Bodily Inscriptions," Judith Butler questions the existence of a body prior to inscription, as if "there is a body that is in some sense there, pregiven, existentially available to become the site of its own ostensible construction" (601). In *Bodies That Matter,* Butler calls for "a return to the notion of matter, not as a site or surface, but as *a process of materialization that stabilizes over time to produce the effect of boundary, fixity, and surface,*" insisting that "these are *both* persistent and contested regions" (66–67). Responding in part to Butler, Kirby nonetheless asks for additional consideration of the "textual adventure of the peristaltic movements of the viscera, the mitosis of cells, the electrical activity that plays across a synapse, the itinerary of a virus" (*Telling Flesh,* 76). She advances the idea of "corporeography," arguing that "the body is more than a visitor to the scene of writing . . . it is the drama of its own remarkability" (154). In *Neural Geographies,* Elizabeth Wilson advocates "readings of biological matter wherein biology is thought as excess to the limits of presence, location and stasis that theories of biological determinism and theories of gender alike have ascribed to it" (65). Butler, Kirby, and Wilson's work, along with that of other feminist scholars such as Susan Bordo (*Unbearable Weight*) and Elizabeth Grosz (*Volatile Bodies*), engage at length with the problematic divide between the body's materiality and its life as an accretion of sociocultural effects.

19 Leading geneticist R. C. Lewontin emphasizes the role of the social in genetic studies: "We are material biological objects developing under the influence of the interaction of our genes with the external world" (*Biology as Ideology,* 122). In an aphoristic pronouncement, he declares, "To be genetic is not to be unchangeable" (35).

20 The terminological slide between "body" and "biology" employed here is common in the sciences, but may require an attitudinal shift for the humanities, which routinely cede the biological organism to the sciences while claiming the social body inhabiting worlds of discourse as its rightful ground. In *Messengers of Sex,* Celia Roberts argues that "shifting meanings of 'biology' and recurrent slippages between biology as a science and biology as body or material flesh" make it "notoriously difficult for both scientists and social theorists" to hold "these two versions of biology apart" (2). I submit that responsible humanistic inquiry into the problem of a good life must recognize and appreciate the informative slippage between body and biology.

21 See Baucom, "The Human Shore."

22 Eagleton, *The Ideology of the Aesthetic,* 13. In a 1993 essay, Terry Eagleton observed, "There will soon be more bodies in contemporary criticism than on the fields of Waterloo" ("It Is Not Quite True," 7). And yet, it is in the work of Eagleton himself and his readings of Frankfurt school aesthetics in several works, including *The Ideology of the Aesthetic,* that links between aesthetics, politics, and sensory cognition were first being elaborated, with suggestive implications for a relinkage of questions of aesthetics, history, and human biology.

23 Among a number of scholars invested in this research, the writings of neurologist Antonio Damasio are often credited with popularizing the idea of embodied cognition and "the brain's body-furnished, body-minded mind" (*Looking for Spinoza,* 206). In an early bid for a recognition of the mind–body nexus, Margaret Cavendish, one of the few women writing on natural philosophy in the early modern period, speculated that "sense and knowledge cannot be bound only to the head or brain" (quoted in Anderson, "Living in a Material World," 192). "I believe," she argued in her 1666 work, *Observations upon Experimental Philosophy,* "that the Eye, Ear, Nose, Tongue, and all the Body, have knowledge as well as the Mind" (115–16, letter 36). Acknowledging the prevalent creed of the time, she writes with some irony thus: "Some learned allow, that all knowledge and perception comes by the sense, and the sensitive spirits; who, like faithful servants, run to and fro, as from the sensitive organs, to the brain and back, to carry news to the mind; and yet they do not grant, that they have any knowledge at all: which shows, they are very dull servants; and I wonder how they can inform the mind of what they do not know themselves" (153).

24 W. J. T. Mitchell argues that as "an imperial practice, aesthetics enlists all the rhetorics of religion, morality, and progressive modernity to pass judgment on the 'bad objects' that inevitably come into view in a colonial encounter" (*Picture Theory,* 147). David Lloyd's discussion of race also incorporates the role of aesthetics in the idea of "normal developmental schema," suggesting that the "racism of culture is . . . an ineradicable effect of its fundamental structures" ("Race under Representation," 63). Lloyd does not use culture to indicate "its generalized sense of the totality of life-forms of a particular society or group," but rather "the sense of *aesthetic culture,*" which functions through "the formulation and development of a *narrative of representation*" (63–64). Simon Gikandi has developed the coimplication of aesthetics and ideology in various pieces from a 1997 article to a 2011 publication, *Slavery and the Culture of Taste.* Gikandi

demonstrates the mutual imbrication of slavery and the development of taste, arenas that are usually segregated in discrete analyses.

25 Put otherwise, *the cultural is racial;* the idea of distinct cultures has been vitally instrumental in the construction of racial categories in the first place. Anthropologist George Stocking argues that early twentieth-century social sciences were dominated by "a vague sociobiological *indeterminism,* a 'blind and bland shuttling between race and civilization,'" with the "Lamarckian notion of acquired characteristics" as "the bridge over which this shuttling took place" (*Race, Culture, and Evolution,* 265). The idea of culture, he observes, "explained all the same phenomenon . . . in strictly non-biological terms," most effectively when it repudiated the "inheritance of acquired characteristics" (265). Pascoe explains that even in the formulations of race scientists, "racial essence stretched seamlessly from physical shape to character, morality, psychology, social organization, even, in the more elaborate schemes, to language. In other words, race scientists invested the term 'race' with all the explanatory power we now associate with the term 'culture'" ("Miscegenation Law," 117). Etienne Balibar mounts a similar argument in discussing cultural differences in neo-racism in "Is There a Neo-Racism?"). Finally, Claude Lévi-Strauss's work in anthropology led him to the conclusion that "far from having to ask whether culture is or is not a function of race, we are discovering that race—or what is generally meant by the term—is one function among others of culture" (*A View from Afar,* 15).

26 Kamala Visweswaran argues that Boas and his students may have fueled "the machine of scientific racism" by "expunging race from social science and assigning it to biology" (*Un/common Cultures,* 53).

27 See Epstein, *The Politics of Difference in Medical Research;* Fausto-Sterling, "Refashioning Race"; Blum, "Racialized Groups"; and Kaplan, "When Socially Determined Categories Make Biological Realities."

28 Fanon declares, "If culture is the combination of motor and mental behavior patterns arising from the encounter of man with nature and with his fellow-man, it can be said that racism is indeed a cultural element" (*Toward the African Revolution,* 32).

29 In "The End of Temporality," Fredric Jameson complains that the proliferation of body theories "replicate[s] the deeper tendency of the socioeconomic order itself, which is a nominalistic one and seeks, in its uniquely historical 'death of the subject,' to reduce the historical dimensions of existential experience" in part through "the reduction to the present and to the body alike" (713). Denouncing "the valorization of the body and its experience as the only authentic form of materialism," Jameson fears that the bodies thus theorized may be evacuated of history (713). Terry Eagleton has also warned against the "new somatics" that fetishize the "libidinal body" over the "labouring" one, within a politics careening between "vacuous universalism and myopic particularism" (*Illusions,* 71, 120). Adorno and Fanon's writings, however, instead of fixating on the present, together situate the politics of the body within a long historical arc on the one hand, and in the context of its manipulation and domination under the rule of capital on the other.

30 See Maurice Merleau-Ponty's *Phenomenology of Perception.* Merleau-Ponty emphasizes the role of the body in human experience and rejects the Cartesian mind–body

split, insisting that "there is no inner man, man is in the world, and only in the world does he know himself" (xi).

31 Although Ehrhard Bahr complains that "the authors [Horkheimer and Adorno] employed a rather naively realistic physiological theory of perception" ("The Anti-Semitism Studies of the Frankfurt School," 132), Adorno's notes on aesthetics in his eighth seminar suggest a broader formulation and a rejection of considerations of "the senses in isolation" and of an "ontology of the senses" in favor of the clear understanding that "the senses are historical" (quoted in Stefan Müller-Doohm, *Adorno,* 140–41).

32 Akira Lippit's exploration of the figure of the animal in modern culture in *Electric Animal* includes many references to the work of Adorno and Horkheimer on the animal as other in the making of the human in philosophical discourses.

33 David Spurr claims, "Under Western eyes, the body is that which is not proper to the primitive, the sign by which the primitive is represented. The body . . . is the essential defining characteristic of primitive peoples" (*Rhetoric of Empire,* 22). Anthropologist David Howes points out that expeditions set out explicitly "to measure primitive predilection for the lower senses (taste, touch, smell) (*Sensual Relations,* 5). He elaborates the sensory foundations of the construction of race thus: "In the very act of measuring the body parts and registering the sensory acuity of 'primitive' peoples, anthropologists were constituting themselves as rational Europeans and their subjects as sensuous savages" (4). Howes's project is invested in seeing how "we learn social divisions, distinctions of gender, color and race, through our senses" and in exploring how "sensual relations are also social relations" (xi). Even though early modern accounts suggest that the European sense of sight was less acute than that of "savages," vision has enjoyed a primacy among the senses in Western culture for a variety of reasons, and with multiple consequences: the long reign of ocular centrism in studies of racial and cultural difference, as well as an associated preoccupation with the more permanent products of human endeavor—written versus oral text, art, painting, architecture, captured sound in visual form as in sheet music and score rather than oral performance. At the same time, imperial eyes have famously indulged selective vision, not seeing so much as producing a landscape available for colonization and the benefit of the colonizer. In other words, the emphasis on visuality is not always indicative of particular acuity or discernment, and is enmeshed in what Pratt has called "the relation of *mastery* predicated between seer and seen" and "explicit interaction between esthetics and ideology" in colonial situations (*Imperial Eyes,* 204–5).

34 Adorno submits that the relation between reflection and reflex is complicated, for "subjects are not only fused with their own physical nature; a consistent legality holds sway also in the psychological realm, which reflection has laboriously divided from the world of bodies" (*Negative Dialectics,* 221).

35 On the topic of *Black Skin, White Masks,* Terry Collits observes, "skin . . . is god-given even if its meanings are social, discursive," while noting that skin and mask are *both* the border that interfaces with the world ("Theorizing Racism," 65).

36 "Does not nature keep nearly everything secret" from man, Nietzsche observes, "even about his own body, in order to hold him fast under the spell of a proud, delusionary consciousness, unmindful of the windings of his entrails, the swift flow of his bloodstream,

the intricate quivering of his tissues!" ("On Truth and Lying in an Extra-Moral Sense," 247). What Damasio calls the body-proper is no longer elided from most accounts of cognition, even if "it is *the body's own tendency toward self-concealment* that allows for the possibility of its neglect or deprecation," as philosopher of medicine Drew Leder points out (*Absent Body,* 69).

37 Bourdieu argues, "Although art obviously offers the greatest scope to the aesthetic disposition, there is no area of practice in which the aim of purifying, refining and sublimating primary needs and impulses cannot assert itself, no area in which the stylization of life, that is, the primacy of forms over function, of manner over matter, does not produce the same effects" (*Distinction,* 5).

38 Neuropsychologist V. S. Ramachandran's groundbreaking essay, "Mirror Neurons and Imitation Learning," on the role of mirror neurons and imitation learning in human evolution inaugurated decades of research on cognition and the role of mirror neurons. Its conclusions are debated and controversial, but Ramachandran's speculations furnish renewed grounds for the significance of mimesis in cultural politics within and among groups in ways not originally intended by the researcher.

39 *Tahzeeb* and *Sabhyata* are Urdu and Hindi language words roughly translated as "etiquette" and "civilization."

40 In a mode reminiscent of Aristotle, Mauss says, "The notion of education could be superimposed on that of imitation." All children go through "the same education, such that we can understand the continuity of the concatenations. What takes place is a prestigious imitation. The child, the adult, imitates actions which have succeeded." Moreover, he notes, a child is apt to imitate those who have authority over him ("Techniques of the Body," 73).

41 Bhabha goes on to speak of "certain kinds of secular, liberal ideas of honor, civility, professional expertise, professional integrity—these too are important community ideals" (quoted in Mitchell, "Translator," 80).

42 Family resemblances extend to the gut. Whether it is for reasons of "diet, human genes or geography," the "gut microbes of people in China are different from those of people in the United States" (Judson, "Microbes 'R' Us").

43 More recently, neuroscientific research has probed the influence of habits on brain plasticity: "If we repeatedly engage in a . . . behavior," neuroscientist Kolb contends, "the behavior itself can alter the brain" (*Brain Plasticity and Behavior,* 5).

44 Lévi-Strauss underscores the biobodily dimensions of our being and becoming, explaining that "cultures leave their mark on the human body: through styles of costume, hair, and ornament, through physical mutilation and through gestures, they mimic differences comparable to those that can exist between races and by favoring certain physical types, they stabilise and even spread them" (*A View from Afar,* 17).

45 See Elias, *The Civilizing Process,* and Bourdieu, *Distinction.* Some half a century before Mauss's influential work on habitus and the body in "Techniques of the Body," French physician turned filmmaker and anthropologist Félix Regnault was also documenting body behavior among different cultures. In "Des attitudes du repos dans les races humaines" and other works, Regnault differentiated between "savages" and the "civilized" through their bodily comportment. In the heyday of racial science, these psychosocial

and biocultural propositions about difference insisted on the relay between biobodily aesthetics, race, and culture, alongside the staples of cranial difference and biological determinism.

46 Hortense Spillers's argument for a reading of the hieroglyphics of flesh as "the concentration of 'ethnicity' that contemporary critical discourses neither acknowledge nor discourse away" makes flesh central in the reading of slavery, in particular through the captive woman's body as abject flesh incarnate ("Mama's Baby, Papa's Maybe," 67). Spillers's distinction between body/flesh is formulated for a particular, historically situated reading, but its larger gesture toward "disjunctures [that] come to be hidden to the cultural seeing by skin color" resonates with my concern that criticism must become attentive to a more extensive semantic range of bodily expressions beyond color and skin in order to better understand the complex registers of difference in racial and cultural politics.

47 Parts of Chirac's speech are available at http://www.youtube.com/watch?v=e4pun9Cdp6Q. The above translation is mine. Explaining the racist behavior of French Communists toward North African immigrants, Memmi refers to the justifications offered for their brutal evictions from public housing in Paris in terms that will seem familiar in Chirac's mobilization of sensory triggers. Apart from taking up space that might have been allotted to young couples, "the immigrants make too much noise in the street at night; their cooking smells up the stairwells of the buildings; they play their music too loud . . . and so on" (Memmi's report of objections against them, *Racism,* 108).

48 William James, arguably the forefather of embodied cognition, claims that "*the phenomena of habit in living beings are due to the plasticity of the organic materials of which their bodies are composed,*" while plasticity implies "the possession of a structure weak enough to yield to an influence, but strong enough not to yield all at once." In this structure, every stable phase of equilibrium "is marked by what we may call a new set of habits. Organic matter, especially nervous tissue, seems endowed with a very extraordinary degree of plasticity of this sort" (*Principles of Psychology,* 105).

49 The suppression of the body and the senses in the history of aesthetics, I would argue, is a symptom of the same anxieties that sundered the mind from the body, leading Baumgarten, the architect of the earliest modern exploration of aesthetics, to worry that "one could accuse him of concerning himself with things unworthy of a philosopher" ' (quoted in Buck-Morss, "Aesthetics and Anaesthetics," 7).

50 Insisting on the banality and primordiality of racism, Memmi warns that *"each time one finds oneself in contact with an individual or group that is different and only poorly understood, one can react in a way that would signify a racism"* because this is a propensity "inherent in the human condition (and perhaps that of animals as well)" (*Racism,* 23).

51 Mauss's distinction between sitting and squatting humankind in "Techniques of the Body" is also suggestive for a consideration of the importance of posture not only with regard to social norms but also because posture and health may be related such that the way we eat, sit, or shit may impact our physical well-being.

52 The description is not his own, but Darwin validates it by failing to question the assumption that the latter characters are Aryan in origin: "A crossed race would ultimately

become homogeneous, though it might not partake in an equal degree of the characters of the two parent-races" (*The Descent of Man,* 241).

53 Nietzsche goes so far as to claim that "all prejudices emanate from the bowels," and that the German spirit "is a case of indigestion, it can never be done with anything" (*Ecce Homo,* 20–21). In a related vein, Kant's "concept of disgust refers just as strongly to the morally disgusting," writes Winfried Menninghaus, explaining that "the defense-reaction of disgust does not only involve the proximity and presence of something repellent; rather, it is also the correlative of an intruding act of consumption" (*Disgust,* 104–5). "The 'nature of disgust,'" he concludes, "is consequently to civilize. Kant perceived this long before Freud and Elias, and erected a politics and morals of disgust upon the insight" (109). Hitler spoke openly of the smell of the Jew, associating it with ghetto East European Jewry in *Mein Kampf:* "I often grew sick to my stomach from the smell of these caftan-wearers. . . . [they] became positively repulsive when, in addition to their physical uncleanness, you discovered the moral stains on this 'chosen people'" (53). According to Jadunath Sinha, classical Indian theory defines disgust (*jugupsā*) "as the shrinking of the mind characterized by hatred." Sinha surveys a long list of Sanskrit theorists whose views together seem to corroborate the association of disgust with shrinking, recoil, revulsion, and contraction. He cites Saradatanaya's division of disgust into *ksobh* and *udvega:* "The former is the shrinking of the mind, while the latter is the shrinking of the body" (*Indian Psychology,* 200). Haidt, McCauley, and Rozin argue that "the most fascinating thing about disgust is that it is recruited to support so many of the norms, rituals, and beliefs that cultures use to define themselves" ("Individual Differences in Sensitivity to Disgust," 186).

54 In his monumental study, *The Civilizing Process,* Norbert Elias explores the reeducation of individuals with regard to bodily functions as well as the development of a series of prohibitions concerning sensory stimuli as foundational to the civilizing process in the West. The regulation of one's own bodily effluences and response to those of others, rules about touching, the sounds one makes or listens to, the sights and smells that are appropriate, what and how to eat, and numerous other prescriptions and proscriptions have been part and parcel of the project of Western civilization. Ascesis, self-cultivation, and repression constitute the underbelly of the cultivation of the self and of taste in the cultured individual. Bourdieu's elaboration of the links between taste, class, and culture, although vigorously debated, nonetheless points to the ways in which aspirations to class mobility in particular allied civilizational aesthetics with bodily ascesis.

55 In *The Color of Angels,* Classen explores the prominence of visualism in shaping the religious and cultural imagination of the West. Smell, once understood as a useful sensory mode of cognition, is now widely disdained, along with the other lower, more animal senses of taste and touch.

56 Colonial discourse habitually characterized the native as animal. To Lord Hastings, governor general of India from 1813 to 1823, for instance, the "Hindoo" appeared to be little more than animal body, "a being nearly limited to mere animal functions, and even in them indifferent . . . with no higher intellect than a dog or an elephant, or a monkey" (*Private Journal,* 17). In her review of "Three [Western] Women's Texts," Gayatri Spivak discusses the construction of the European self as premised on rendering

"indeterminate the boundary between human and animal" with regard to the native to withhold full humanity from its other (249).

57 Kürnberger, quoted in the opening epigraph of Adorno's *Minima Moralia.*

58 Genealogical obfuscation caused by lost records and the practice of christening native converts with Christian names make it extremely difficult to establish boundaries between Anglo-Indian and native Christian converts. Moreover, genealogical researchers repeatedly find gender trouble in the archive. In archival work on interracial relationships, Durba Ghosh says she looks out "for subjects with incomplete or partial names because the lack of a complete name signaled the presence of a native female" ("Decoding the Nameless," 301). Moreover, Buettner notes an 1891 census report citing problems of categorization given "the tendency for Eurasians to enter the European group, and for native Christians to be returned as Eurasians" ("Problematic Spaces, Problematic Races," 280). Although it is more common to encounter narratives of Anglo-Indians passing for white, passing as Anglo-Indian by native converts to Christianity constitutes an intriguing phenomenon in its own right. The Anglo-Indian community has tried to distinguish itself from Indian Christian converts, continuing the separation into "the graveyards" (Younger, *Neglected Children of the Raj,* 41).

59 Schedule 366 (2) of the 1950 Constitution of India states, "an Anglo-Indian means a person whose father or any of whose other male progenitors in the male line is or was of European descent but who is domiciled within the territory of India and is or was born within such territory of parents habitually resident therein and not established there for temporary purposes only" (quoted in Anthony, *Britain's Betrayal in India,* 5). In a long list of sliding monikers, this figure has been known euphemistically in the Indian context as "Domestic Occurrence" and "Rear rank European" (Lahiri-Dutt, *In Search of a Homeland,* 16); colloquially as "Tansh," "Albino," "chi-chi," "mongrel," "pariah," "blackie-white," "Anglo-Banglo," "Wog," "Nigger," "Char Anna," "Eight Anna" (Gabb, *Anglo-Indian Legacy,* 22); multilingually as *Mestizo, Oolandez, Wallendez, Mustees, Metis, Fringy;* and in colonial documents as "Half-caste," "Indo-Briton," "East Indian," "Anglo-Asian," "Asiatick," "Asiatick Briton," and "Britasian." The Anglo half (quarter, eighth, total) could be English (Scottish, Welsh, Irish, or a hybrid of any or all of these), Portuguese, French, Dutch, Spanish. or any other sort of European male on an extended or short tour through colonial India. The Indian half of "Anglo-Indian" could be Burmese, Bangladeshi, Nepali, Pakistani, Sri Lankan, Malay, immigrant Chinese, Anglo-Indian, or any other Indian hybrid. "Anglo-Indian," a plurisignifying term, speaks to the question of the provisionality of language and identity, but no less of hybrid histories that develop through the truck of languages as well as bodies. A series of misnomers finally culminate in a stabilized legal statute constituting a person based on a particular genealogy in the constitutional writ quoted above. To compound the confusions associated with the term, "Anglo-Indian" was also used to designate Englishmen resident in India.

60 For a detailed study of Anglo-Indians in literature, see Glenn D'Cruz's *Midnight's Orphans* and Shuchi Kapila's *Educating Seeta.*

61 Now firmly associated with India, the term "caste" itself is borrowed from the Latin *castus,* meaning "pure," "unpolluted": "Apparently at first from Spanish; but in its Indian

application from the Portuguese, who had so applied it about the middle of the 16th cent. (Garcia 1563)" (*Oxford English Dictionary Online*, s.v. "caste"). Born in confusion, the idea of caste "has been retained in English under the supposition that it was the native name" (Yule and Burnell, *Hobson-Jobson*, 170). The enormous complexity of the Hindu social order was simplified in the process of translation for Europe, and indeed for modern Indians, such that many Indians now refer to the caste system without qualifying the term. Some of the simplification in most renditions of the caste system stems from European reliance on written Sanskrit sources because the intricacies of the social system in the realm of everyday practice were unavailable to Western scholars. Nicholas Dirks has argued in "Castes of Mind" for an understanding of the idea of caste as a colonial form of knowledge.

62 According to Buettner, "nearly half of the Europeans in late nineteenth-century India fell into the category of 'poor whites' " ("Problematic Spaces, Problematic Races," 279).

1. "No Escape from Form"

1 It is possible to question Saleem's account of his parentage and how he can so confidently assert a line of descent from Methwold. Whether or not this account is true, or indeed his account of anything at all in the novel, in drawing attention to the encounter, Saleem points to a usually unclaimed fragment of hegemonic accounts of the nation, which rarely acknowledges its racially hybrid population in any significant way.

2 In "Outside the Whale," Rushdie argues, "if a rape must be used as the metaphor of the Indo-British connection, then surely, in the interests of accuracy, it should be the rape of an Indian woman by one or more Englishmen of whatever class" (*Imaginary Homelands*, 89).

3 Abandoned by European sires, the British government, and subsequently the independent nations of Pakistan and India, the residue of imperial desire demands but rarely receives due recognition in our theories of hybridity, or indeed in accounts of the nation. The prominent Anglo-Indian Sir Henry Gidney once said, "We represent in our very bodies a synthesis of India and Britain as no other people do or can do, a fusion of East and West" (quoted in Blunt, *Domicile and Diaspora*, 42). Anglo-Indians at empire's end, incidentally, had also intermingled with the Burmese and Chinese diasporas. Indian historiography rarely includes these minor characters on the national stage. The deliberate marginalization of Anglo-Indians under the British, and their subsequent absence from mainstream narratives of the Indian nation, is abundantly recorded in studies of the community. Saleem Saleem's fanciful assumption of the role of mouthpiece for midnight's children ironically emphasizes this history of erasure. Nor has postcolonial theory accorded Anglo-Indians and other racial hybrids a starring role in the long-running, blockbuster concept of hybridity, even though they might be considered its exemplary embodiment by almost every available definition, whether based in biology as conventionally understood, or in culture, or in the third space between identities. Furthermore, Anglo-Indian lifestyles represented vernacular forms of *Weltbürgertum* (cosmopolitanism) that had developed in the Global South in cities such as Canton and Calcutta. Routinely upstaged in postcolonial theory by other formulations, the unclaimed hybridity and cosmopolitanism characteristic of this community have

gone largely unremarked. This betrayal is commemorated in historical, autobiographical, and literary narratives with titles that point to it with incantatory insistence. Among them are Stark's *Hostages to India; or, the Life-Story of the Anglo-Indian Race,* Anthony's *Britain's Betrayal in India: The History of the Anglo-Indian Community,* Hawes's *Poor Relations,* Gist and Wright's *Marginality and Identity: Anglo Indians as a Racially-Mixed Minority in India,* and Lahiri-Dutt's *In Search of a Homeland.*

4 The revelation of Saleem's true genealogy and its quick dismissal ("it *made no difference!*") can leave readers disappointed that a canonical literary text in postcolonial fiction about India should have tantalized us with the promise of a bona fide racially hybrid Anglo-Indian as the voice of the nation, and then diffused his story into a sea of others beset by their own anxieties of belonging and disenfranchisement (136). Critics invested in a spatio-temporally situated history of racial hybrids complain that the racial hybrid in Rushdie's fiction is reduced to a trendy trope for in-betweenness reliant on "notions of hybridity severed from history" in a mode familiar from influential formulations of hybridity in postcolonial theory (Mijares, "You Are an Anglo-Indian?," 130; D'Cruz, *Midnight's Orphans*).

5 Coralie Younger writes of a series of colonial ordinances designed to keep the community underdeveloped: a 1786 order prohibited wards of the upper orphanage school at Calcutta from proceeding to England to complete their education; a 1791 ordinance barred them from the company's civil, military, or marine services; by 1795, persons of mixed blood could only serve in the army as fifers, drummers, and farriers; an 1813 order prohibited them from holding or purchasing land, or living farther than ten miles from a company settlement without sanction of the chief secretary (*Anglo-Indians,* 12).

6 Part of this diaspora was linked to the slave trade in South Asia, a history that is underexplored and insufficiently documented. In "The African Diaspora of the Indian Subcontinent," Mampilly reports, "little is known about Africans who moved from the African continent to the Indian subcontinent, some as slaves, but others purposefully and freely." Traders, warriors, sailors, mercenaries, prisoners of war of the Muslim rulers, "Africans also came as midwives and herbalists, and as musicians, sailors and merchants." Today, Mampilly speculates, "under the extensive Indian affirmative action programs, most Indo-Africans are classified as scheduled tribes, which entitles them to reservations in university seats and other government support." Sudipta Sen notes that it "was only in 1789 that the East India Company stopped transporting slaves from Africa to the Indian Malabar coast" (*Distant Sovereignty,* 17). Linguistic traces of this diaspora survive in sound bites encoding complicated histories in words such as *habshi, sidi,* and *kafir* (Pankhurst, "The Ethiopian Diaspora," 190). For further information, see *African Diaspora,* especially essays by Pankhurst, Basu, and Jayasuriya.

7 The nominal "Caucasian," however, is arguable, and the designation, when used, was usually limited to upper-caste Brahmins of the North.

8 Hegel, who otherwise relied heavily on James Mill's assessment of Indian art as "rude" and poorly formed, would nonetheless declare in *Philosophy of History* that "no language can be regarded as more fully developed than the Sanscrit," pointing, like Schlegel and others, to a profound linkage between this tongue and those of Europe: "Greek, Latin, and German" (162, 142).

9 For an understanding of the complexities of defining white identity, it is instructive to consider the landmark case of an Indian man named Bhagat Singh Thind in American history. His petition for American citizenship prompted the question: "Is a high caste Hindu of full Indian blood, born at Amrit Sar, Punjab, India, a white person within the meaning of section 2169, Revised Statutes?" In a convoluted opinion, Justice Sutherland "clarifies" the matter thus: "Caucasian is a conventional word of much flexibility, as a study of the literature dealing with racial questions will disclose, and while it and the words 'white persons' are treated as synonymous for the purposes of that case, they are not of identical meaning. . . . The words of the statute are to be interpreted in accordance with the understanding of the common man from whose vocabulary they were taken. . . . It may be true that the blond Scandinavian and the brown Hindu have a common ancestor in the dim reaches of antiquity, but the average man knows perfectly well that there are unmistakable and profound differences between them today" ("Not All Caucasians Are White").

10 Longtime resident of India, missionary Bishop Caldwell, on the other hand, notes, "The condition of the Indo-Aryans, in point of intellect and culture, differs [so] widely from that . . . [of] aboriginal tribes . . . that it is difficult to realise the fact that both races have lived together for ages" (7–8). On their physical appearance, he observes "many differences in complexion and type of feature, and also many differences in culture and mental and moral characteristics" ("Languages," 9). He speaks approvingly of Brahmans who "rank at the head of native society as a sacred, priestly aristocracy, which has not degraded itself by a single intermarriage with the classes beneath it for 2,500 years" (*Lectures,* 38).

11 As American writer and planter Alfred Stone points out, theories about racial affinities in India met their limits in the fray: "The British scientist may tell the British soldier in India that the native is in reality his brother, and that it is wholly absurd and illogical and unscientific for such a thing as 'race prejudice' to exist between them. Tommy Atkins simply replies with a shrug that to him and his messmates the native is a 'nigger'; and in so far as their attitude is concerned, that is the end of the matter" ("Conflict and Accommodation," 632).

12 Partha Mitter argues that without the notion of the Aryan thesis and its geographical coordinates in Asia, it would not have been possible to generate the idea of Africa as an absolute other to imperial Europe. It was this myth, he argues, that "provided ammunition for the racial classification of mankind" ("Greece, India, and Race among the Victorians," 57).

13 In the *internal* hierarchies produced by the fertilization of indigenous prejudices with colonial thought, aboriginals, for instance, understood as "*jungle*-dwellers," were aligned with "all that was deemed wild, uncivilized and uncouth" (Arnold, "Race, Place, and Bodily Difference," 266). Arnold explains: "Because the British sense of national superiority had become so marked by the eighteen-thirties, it was possible to deploy a language and typology of race not so much to police a racial frontier between Britons and others as to differentiate among Indians themselves . . . on the basis of their appearance as if at some eternal beauty contest" (263). In a rich comment on the diversity of Indian colonial experiences, Dipesh Chakrabarty justifiably argues for a variable schedule

of colonization in the Indian experience: "There were spaces in our lives—so-called classical music would be a case in point—where we could use European institutional forms, syllabi, etc. (Bhatkhande [lawyer and musician who committed the tenets of classical Indian music to text and initiated a modernized system of musical education] would be a case in point) to our advantage without feeling deeply colonized. Aboriginal societies were just pulverized and sometimes wiped out. I do not think we—again, I mean the middle classes—suffered anything like that" (in Ghosh, "Reflections," 159).

14 Elsewhere, Rushdie exposes the limits of both the liberal narrative and that of Marxism when transported into a racially charged colonial context. In *The Moor's Last Sigh*, educated Communist Camoens learns the racial limits of Marxism when he invites "a genuine, card-carrying member of the Special Lenin Troupe" to visit what he hopes will be "the Troupe's new Cochin Branch" (30). The comrade, however, is outraged by the audacity of the Red spirit in black bodies: "These persons have blackness of skin and their features are not his," he complains through a translator (30). Liberal ideology or communism, what Ghosh calls the +R, the fact of race, points to the wrongness of the body that attempts to enact ostensibly humanist programs that claim to transcend social and racial hierarchies.

15 Indian historiography has not been as silent on the subject of race as Ghosh implies. In *Racism, Struggle for Equality*, Nemai Sadhan Bose studies the "dominant racial element" of various colonial legal acts and agitations against them (xvii). Bose bluntly equates civilizational and racial prejudice: "The European who viewed the Indians with hatred, contempt, dislike and distrust and boasted of his inherent all-round superiority in justification of his political domination was as much a racist as one who, while abandoning the concept of genetic superiority, was obsessed with the idea of the absolute superiority of his own culture, civilization, education, morality, and ways of life" (xv).

Bose speaks of segregation and virtual apartheid between colonizer and colonized in the cities, and suggests, moreover, that both ruler and ruled perceived the other as different: "To an Indian living in the nineteenth century the Europeans appeared, without a shadow of doubt, as belonging to a distinct and different race" (xiii). During colonialism, several thinkers drew attention to colonial racism. Kshirod Chandra Sen, follower of reformist Keshab Chandra Sen, admonishes his readership to recall the racial divide between ruler and ruled: "Intellectual eminence, learning and wealth possessed by individuals belonging to a subject race can not compensate for general national degradation expressed in submission to foreign domination. A Hindu Peer, a Hindu Councillor or a Hindu Chief Justice—they are very admirable persons taken as individuals,—but does their high position affect their nationality, their positions as members of a subject race?" (*The Gita and the Castes*, 13–14). However, what V. S. Naipaul describes in *India: A Wounded Civilization* as a peculiar Indian "gift for cultural synthesis" could explain in part why it sometimes seems that "the racial sense is alien to Indians," permitting us to forget that Gandhi, "until middle age . . . was literally a racial leader, fighting racial battles; and it was as a racial leader that he returned to India" (112, 141, 143).

16 According to some sources, the *chi chi* accent referred to "the sing-song, almost Welsh accent of the 'Anglo-Indian' community at large" (quoted in Buettner, "Problematic Spaces, Problematic Races," 285).

17 The offensive "chee chee," often used for Anglo-Indian girls, does not survive in American argot today but features suggestively in the following advertisement copy for the MGM adaptation of John Masters's novel *Bhowani Junction* starring Ava Gardner and Stewart Granger in *Life* magazine's June 11, 1956, issue: "A Land—and three lovers—of violent contrasts! Turbulent India is mirrored in the stormy love affairs of a 'chee chee' beauty with an Indian, a white man, and a half-caste" (115). Colonial texts frequently alluded to the beauty of Eurasian women while commenting on their verbal deficiencies and "tchi-tchi tongue": "The Eurasian girl is often pretty and graceful; and, if the solution of India in her veins be weak, there is an unconventionality and *naïveté* sometimes which undoubtedly has a charm; and which, my dear friend, J.H——, of the 110th Clodhoppers (Lord Cardwell's Own Clodhoppers) never could resist: 'What though upon her lips there hung the accents of the tchi-tchi tongue'" (Aberigh-Mackay, *Twenty-One Days in India*, 121–22).

18 Many years later, in a hip-hop inspired dancing number designed for the nation's gilded clubbers in Disney's 2014 remake of a popular Hindi film *Khoobsurat* [Beautiful], the allegedly feminist heroine dares someone to take her on; the world rests, she says, at the tip of her Jimmy Choo shoes. In the song's catchy refrain, *abhi toh party shuru hui hai;* in other words, and in more ways than one, as the English translation suggests, "the party's only just begun."

19 The legacy of English and liberal education manifests diversely in India today. *New York Times* writer Manu Joseph observes: "Hindi films are now written in English—the instructions in the screenplays are in English, and even the Hindi dialogue is transcribed in the Latin alphabet. Mumbai's film stars, like most educated Indians, find it easier to read Hindi if it is written this way. Almost all advertising billboards in India are in English. There is not a single well-paying job in the country that does not require a good understanding of the language. Higher education here is conducted entirely in English." "What is indisputable is that in India today," Joseph writes, "English has the force and quality of a national language." True to Indian form, there is a Goddess of English in Northern India, dedicated to the advancement of the untouchable population: "Modelled on the American Statue of Liberty, she is pictured against a map of India, wearing a sari and an English straw hat, standing on a computer and holding aloft a giant pink pen." Chandra Bhan Prasad, the entrepreneurial untouchable who proposed and built the temple in which she is housed, recommends the following ritual offering for couples during their wedding ceremony: signing the letters A, B, C, and D on a piece of a paper. "That would be a promise they make that they will teach their children English," he is reported to have said. He also plans to adopt an Islamic tradition and fix a loudspeaker in the temple from which a recorded voice would chant the English alphabet, from A to Z, every day at five o'clock in the morning (Joseph, "India Faces a Linguistic Truth"). On October 25, Prasad and other devotees allegedly gather to celebrate the birthday of Macaulay, the man who is considered the architect of English language and literature education in India. One hundred seventy-eight years later, after

the proclamation of the famous minute, Prasad preaches a version of Macaulay's dream. Celebrations include a hymn of praise to the new deity: "Oh Devi Ma, please let us learn English! Even the dogs understand English" (Masani, "English or Hinglish"). In response to a national fever for learning English, schools with indifferent instructional quality have mushroomed all over India.

20 In an early draft of *Midnight's Children,* Rushdie considered "From Monkey to Rhesus" as an alternative title to chapter 16 (Draft, 16.218). In the draft as in the final published version, he refers to "rhesus, which is also a type of monkey" (Draft, 16.221). The connections between race, blood, civilization, and those between apes, aping, and native mimicry are more than explicit in several such references.

21 Saleem displays precocious understanding of a similar rage in Mr. Emil Zagallo, his teacher, who "claimed to be Peruvian, and was fond of calling us jungle-Indians, bead-lovers" (*Midnight's Children,* 275). Saleem volunteers this assessment of the teacher who cruelly uses him for a human geography lesson: "We called him Pagal-Zagal, crazy Zagallo, because for all his talk of llamas and conquistadores and the Pacific Ocean we knew, with the absolute certainty of rumour, that he'd been born in a Mazagaon tenement and his Goanese mother had been abandoned by a decamped shipping agent; so he was not only an 'Anglo' but probably a bastard as well. Knowing this, we understood why Zagallo affected his Latin accent, and also why he was always in a fury, why he beat his fists against the stone walls of the classroom; but the knowledge didn't stop us being afraid" (275).

22 The chemically tactile impact of smell violates the regime of tact that requires distance and alienation. Horkheimer and Adorno explain that the civilized individual indulges in the pleasure of smell only in the guise of mocking it, in the form of a joke, for instance, in "a wretched parody of fulfillment" that evades the prohibition of forbidden impulse by identifying with the authority that forbids it: "Anyone who sniffs out 'bad' smells in order to extirpate them may imitate to his heart's content the snuffling which takes its unrationalized pleasure in the smell itself" (*Dialectic of Enlightenment,* 151).

23 Kant isolates smell for its capacity to invade us willy-nilly: "Smell is, so to speak, taste at a distance, and other people are forced to share a scent whether they want to or not. Hence, by interfering with individual freedom, smell is less sociable than taste; when confronted with many dishes and bottles, one can choose that which suits his pleasure without forcing others to participate in that pleasure. Filth seems to awaken nausea less through what is repulsive to eye and tongue than through the stench associated with it. Internal penetration (into the lungs) through smell is even more intimate than through the absorptive vessels of mouth or gullet" (*Anthropology,* 45). In "Determination of the concept of a Human Race," Kant makes a link between innate and purposive design and the significance of smell in the "negro": "it was a very wisely designed device of Nature so to constitute their skin that the blood, as it cannot dispose of enough phlogiston through the lungs, can dephlogisticate itself through the skin much better than it can in our case" (quoted in Greene, "Some Early Speculations," 38). Bernard Cohn's notes on European views of Indian sweat and skin suggest a similarity with the notion of phlogiston: "The Indian's skin and the whole process of perspiring are different from that of

the Europeans. Indian skins 'secrete a very different kind of fluid being more of an oily and tenacious nature than the sweat of the European'" (*Colonialism and Its Forms of Knowledge,* 156). Kant's emphasis on this wise arrangement of nature, the notion that smell is *purposive* in a particular group is an early example of the connection between aesthetics and racial distinctions. Also remarkable in this writing is the quasi-biologistic idea of innate and determinate purpose in terms analogous to his arguments about indeterminate purposiveness as a feature of beauty in art and nature in the foundational text of aesthetic theory, *Critique of Judgment* (1790), a book initially announced under the title *Critique of Moral Taste.* Kant's disquisition on teleological judgment in the text grounds his critical project in a commitment to purposiveness or teleology as the link between aesthetics and biology. As Hannah Arendt points out, moreover, the counterpoint to beauty in this foundational text on aesthetics is not ugliness but "that which excites disgust" (*The Life of the Mind,* 2). Kant's disgust-taboo imbues his otherwise neutral observation about biological functions such as sweating with aesthetic and moral judgment.

24 See Alison Blunt's discussion of the sexualization of Anglo-Indian women in *Domicile and Diaspora,* especially 156–57. In Amina's estimation, Mary's sister—like her husband's other female employees—represents the national "stereotype of the Anglo-Indian *tnyas* (half-breed)—Westernized and common at the same time," in the words of Partha Chatterjee (*The Nation and Its Fragments,* 132). Amina's outburst indicts the whole tribe: "'Those Anglos with their funny names, Fernanda and Alonso and all, and surnames, my God! Sulaca and Colaco and I don't know what. . . . Cheap type females. I call them all his Coca-Cola girls—that's what they all sounded like'" (*Midnight's Children,* 155). As Partha Chatterjee notes, the Westernized and lower-class half-breed was "the most extreme object of contempt for the nationalist" (*The Nation and Its Fragments,* 132). Moreover, Nirad Chaudhuri writes that "Hindus who are on the sensual quest" are apt "to look upon all Eurasian girls, irrespective of their conduct, as fair prey" based on the assumption that "in the British days it was the women of this class who mostly supplied *prostitutes* for the White Man in India" (*The Continent of Circe,* 264, 260). Historically, a combination of "educational and occupational handicaps" effectively confined Anglo-Indian women to a predictable range of usually underpaid jobs where they would be exposed to male advances (Gist and Wright, *Marginality and Identity,* 58). Skirt-wearing Anglo-Indian women, seen as available bodies, were stereotyped in an India accustomed to its traditional women working within the home rather than in the world beyond, and remaining covered and thus socially shielded from unwanted advances. The Helens, Julies, Monas, and Rosies of early Bollywood cinema occupy the cultural space of promiscuous women in their roles as cabaret queens, dancers, and gangsters' molls, sometimes redeemed by a golden heart but seldom by rehabilitation into the fabric of the national imagination.

25 Earlier in the narrative, bragging about his nasal competence, Saleem tells us that "long before the American commentator Herbert Feldman came to Karachi to deplore the existence of a dozen aerated waters in a city which had only three suppliers of bottled milk, I could sit blindfolded and tell Pakola from Hoffman's Mission, Citra Cola from Fanta. Feldman saw these drinks as a manifestation of capitalist imperialism; I, sniffing

out which was Canada Dry and which 7-Up, unerringly separating Pepsi from Coke, was more interested in passing their subtle olfactory test" (*Midnight's Children,* 379). Rushdie's comment on the "Coca-Colonization of the planet" joins imperialism with capitalist intrusion into the native marketplace, but read alongside Saleem's acute sensitivity to the array of carbonated drinks on offer in colonial South Asia also implicates their ingestion with a recalibration of the sensorium (*The Satanic Verses,* 406).

26 *Malasana,* the name of this yoga pose, is one that many non-Westerners and modern Indians are unable to perform because they are no longer habituated to sitting on their haunches.

27 While in animals, "squat urination and defecation probably have scent-marking as well as eliminative functions," several researchers note their benefits for humans (Lopez, *Of Wolves and Men,* 49). Progressive medicine cites lower incidences of hemorrhoids among squatters. Medical biologist Sikirov contends: "The only natural defecation posture for a human being is squatting. The alignment of the recto-anal angle associated with squatting permits smooth bowel elimination. This prevents excessive straining with the potential for resultant damage to the recto-anal region and, possibly, to the colon and other organs" ("Primary Constipation," 71).

2. Shibboleth

1 In *In Search of a Homeland,* Kuntala Lahiri-Dutt describes the failed attempt of the Anglo-Indian community to create a homeland within India in McCluskiegunge, a town in the state of Jharkhand. A mere handful of the community remains in McCluskiegunge, most having migrated to England and other countries, but this dream of a homeland within the nation offers an intriguing study of internal diaspora. Geographer Alison Blunt summarizes the attitudes of the community in the following words: "Although Anglo-Indians were 'country-born' and domiciled in India, many imagined Britain as home and identified with British life even as they were largely excluded from it. In many ways, Anglo-Indians imagined themselves as part of an imperial diaspora in British India" (*Domicile and Diaspora,* 2).

2 Over time, moreover, the love of leavened bread has grown exponentially in South Asia, along with the number of artisanal bakeries, requiring us to reckon with new forms of alimentary conversion.

3 Several pieces of official communication disclose a disinclination to absorb Anglo-Indian migrants into the "home" country, unless they were of substantial means. A July 21, 1947, dispatch from L. A. C. Fry to C. A. Gault, counsellor to the general secretary, the European Association, Calcutta, indicated a disinclination to invite emigration from Anglo-Indians: "Applications from Anglo-Indians for special facilities to remove themselves to the United Kingdom are not to be encouraged or accepted," in part because the association "will not sponsor any emigration scheme." Moreover, emigration by British subjects is to be "dissuade(d) . . . unless they have good prospects of being able to support themselves there and realize fully the climatic and other austerities which they would have to face" (Fry to Gault, letter). A cypher telegram on the subject of "Repatriation of Europeans," from the U.K. high commissioner in New Delhi, India, to the Cabinet Office, August 12, 1947, discloses the government's position in the voice of

its representative: "I do not however intend (vide paragraph 1 of your telegram No. 485 of 25th July 1947) to mention Anglo-Indians in this communiqué as to do so would encourage them to seek repatriation which would be contrary to provisions of paragraph 2 (d) of your dispatch No. 13 dated 22nd May 1947" (U.K. high commissioner). The telegram goes on to clarify that "Any Anglo Indians who do travel under their own resources will be included in ship by ship forecasts," while bemoaning the "difficulties in obtaining all this information particularly in making accurate differentiation between Europeans and Anglo Indians, as latter so often claim without justification to be pure British Europeans" (2). At the same time, another secret cypher telegram dispatched by O. T. P. from the Cabinet Office to the U.K. high commissioner in New Delhi, India, on July 24, 1947, underlined the problem of resources thus: "His Majesty's Govt wish . . . to make it clear that there is no barrier to the emigration to this country of domiciled [this word crossed out in pencil] Europeans and Anglo Indians who can pay their own way" (Cabinet Office).

4 In *Carnal Knowledge and Imperial Power,* Stoler argues for a better understanding of how "the making of race has figured in placing sexuality at the center of imperial politics" (141). Stoler (in "Sexual Affronts and Racial Frontiers"), Kenneth Ballhatchet (in *Race, Sex, and Class*), and others expose miscegenation and the fear of "sexual affronts" as the very engine of empire in the Asian theater of colonialism.

5 Bradley Shope explains that Portuguese Goans and Anglo-Indians were "especially involved" in Western music performance culture to satisfy British and American "nostalgia for live performance of the foxtrot, the tango, the waltz, the rumba, big-band music, and Dixieland." Shope claims, "For these two groups, it served to assert their identities as distinct from other South Asians and highlighted that their taste for music reached beyond the geographical boundaries of India" ("Anglo-Indian Identity, Knowledge, and Power," 167).

6 Rejecting Malayalam-speaking mixed-race individuals of Portuguese extraction in Kerala, prominent Anglo-Indian leader Frank Anthony insisted on the community as a "homogenous racial-cum-linguistic-cum-cultural entity" (quoted in Younger, *Anglo-Indians,* 23). In his 1974 definition, W. T. Roy insists that the Anglo-Indian "is a member of a group possessing a distinctive subculture whose characteristics are that all of its members are Christians of one denomination or another, speak English, wear European clothes on almost all occasions, have substantially European dietary habits (but are addicted to the fairly lavish use of Indian spices), are occupationally engaged in a restricted number of trades and professions, and are by and large endogamous ("Hostages to Fortune," 56). Using similar criteria and deploying an intriguing comparison with the Indian caste system, Mark Naidis claims that "Anglo-Indians came to resemble an exterior caste, if one defines such a group by rules of endogamy, craft exclusiveness and commensality" (quoted in Younger, *Anglo-Indians,* 42).

7 As one Anglo-Indian reported: "I was born an Anglo-Indian and my heritage from my far removed Indian forbear was the olive hue of my skin; but there my Indian heritage ceased, for I was taught the language of the Englishman, his manners, his tastes, his traditions, his history and religion . . . the history of England was taught to me as the history of my country" ("Anglo-Indian"). With regard to the community's adherence to

English, it is interesting to note that a new wave of migration out of India began in the 1960s after attempts to impose regional languages in Anglo-Indian schools in India.

8 On the eve of the partition and independence of British India, the *Glasgow Herald* carried the following story under the headline "Anglo-Indian Exodus," August 2, 1947: "Hundreds of Anglo-Indian families are leaving India shortly to settle in Britain and Australia. The exodus starts on Sunday, when the first batch of 630—the majority from Bengal, Madras, and the Central Provinces—leaves Bombay on board the Australian ship Manoora, for Sydney. Over 4,000 Anglo-Indians have so far registered for passage to Australia. The sailings to Britain will begin with the departure of the Franconia in the second week of August and the Strathmore in the following week."

9 Speaking of those other Indians, the narrator confides: "We're not the only ones. They want to go too. You read their matrimonial columns, American Green Card Holder preferred, only doctor or engineer settled in U.S.A., Canada, Australia" (*The Trotter-Nama,* 574). Sealy underscores desires for the West and a Western lifestyle shared by the two groups.

10 Younger writes: "Many Anglo Indians who migrated integrated well into their new countries and preferred to forget their Indian connection and mixed blood. This often motivated them into cutting all ties with parents and family who still remained here [India] and so pretending they were of pure white blood"; "some Anglo Indians mentioned they met Anglo Indians in the streets and . . . feigned unfamiliarity" (*Anglo-Indians,* 94, 50).

11 Australian policies regarding the admission of persons of mixed race required the individual to demonstrate "by appearance, education, upbringing, outlook, mode of dress and way of living, that he is capable of ready integration into the Australian community" ("Policy for Admission").

12 Anglo-Indians frequently comment on the coming extinction of the community's racial and cultural distinctiveness as they dissolve into larger national, cultural, genetic, and racial groups that dominate in the countries of their residence. "Today we watch the rapid demise of the Anglo-Indians as we know them to be," notes Patricia Brown, writer of a chatty book titled *Anglo-Indian Food and Customs*. "Future generations will be assimilated into other cultures, and during the next century they will no doubt be totally absorbed by the global melting pot. Finally, to be swept away, without a trace, by the tide of time," she notes poetically (10–11).

13 During its early years, the East India Company had encouraged Anglo-Indian "unions by granting five rupees per month for each child born to British soldiers" (Gist and Wright, *Marginality and Identity,* 10). Anglo-Indian historian Herbert A. Stark comments on the advantages of these alliances for the company: "The children grew up in attachment to, and in dependence upon, the nation of their fathers. Their mothers having been cast out by their Indian relatives, the children formed the beginnings of a new race standing in detachment from the people of the soil, and separated from them by speech, religion, dress, customs and habits—by those fundamentals which go to constitute nationality" (*Hostages to India,* 30).

14 Colonial writer George Aberigh-Mackay notes the heterogeneity of the Anglo-Indian population, which he refers to as Eurasian: "There is no proper classification of the

mixed race in India as there is in America. The convenient term *quadroon,* for instance, instead of 'four annas in the rupee,' is quite unknown; the consequence is that every one—from Anna Maria de Souza, the 'Portuguese' cook, a nobleman on whose cheek the best shoe-blacking would leave a white mark, to pretty Miss Fitzalan Courtney, of the Bombay Fencibles, who is as white as an Italian princess—is called an 'Eurasian'" (*Twenty-One Days in India,* 124).

15 Neurological research in acoustic arousal links sound and responses of pleasure or irritation depending on early training in both music and language. Colonial travel literature is rife with references to native music as the annoying sound of difference. See Mill, *The History of British India.* Synaptic pruning in the process of learning arguably plays a role in developing an appreciation for a given range of intonations, whether in music or language. See Douglas Brown, "Cognitive Pruning."

16 The idea of the encephalization quotient (EQ)—relative brain size defined as the ratio between actual brain mass and predicted brain mass for an animal of a given size—hypothesized to be a rough estimate of the intelligence of the animal, long dominated studies of human evolution. Current research suggests "brain evolution was not merely a matter of enlargement, but involved changes at all levels of organization that have been examined. These include the cellular and laminar organization of cortical areas; the higher order organization of the cortex, as reflected in the expansion of association cortex (in absolute terms, as well as relative to primary areas); the distribution of long-distance cortical connections; and hemispheric asymmetry" (Preuss, "The Human Brain," 1). Preuss questions what really happens when the brain enlarges. Recent discoveries concerning the Cetacean brain and bird intelligence decrease confidence in the usefulness of brain size as an indicator of intelligence, but belief persists in the theory that greater ratios of brain to body mass may increase the amount of brain mass available for more complex cognitive tasks and for distinctively human specialization. Cruder predecessors of this science had equated brain size and the encephalization quotient with intelligence.

17 In his discussion of racialized sexuality as a product of "stereotypic, symbolizing, and condensing discursivity," Abdul JanMohamed suggests that "it is the hystericized, oversexualized body of the black male that is used by the discourse of racialized sexuality to reinforce the hysterical boundaries between the two racialized communities ("Sexuality," 105–6). The "open secret" of the white master's desire for the female sexual slave, on the other hand, is characterized by a "peculiar silence" (104, 94). This silence and Foucault's "bracketing of the circuit of power at the macro and micro ends," JanMohamed complains, prevent "the development of the kind of confessional and 'scientific' discursivity central to the deployment of sexuality as Foucault defines it" (97, 104).

3. Doyle Plays Sherlock

1 Rosemary Jann points to the "narrative manipulation necessary to guarantee his [Holmes's] positivistic triumphs," citing several critics who expose the rigging of the facts such that they can only point to the inevitable conclusion Holmes arrives at ("Sherlock Holmes Codes," 685).

2 Barnes suggests, with support from biographical accounts, that it was in the aftermath of the death of Doyle's first wife that the famous detective came upon a file of cuttings from a scandal sheet, *The Umpire,* with a letter signed "George Edalji," "a name that means absolutely nothing to him" (*Arthur and George,* 254).

3 In her reading of the story in *Anxieties of Empire and the Fiction of Intrigue,* Yumna Siddiqi suggests that "imperial territories are irrevocably alien and ungovernable," and likens Miss Warrender both to Virender in Wilkie Collins's *The Moonstone* and to "the figure of the indigent returned colonial" that "recurs in Doyle's fiction" (41). Siddiqi locates the story's anxieties in the recalcitrance and resistance of the colony to education and the empire's production of cultural and economic misfits. Siddiqi proposes that "the nexus between anthropology and the rationality of government" is a theme in this and other stories by Doyle, Collins, and Kipling (49). Miss Warrender could be a fictional counterpart, Siddiqi suggests, for the historical figures of servant Indians in England or a colonial returnee, as she develops an intricate argument about governmentality and corruption by empire.

4 Like Holmes, the narrator of the story, Hugh Lawrence, has lodgings on Baker Street, while his friend John H. Thurston shares Watson's first name and initial along with a tendency to admire beautiful women and to miss the point by a wide margin. Thurston's interest in chemistry would later be transferred to Holmes and Lawrence's in medicine to Watson. Haining points out other parallels: "Lawrence, like Holmes, makes a practice of studying people to discern their characters, is good at cross-examination, and is quite indifferent to the charms of women. He is also strong, brave and resourceful and prefers to solve the mysterious goings-on in the household himself rather than call in the police" (*The Final Adventures of Sherlock Holmes,* 35). Owen Dudley Edwards says: "It is amusing to see how Doyle was switching attributes between his Holmes-type and Watson-type. . . . Thurston is largely required to bring Lawrence in, to provide the link with the mysterious household and be in mortal danger as its legatee, and to supply background briefing" (*The Quest for Sherlock Holmes,* 120). These and other parallels, Haining argues, make the otherwise little-known story a "legitimate precursor to . . . [*A Study in Scarlet*] . . . qualifying it for a place in the [Holmes] canon" (*The Final Adventures of Sherlock Holmes,* 35). For reasons not fully known, Doyle never allowed the story to be reprinted (Fleissner, *A Rose by Another Name,* 49).

5 Jann suggests that the detective routinely relied on physiognomic information, incorporating it into his deductive method in many of his stories: "The myth of rationality that Doyle constructs in the Holmes stories relies heavily on the posited but seldom tested validity of indexical codes of body and behavior that allow Holmes infallibly to deduce character and predict actions from gesture and appearance" ("Sherlock Holmes Codes," 686). Holmes, however, does not seem to employ physiognomic and phrenological evidence consistently. In *The Sign of Four,* he declares: "A client to me is a mere unit, a factor in a problem. The emotional qualities are antagonistic to clear reasoning. I assure you that the most winning woman I ever knew was hanged for poisoning three little children for their insurance-money, and the most repellent man of my acquaintance is a philanthropist who has spent nearly a quarter of a million upon the London poor" (31).

6 In their investigation of the concept of enlightenment, Horkheimer and Adorno explain the role of primitivism in the casting of self and other in the following terms: "The cry of terror called forth by the unfamiliar becomes its name. It fixes the transcendence of the unknown in relation to the known, permanently linking horror to holiness . . . *mana,* the moving spirit, is not a projection but the echo of the real preponderance of nature in the weak psyches of primitive people. The split between animate and inanimate, the assigning of demons and deities to certain specific places, arises from this preanimism. Even the division of subject and object is prefigured in it" (*Dialectic of Enlightenment,* 10–11).

7 In Kipling's "Beyond the Pale," described by Kingsley Amis as "one of the most terrible stories in the language" (*Rudyard Kipling and His World,* 48), we see a matter-of-fact reference to ungovernable impulses among Orientals: "Much that is written about 'Oriental passion and impulsiveness,'" writes Kipling, "is exaggerated and compiled at second-hand, but a little of it is true; and when an Englishman finds that little, it is quite as startling as any passion in his own proper life" (*Plain Tales,* 176). The story is intended as a warning to a would-be suitor of an Oriental beauty, announcing its purpose quite clearly in a prefatory note: Kipling writes, "A man should, whatever happens, keep to his own caste, race and breed. Let the White go to the White and the Black to the Black" (171). The very next sentence announces the foregone conclusion: "This is the story of a man who willfully stepped beyond the safe limits of decent every-day society, and paid for it heavily. . . . He took too deep an interest in native life; but he will never do so again" (171).

8 George recalls the catechism vividly, chapter and verse, "Galatians, chapter five—they begin with Adultery, Fornication, Uncleanness and Lasciviousness" (*Arthur and George,* 82): "Christianity," Horkheimer and Adorno argue, "declared the flesh to be the root of all evil" (*Dialectic of Enlightenment,* 231).

9 According to Risinger, Horace "married Ann Gertrude Magee, an Ulster woman, in Hereford in 1910. Adopting her name, he moved as Horace Edward Magee to Belfast, and later to Dublin, where he lived in the prosperous suburb of Blackrock. After changing his name he broke completely with his family. He died in a Dublin nursing home in 1953" ("Boxes in Boxes," 89n520). Other sources clarify that he returned for his father's and aunt's funerals, but his alienation from the family began when he offered to cooperate in the legal proceedings and suggested that George may have written some of the scurrilous letters associated with the case. His mother and aunt subsequently wrote him out of their wills. See Roger Oldfield's *Outrage.*

10 Reading his autobiography some years after the distinguished writer chose to insert himself into the case of the Great Wyrley Outrages, George comes across these sentences about his father and his family: "Perhaps some Catholic-minded patron wished to demonstrate the universality of the Anglican Church. The experiment will not, I hope, be repeated, for though the Vicar was an amiable and devoted man, the appearance of a coloured clergyman with a half-caste son in a rude, unrefined parish was bound to cause some regrettable situation" (*Arthur and George,* 414). George resents the description of him as "half-caste," for "Was there not a better way of putting it? Perhaps his father, who believed that the world's future depended upon the harmonious commingling

of the races, could have come up with a better expression" (414). George not only resents the freighted term "half-caste," but also the distinguished writer's disinterest in George's elaborate account of his father's conversion. The denial of George's account and the use of vocabulary associated with a far less enlightened attitude toward race suggest that the writer, so ardent a believer in justice for the hapless barrister, was nonetheless reproducing the sort of prejudice that informs his depiction of empire's others in his fictions, despite his knowledge of objective facts about George and his family.

11 Classen claims that "the 'male' senses of sight and hearing were classified as 'distance' senses and the 'female' senses of smell, taste, and touch were characterized as 'proximity' senses" (*The Color of Angels,* 66). Friedrich Schiller explains that nature furnishes man "with two senses which lead him to knowledge of the real world through semblance alone. In the case of the eye and the ear, she herself has driven importunate matter back from the organs of sense, and the object, with which in the case of our more animal senses we have direct contact, is set at a distance from us" (*On the Aesthetic Education of Man,* 195). The alliance of vision, distance, and perspective with superior aesthetic capacity follows: "What we actually see with the eye is something different from the sensation we receive; for the mind leaps out across light to objects. The object of touch is a force to which we are subjected; the object of eye and ear a form that we engender. As long as man is still a savage he enjoys by means of these tactile senses alone, and at this stage the senses of semblance are merely the servants of these. . . . Once he does begin to enjoy through the eye, and seeing acquires for him a value of its own, he is already aesthetically free and the play-drive has started to develop" (195). Elias argues that in place of smell, "we see one of the interconnections through which a different sense organ, the eye, has taken on a very specific significance in civilized society. In a similar way to the ear, and perhaps even more so, it has become a mediator of pleasure, precisely because the direct satisfaction of the desire for pleasure has been hemmed in by a multitude of barriers and prohibitions" (*The Civilizing Process,* 17). Herzfeld explains that while Aristotle "considered sight to be the most highly developed of the senses," "the gradual European abandonment of smell and increasing emphasis on vision is directly linked to the technologies of literacy and to the expansion of social relations beyond the face-to-face" (*Anthropology,* 244).

12 Robert Young argues that Englishness should be understood as a "heterogenous, conflictual composite of contrary elements" that are internally riven (*Colonial Desire,* 3).

13 Doyle offers his own version of "the White Man's Burden" in "A Hymn of Empire, Coronation Year, 1911": "God guard our Indian brothers, / The Children of the Sun / Guide us and walk beside us / Until Thy will be done. / To all be equal measure / Whate'er his blood or birth" (*Songs of the Road,* 66).

14 Although several Parsis participated in the struggle for Indian freedom, Parsi Anglophilia was a recognized phenomenon. Writers Bapsi Sidhwa and Salman Rushdie both comment on it in their novels. In Rushdie's *The Ground beneath Her Feet,* the role of resident Anglophile is filled by Ormus Cama's father, Sir Darius Xerxes Cama, a secularized Parsi: "Brace up! Do yourselves justice!" he declaims, "The British are watching" (28). Sir Darius's dreams are English dreams: "Whenever he dreamed, he dreamed of

England: England as a pure, white Palladian mansion set upon a hill above a silver winding river, with a spreading parterre of brilliant green lawns edged by ancient oaks and elms, and the classic geometry of flower beds orchestrated by unseen master gardeners into a four-seasons symphony of colour" (86).

15 British physician Hector Gavin said that the air in poor homes in England was "so saturated with putrescent exhalations, that to breathe it was to inhale a dangerous, perhaps fatal, poison" (*Sanitary Ramblings,* 69). A major campaign to promote bathing and cleanliness in the nineteenth century in England, resisted stoutly by the poor, would have either sensitized the overseas English nose even more keenly to bad odors in India and other colonies or activated animus against unfamiliar smells on the grounds that they were unfamiliar, and therefore bad; arguably, it may have taught them to relegate native smells to the class of odors the English abroad had learned to associate with the poor, uncultivated masses in their own homeland. Orwell reveals "the real secret of class distinctions in the West. . . . It is summed up in four frightful words which people nowadays are chary of uttering. . . . The words were: *The lower classes smell*" (*The Road to Wigan Pier,* 129).

16 Biologists are less likely to credit human exceptionalism on the traditional grounds used by philosophers. If ribosomatic structure and molecular/cellular form were the criteria, they claim, we would have more in common with mice and yeast than with apes: "Humans are a lot like yeast. . . . Humans also are a lot like fruit flies, mice, and other animals and organisms that have *eukaryotic* . . . cells" (Goldstein and Schneider, *Stem Cells for Dummies,* 12). At the cellular level, the authors claim, "nature uses many of the same blueprints and mechanisms" (12). In "Microbes 'R' Us," biologist Olivia Judson writes: "On a cell-by-cell basis, then, you are only 10 percent human. For the rest, you are microbial."

17 At the law firm, George is persecuted precisely on this point by his fellow workers Greenway and Stentson, who want to know "where do you *really* come from. . . . Have you got a girl, George?" (*Arthur and George,* 70). When he makes up a "Dora Charlesworth," a Dora worthy of a Charles in what might be an unwitting invocation of Dickens's world and the place of women in it, George is asked, "Is she a darkie?" (71). When he responds, "She's English, just like me," they taunt him: "Just like you, George, *Just* like you? . . . I bet she's a Bechuana girl" (71).

Epilogue

1 Balibar's exploration of contemporary forms of "racism without races" prompts a reevaluation of the dispersal of racism into displaced forms ("Is There a Neo-Racism?," 21). I submit that this evaluation should include an understanding of the logic of dominative and instrumental rationality, so illuminatingly elaborated in Frankfurt school critical theory, and the emplacement of this discussion in the larger context of the civilizing process in Europe and beyond with due attention to its repressive bio-logic.

2 In *Lifebuoy Men, Lux Women,* Timothy Burke explores the nexus between colonialism and global capitalism by analyzing the growth of advertising and changing patterns of consumption, especially of cosmetic products, in modern Zimbabwe, in part through a social history of hygiene.

3 As Tim Armstrong points out, modernity offers a conception of the body as lack, to be remedied, and compensated "as a part of capitalism's fantasy of the complete body: in the mechanisms of advertising, cosmetics, cosmetic surgery . . . all prosthetic in the sense that they promise the perfection of the body" (*Modernism, Technology, and the Body,* 3).

4 Žižek exposes "the universality of capitalism," which is no longer "a name for a civilization, for a specific cultural-symbolic world," but rather "the name for a truly neutral economico-symbolic machine which operates with Asian values as well as with others." The problem with capitalism, Žižek avers, "is not its secret Eurocentric bias, but the fact that it really is universal, a neutral matrix of social relations." Although it may not "inscribe itself into the totality of their lifeworlds in the same way, it generates the same formal set of social relations" with "the same profit-oriented matrix" (quoting himself in "Tolerance as an Ideological Category," 673).

5 Mahatma Gandhi's reference to the "raw kaffir" in South Africa is discussed briefly in the first chapter of this book. James Mill's verdict on Indian art and its people as rudely formed can be found in his 1817 six-volume *History of British India.* In this work, James Mill, father of John Stuart Mill, countered positive evaluations of Indian civilization by Western scholars such as Sir William Jones on the grounds of their having been misinformed and inadequately critical. In an aggressive deployment of the hierarchy of the senses to discount evidence of civilizational excellence even where others had found beauty, the text repeatedly refers to Hindus and Hindu art and architecture as rude and barbaric.

6 The dream of a return to national culture is a bootless quest in the struggle for liberation, Fanon argues, since the native intellectual finds that what he wishes to stamp "with a hallmark [of the] national . . . is strangely reminiscent of exoticism" (*The Wretched of the Earth,* 223). And yet, "the withering away of the reality of the nation and the death pangs of national culture are linked to each other in mutual dependence," which is why, he insists, "it is of capital importance to follow the evolution of these relations" (238). At the same time that he recognizes that art forms infused with "the will to liberty" can generate a "new movement" which could give "rise to a new rhythm of life and to forgotten muscular tensions . . . [developing] the imagination," as in the rejuvenation and reconstitution of epic storytelling in Algeria in the early 1950s, the "fundamental tasks" pressing on the nation, he insists, require not "proclamation[s] concerning culture," but "the liberation of the national territory" and "a continual struggle against colonialism in its new forms" (*The Wretched of the Earth,* 240–41, 235). Fanon implies that it is the task of liberating the nation and its peoples from all forms of exploitation that produces a worthwhile form of culture.

7 Malabou's 2008 iteration of plasticity in *What Should We Do with Our Brain?* addresses neuroplasticity and cognitive science in an attempt to explore "the possibility of saying no to afflicting economic, political, and mediatic culture that celebrates only the triumph of flexibility, blessing obedient individuals who have no greater merit than that of knowing how to bow their heads with a smile" (79). For Malabou, brain plasticity involves "not only the creation of form but also an agency of disobedience to every constituted form, a refusal to submit to a model" (6). The "agency of disobedience" is an

enticing prospect, arguably compromised, I suggest, by seductive models of Capitalist personhood and affective histories of the manipulation of feelings of inferiority.

8 Modernity undoubtedly brings advances in medicine, connectivity, and the possibility of positive collective action, but the countervailing forces of domination proliferate at an even greater pace. Lifesaving and enhancing technologies are continually produced, but enmeshed in profit-centered industries that limit their potential, while the imponderable cost of environmental destruction on individual lives, human and nonhuman, grows exponentially.

9 Derrida points out that Nazi pseudozoophilia and Hitler's dogged vegetarianism only serve to reveal the tension between the impulse to stroke one animal and victimize another in whom the animal is perceived (*Paper Machine,* 180).

BIBLIOGRAPHY

Aberigh-Mackay, George. *Twenty-One Days in India; or, The Tour of Sir Ali Baba, K.C.B.* London: W. H. Allen, 1881.

Adorno, Theodor W. *Aesthetic Theory.* Translated by Robert Hullot-Kentor. Minneapolis: University of Minnesota Press, 1997.

———. *The Culture Industry: Selected Essays on Mass Culture.* Edited by J. M. Bernstein. London: Routledge, 1991.

———. "Marginalia to Theory and Praxis." In *Critical Models: Interventions and Catchwords,* translated by Henry W. Pickford, 259–78. New York: Columbia University Press, 1998.

———. *Metaphysics: Concept and Problems* (1965). Edited by Rolf Tiedemann. Translated by Edmund Jephcott. Stanford, Calif.: Stanford University Press, 2001.

———. *Minima Moralia: Reflections on a Damaged Life.* Translated by Edmund Jephcott. London: Verso, 2005.

———. *Negative Dialectics.* Translated by E. B. Ashton. New York: Continuum, 1999.

———. *Negative Dialektik.* Frankfurt: Suhrkamp, 1966.

———. "On Jazz" (1936). Translated by Jamie Owen Daniel. *Discourse* 12, no. 1 (1989–1990): 45–69.

———. *Prisms.* Translated by Samuel Weber and Shierry Weber. Cambridge, Mass.: MIT Press, 1981.

Adorno, Theodor W., and Max Horkheimer. "Towards a New Manifesto?" *New Left Review* 65 (September–October 2010): 33–61.

Ahmad, Aijaz. "Postcolonial Theory and the 'Post-' Condition." *Socialist Register* 33 (1997): 353–81.

Ahmed, Sara. " 'She'll Wake Up One of These Days and Find She's Turned into a Nigger': Passing through Hybridity." *Theory, Culture & Society* 16, no. 2 (April 1999): 87–106.

Akbar, M. J. "Living with the Difference." *Khaleej Times,* July 30, 2012. http://www.khaleej times.com/kt-article-display-1.asp?xfile=/data/opinion/2012/July/opinion_July97.xml&section=opinion.

Amis, Kingsley. *Rudyard Kipling and His World.* London: Thames & Hudson, 1975.

Anderson, Misty G. "Living in a Material World: Margaret Cavendish's *The Convent of Pleasure*." In *Sensible Flesh: On Touch in Early Modern Culture,* edited by Elizabeth D. Harvey, 187–204. Philadelphia: University of Pennsylvania Press, 2003.

"Anglo-Indian: XXIII: 1, Jan 1930." Quoted in Hawes Private Papers; Mss Eur F 531/54, 5. India Office Collection, British Library, London.

"Anglo-Indian Exodus." *Glasgow Herald,* August 2, 1947. Microfiche, Emory University Library.

Anthony, Frank. *Britain's Betrayal in India: The Story of the Anglo-Indian Community.* Delhi: Allied, 1969.

Arendt, Hannah. *The Life of the Mind.* New York: Harcourt, 1978.

Aristotle. *The Rhetoric of Aristotle.* Vol. 2. Commentary by Edward Meredith Cope. Cambridge: Cambridge University Press, 1877.

Armstrong, Tim. *Modernism, Technology and the Body: A Cultural Study.* Cambridge: Cambridge University Press, 1998.

Arnold, David. "Race, Place, and Bodily Difference in Early Nineteenth-Century India." *Historical Research* 77, no. 196 (May 2004): 254–73.

Ashcroft, Bill, Gareth Griffiths, and Helen Tiffin, eds. *The Post-Colonial Studies Reader.* London: Routledge, 1995.

Attridge, Derek, Geoff Bennington, and Robert Young. *Post-Structuralism and the Question of History.* Cambridge: Cambridge University Press, 1987.

Bahr, Erhard. "The Anti-Semitism Studies of the Frankfurt School: The Failure of Critical Theory." *German Studies Review* 1, no. 2 (May 1978): 125–38.

Bahri, Deepika. "Hybridity, Redux." *PMLA* 132, no. 1 (January 2017): 142–48.

Bakhtin, M. M. *The Dialogic Imagination: Four Essays.* Translated by Caryl Emerson and Michael Holquist. Austin: University of Texas Press, 1981.

Bald, Vivek. *Bengali Harlem and the Lost Histories of South Asian America.* Cambridge, Mass.: Harvard University Press, 2013.

Balibar, Etienne. "Is There a Neo-Racism?" In *Race, Nation, Class: Ambiguous Identities,* edited by Etienne Balibar and Immanuel Wallerstein, 17–28. New York: Verso, 1991.

Ballhatchet, Kenneth. *Race, Sex, and Class under the Raj: Imperial Attitudes and Their Critics, 1793–1905.* London: Weidenfeld, 1980.

Barad, Karen. *Meeting the Universe Halfway: Quantum Physics and the Entanglement of Matter and Meaning.* Durham, N.C.: Duke University Press, 2007.

Barkan, Elazar. *The Retreat of Scientific Racism.* Cambridge: Cambridge University Press, 1992.

Barnes, Julian. *Arthur and George.* New York: Vintage, 2005.

Barthes, Roland. *The Pleasure of the Text.* Translated by Richard Howard. New York: Hill and Wang, 1975.

Basham, A. L. *The Wonder That Was India.* London: Picador, 2004.

Basu, Helen, and Shihan de Silva Jayasuriya. "Slave, Soldier, Trader, Faqir: Fragments of African Histories in Western India (Gujarat)." In *The African Diaspora in the Indian Ocean,* edited by Shihan de Silva Jayasuriya and Richard Pankhurst, 223–49. Trenton, N.J.: Africa World Press, 2003.

Baucom, Ian. "The Human Shore: Postcolonial Studies in an Age of Natural Science." *History of the Present* 2, no. 1 (2012): 1–23.

Bauman, Zygmunt. *Modernity and Holocaust*. Ithaca, N.Y.: Cornell University Press, 2001.

Benjamin, Walter. *Illuminations: Essays and Reflections*. Translated by Harry Zohn. New York: Schocken Books, 1968.

———. *Reflections: Essays, Aphorisms, and Autobiographical Writings*. Translated by Peter Demetz and Jephcott Edmond. New York: Schocken Books, 1986.

Bennington, Geoff, and Robert Young. "Introduction: Posing the Question." In *Post-Structuralism and the Question of History*, edited by Derek Attridge, Geoff Bennington, and Robert Young, 1–14. Cambridge: Cambridge University Press, 1987.

Bernal, Maurice. *Black Athena: The Fabrication of Ancient Greece, 1785–1985*. New Brunswick, N.J.: Rutgers University Press, 1987.

Bhabha, Homi K. "Black and White and Read All Over." *Artforum* 34, no. 2 (October 1995): 16–17, 114, 116.

———. "DissemiNation." In *Nation and Narration*, edited by Homi K. Bhabha, 291–322. London: Routledge, 1995.

———. *The Location of Culture*. London: Routledge, 1994.

———. "Signs Taken for Wonders: Questions of Ambivalence and Authority under a Tree outside Delhi, May 1817." Special issue, *Critical Inquiry* 12, no. 1 (Autumn 1985): 144–65.

———. "The Third Space": Interview with J. Rutherford. In *Identity, Community, Culture, Difference*, 207–21. London: Lawrence and Wishart, 1990.

Bhowani Junction. Advertisement. *Life*, June 11, 1956, 115.

Bhowani Junction. Directed by Georg Cukor. Hollywood, Calif.: MGM, 1956.

Blaise, Clark. "A Novel of India's Coming of Age." Review of *Midnight's Children* by Salman Rushdie. *New York Times Book Review*, April 19, 1981. https://www.nytimes.com/books/98/12/06/specials/rushdie-children.html.

Blum, Lawrence. "Racialized Groups: The Sociohistorical Consensus." *The Monist* 93, no. 2 (2010): 298–320.

Blunt, Alison. *Domicile and Diaspora: Anglo-Indian Women and the Spatial Politics of Home*. Malden, Mass.: Blackwell, 2005.

Booth, Martin. *The Doctor and the Detective: A Biography of Sir Arthur Conan Doyle*. New York: Dunne, 1997.

Bordo, Susan. *Unbearable Weight: Feminism, Western Culture, and the Body*. Berkeley: University of California Press, 1993.

Bose, Nemai Sadhan. *Racism, Struggle for Equality, and Indian Nationalism*. Calcutta: Firma KLM, 1981.

Bourdieu, Pierre. *Distinction: A Social Critique of the Judgement of Taste*. Cambridge, Mass.: Harvard University Press, 1984.

Boyarin, Daniel. "Hybridity and Heresy: Apartheid Comparative Religion in Late Antiquity." In *Postcolonial Studies and Beyond*, edited by Ania Loomba et al., 339–58. Durham, N.C.: Duke University Press, 2005.

Brinton, Daniel Garrison. *The Basis of Social Relations: A Study in Ethnic Psychology*. New York: Knickerbocker Press, 1902.

Brown, Douglas. "*Cognitive Pruning* and Second Language Acquisition." *Modern Language Journal* 56, no. 4 (April 1972): 218–22.

Brown, Patricia. *Anglo-Indian Food and Customs.* New Delhi: Penguin, 1998.

Brynie, Faith Hickman. *Brain Sense: The Science of the Senses and How We Process the World around Us.* New York: Amacom, 2009.

Buck-Morss, Susan. "Aesthetics and Anaesthetics: Walter Benjamin's Artwork Essay Reconsidered." *October* 62 (Autumn 1992): 3–41.

Buettner, Elizabeth. "Problematic Spaces, Problematic Races: Defining 'Europeans' in Late Colonial India." *Women's History Review* 9, no. 2 (2000): 277–98.

Burke, Timothy. *Lifebuoy Men, Lux Women: Commodification, Consumption, and Cleanliness in Modern Zimbabwe.* Durham, N.C.: Duke University Press, 1996.

Butler, Judith. *Bodies That Matter: On the Discursive Limits of "Sex."* New York: Routledge, 1993.

———. "Foucault and the Paradox of Bodily Inscriptions." *Journal of Philosophy* 86, no. 11 (November 1989): 601–7.

Cabinet Office to U.K. High Commissioner in New Delhi, IOR POL 9064/47. India Office Collection, British Library, London.

Caldwell, Robert. "The Languages of India, in Their Relation to Missionary Work." Speech delivered at the Annual Meeting of the Society for the Propagation of the Gospel in Foreign Parts, April 28, 1875. MSS Eur P/T586, India Office Collection, British Library, London.

———. *Lectures on the Tinnevelly Missions, Descriptive of the Field, the Work, and the Results; With an Introductory Lecture on the Progress of Christianity in India.* London: Bell & Daldy, 1857.

Cavendish, Margaret. *Observations upon Experimental Philosophy* (1666). Edited by Eileen O'Neill. Cambridge: Cambridge University Press, 2001.

Chalmers, David. Foreword to *Supersizing the Mind: Embodiment, Action, and Cognitive Extension,* by Andy Clark, ix–xvi. New York: Oxford University Press, 2011.

Chandra, Vikram. *Red Earth and Pouring Rain.* Winchester: Faber, 1995.

Chatterjee, Partha. *The Nation and Its Fragments: Colonial and Postcolonial Histories.* Princeton, N.J.: Princeton University Press, 1993.

Chaudhuri, Nirad. *The Continent of Circe: An Essay on the Peoples of India.* London: Chatto & Windus, 1965.

Clark, Andy. *Being There: Putting Brain, Body, and World Together Again.* Cambridge, Mass.: MIT Press, 1997.

———. *Supersizing the Mind: Embodiment, Action, and Cognitive Extension.* Oxford: Oxford University Press, 2008.

Classen, Constance. *The Color of Angels: Cosmology, Gender and the Aesthetic Imagination.* London: Routledge, 1998.

Coelho, Gail. "Anglo-Indian English: A Nativized Variety of Indian English." *Language in Society* 26, no. 4 (December 1997): 561–89.

Cohn, Bernard. *Colonialism and Its Forms of Knowledge: The British in India.* Princeton, N.J.: Princeton University Press, 1996.

Collins, Wilkie. *The Moonstone.* London: J. M. Dent, 1944.

Collits, Terry. "Theorizing Racism." In *Describing Empire, Postcolonialism, and Textuality,* edited by Chris Tiffin and Alan Lawson, 61–69. London: Routledge, 1994.

Corbin, Alain. *The Foul and the Fragrant: Odor and the French Social Imagination.* Cambridge, Mass.: Harvard University Press, 1986.

Cox, Jack. *Take a Cold Tub, Sir! The Story of the Boy's Own Paper.* Guildford, U.K.: Lutterworth Press, 1982.

Cuningham, Henry. "Sherlock Holmes and the Case of Race." *Journal of Popular Culture* 28, no. 2 (1994): 113–25.

Dalrymple, William. *White Mughals: Love and Betrayal in Eighteenth-Century India.* New York: Penguin, 2002.

Damasio, Antonio. *The Feeling of What Happens: Body and Emotion in the Making of Consciousness.* New York: Harcourt, 1999.

———. *Looking for Spinoza: Joy, Sorrow, and the Feeling Brain.* Orlando, Fla.: Harcourt, 2003.

Darwin, Charles. *The Descent of Man, and Selection in Relation to Sex.* London: John Murray, 1871.

Davis, Lennard J., and David B. Morris. "Biocultures Manifesto." *New Literary History* 38, no. 3 (Summer 2007): 411–18.

D'Cruz, Glenn. *Midnight's Orphans: Anglo-Indians in Post/colonial Literature.* Bern: Peter Lang, 2006.

Derrida, Jacques. *The Animal That Therefore I Am.* Edited by Marie-Louise Mallet. Translated by David Wills. New York: Fordham University Press, 2008.

———. *Archive Fever: A Freudian Impression.* Translated by Eric Prenowitz. Chicago: University of Chicago Press, 1996.

———. "But, beyond . . . (Open Letter to Anne McClintock and Rob Nixon)," translated by Peggy Kamuf. In *"Race," Writing, and Difference,* edited by Henry Louis Gates Jr., 354–69. Chicago: University of Chicago Press, 1985.

———. *Paper Machine.* Translated by Rachel Bowlby. Stanford, Calif.: Stanford University Press, 2005.

Dewey, John. *Experience and Nature* (1925). Vol. 1, In *The Later Works, 1925–1953.* edited by Jo Ann Boydston. Carbondale: Southern Illinois University Press, 1981.

DiGregorio, Sarah. "Mind Your Manners: Eat with Your Hands." *New York Times Online,* January 17, 2012. http://www.nytimes.com/2012/01/18/dining/mind-your-manners-eat-with-your-hands.html.

Dirks, Nicholas. "Castes of Mind." *Representations* 37 (1992): 56–78.

Dover, Cedric. *Know This of Race.* London: Secker & Warburg, 1939.

Doyle, Arthur Conan. *Memories and Adventures.* Cambridge: Cambridge University Press, 2012.

———. "On the Slave Coast with a Camera." In *Essays on Photography: The Unknown Conan Doyle,* edited by John Michael Gibson and Richard Lancelyn Green, 13–22. London: Secker, 1982.

———. *The Sign of Four.* London: Spencer Blackett, 1890.

———. *Songs of the Road.* Garden City, N.Y.: Doubleday, 1911.

———. *A Study in Scarlet* (1887). Reprint, London: Penguin, 1981.

———. "Uncle Jeremy's Household." In *The Final Adventures of Sherlock Holmes: Completing the Canon by Sir Arthur Conan Doyle,* collected and introduced by Peter Haining, 41–79. Secaucus, N.J.: Castle, 1981.

Eagleton, Terry. *The Ideology of the Aesthetic.* Malden, Mass.: Blackwell, 1990.

———. *The Illusions of Postmodernism.* Oxford: Blackwell, 1996.

———. "It Is Not Quite True That I Have a Body, and Not Quite True That I Am One Either." *London Review of Books* 25, no. 10 (May 27, 1993): 7–8.

Easthope, Anthony. "Bhabha, Identity, and Hybridity." *Textual Practice* 12, no. 2 (1998): 341–48.

Edwards, Owen Dudley. *The Quest for Sherlock Holmes: A Biographical Study of Arthur Conan Doyle.* Totowa, N.J.: Barnes & Noble, 1983.

Elias, Norbert. *The Civilizing Process: Sociogenetic and Psychogenetic Investigations.* Translated by Eric Dunning, Johan Goudsblom, and Stephen Mennell. Malden, Mass.: Blackwell, 2000.

Epstein, Steven. *Inclusion: The Politics of Difference in Medical Research.* Chicago: University of Chicago Press, 2007.

Fanon, Frantz. *Black Skin, White Masks.* Translated by Charles Lam Markmann. New York: Grove, 1967. Originally published as *Peau noire, masques blancs* (Paris: Editions du Seuil, 1952).

———. *A Dying Colonialism.* Translated by Haakon Chevalier. New York: Grove, 1965.

———. *Toward the African Revolution.* Translated by Haakon Chevalier. New York: Grove, 1988.

———. *The Wretched of the Earth.* Translated by Constance Farrington. New York: Grove, 1963.

Farwell, Byron. *Mr. Kipling's Army: All the Queen's Men.* New York: Norton, 1987.

Fausto-Sterling, Anne. "Refashioning Race: DNA and the Politics of Health Care." *differences: A Journal of Feminist Cultural Studies* 15, no. 3 (2004): 1–37.

Fleissner, Robert F. *A Rose by Another Name: A Survey of Literary Flora from Shakespeare to Eco.* West Cornwall, Conn.: Locust Hill Press, 1989.

Foucault, Michel. *Discipline and Punish: The Birth of the Prison.* Translated by Alan Sheridan. New York: Random House, 1977.

———. *The History of Sexuality.* Vol. 1. Translated by Robert Hurley. New York: Vintage, 1980.

———. "Nietzsche, Genealogy, History." In *The Foucault Reader,* edited by Paul Rabinow, 76–100. New York: Pantheon, 1984.

Freud, Sigmund. *The Complete Letters of Sigmund Freud to Wilhelm Fliess, 1887–1904.* Translated by Jeffrey Moussaieff Masson. Cambridge, Mass.: Harvard University Press, 1985.

———. *The Standard Edition of the Complete Psychological Works of Sigmund Freud.* 24 vols. Edited by James Strachey. London: Hogarth, 1953–1974.

———. "The Unconscious" (1915). In *The Standard Edition of the Complete Psychological Works of Sigmund Freud,* vol. 14, edited by James Strachey, 159–215. London: Hogarth, 1957.

Friedman, Jonathan. "Global Crises, the Struggle for Cultural Identity and Intellectual Porkbarrelling: Cosmopolitans versus Locals, Ethnics and Nationals in an Era of De-Hegemonisation." In *Debating Cultural Hybridity: Multi-Cultural Identities and the*

Politics of Anti-Racism, edited by P. Werbner and T. Modood, 70–89. London: Zed, 1997.

Fry to Gault. Letter. POL 9198/47, India Office Collection, British Library, London.

Gabb, Alfred D. F. *Anglo-Indian Legacy: A Brief Guide to British Raj India History, Nationality, Education, Railways, and Irrigation, 1600–1947.* York: Quacks, 1998.

Gallese, Vittorio, and George Lakoff. "The Brain's Concepts: The Role of the Sensory-Motor System in Reason and Language." *Cognitive Neuropsychology* 22 (2005): 455–79.

Gates, Henry Louis, ed. *"Race," Writing, and Difference.* Chicago: University of Chicago Press, 1986.

Gavin, Hector. *Sanitary Ramblings: Being Sketches and Illustrations of Bethnal Green.* London: John Churchill, 1848.

Ghosh, Amitav, and Dipesh Chakrabarty. "Reflections: A Correspondence on Provincializing Europe." *Radical History Review* 83 (2002): 146–72.

Ghosh, Durba. "Decoding the Nameless: Gender, Subjectivity, and Historical Methodologies in Reading the Archives of Colonial India." In *A New Imperial History: Culture, Identity, Modernity, 1660–1840,* edited by Kathleen Wilson, 297–316. Cambridge: Cambridge University Press, 2004.

Gibson, John Michael, and Richard Lancelyn Green, eds. *Essays on Photography: The Unknown Conan Doyle.* London: Secker, 1982.

Gikandi, Simon. "Aesthetic Reflection and the Colonial Event: The Work of Art in the Age of Slavery." *Journal of the International Institute* 4, no. 3 (Summer 1997). https://quod.lib.umich.edu/j/jii/4750978.0004.306/--aesthetic-reflection-and-the-colonial-event-the-work-of-art?rgn=main;view=fulltext.

———. *Maps of Englishness: Writing Identity in the Culture of Colonialism.* New York: Columbia University Press, 1996.

———. "Race and the Idea of the Aesthetic." *Michigan Quarterly Review* 40 (2000): 318–50.

———. *Slavery and the Culture of Taste.* Princeton, N.J.: Princeton University Press, 2011.

Gilroy, Paul. *Against Race: Imagining Political Culture beyond the Color Line.* Cambridge, Mass.: Harvard University Press, 2000.

Gist, Noel P., and Roy Dean Wright. *Marginality and Identity: Anglo-Indians as a Racially-Mixed Minority in India.* Leiden: E. J. Brill, 1973.

Godzich, Wlad. *The Culture of Literacy.* Cambridge, Mass.: Harvard University Press, 1994.

Goetz, Hermann. *The Art of India: Five Thousand Years of Indian Art.* New York: Greystone Press, 1964.

Goldstein, Lawrence S. B., and Meg Schneider. *Stem Cells for Dummies.* Hoboken, N.J.: Wiley, 2010.

Greene, John C. "Some Early Speculations on the Origin of Human Races." *American Anthropologist,* n.s., 56, no. 1 (February 1954): 31–41.

Grosz, Elizabeth. *Volatile Bodies: Towards a Corporeal Feminism.* London: Routledge, 1994.

Guha, Ranajit. *Elementary Aspects of Peasant Insurgency in Colonial India.* Durham, N.C.: Duke University Press, 1999.

Gunew, Sneja Marina. "Feminism and the Politics of Irreducible Differences: Multiculturalism/Ethnicity/Race." In *Feminism and the Politics of Difference,* edited by Sneja Gunew and Anna Yeatman, 1–34. Boulder, Colo.: Westview, 1993.

———. "Technologies of the Self: Corporeal Affects of English." *South Atlantic Quarterly* 100, no. 3 (Summer 2001): 729–47.

Haidt, J., C. McCauley, and P. Rozin. "Individual Differences in Sensitivity to Disgust: A Scale Sampling Seven Domains of Disgust Elicitors." *Personality and Individual Differences* 16 (1994): 701–13.

Haining, Peter, ed. *The Final Adventures of Sherlock Holmes: Completing the Canon by Sir Arthur Conan Doyle.* Secaucus, N.J.: Castle, 1981.

Hardt, Michael, and Antonio Negri. *Empire.* Cambridge, Mass.: Harvard University Press, 2000.

Hastings, Francis Rawdon. *The Private Journal of the Marquess of Hastings* [1858]. Edited by the Marchioness of Bute. Allahabad: L. M. Basu, 1907.

Hawes, Christopher. *Poor Relations: The Making of a Eurasian Community in British India, 1773–1833.* Richmond, Va.: Curzon, 1996.

Hegel, Georg Wilhelm Friedrich. *Lectures on the Philosophy of History.* Translated by Hugh B. Nisbet. Cambridge: Cambridge University Press, 1975.

———. *Philosophy of History* (1822). Translated by John Sibree. Reprint, New York: Dover, 1956.

Herzfeld, Michael. *Anthropology: Theoretical Practice in Culture and Society.* Malden, Mass.: Wiley-Blackwell, 2001.

Hitler, Adolf. *Mein Kampf.* Translated by R. Manheim. Boston: Houghton Mifflin, 1943.

Hodgson, Brian Houghton. *On the Aborigines of India: The Kocch, Bódo and Dhimál Tribes.* Calcutta: J. Thomas, 1847.

"Hong Kong History: Margaret Thatcher 1982." http://www.timeout.com.hk/big-smog/features/41918/hong-kong-history-margaret-thatcher-1982.html.

Horkheimer, Max, and Theodor Adorno. *Dialectic of Enlightenment: Philosophical Fragments.* Edited by Gunzelin Schmid Noerr. Translated by Edmund Jephcott. Stanford, Calif.: Stanford University Press, 2002.

Howes, David. *Sensual Relations: Engaging the Senses in Culture and Social Theory.* Ann Arbor: University of Michigan Press, 2003.

Hutnyk, John. *Critique of Exotica: Music, Politics, and the Culture Industry.* London: Pluto, 2000.

James, William. *The Principles of Psychology.* Toronto: Henry Holt, 1910.

———. *Some Problems of Philosophy* (1910). Reprint, Cambridge, Mass.: Harvard University Press, 1979.

———. "What Is an Emotion?" *Mind* 9 (1884): 188–205.

Jameson, Fredric. *Archaeologies of the Future: The Desire Called Utopia and Other Science Fictions.* London: Verso, 2005.

———. "The End of Temporality." *Critical Inquiry* 29, no. 4 (Summer 2003): 695–718.

———. *Singular Modernity: Essay on the Ontology of the Present.* London: Verso, 2002.

JanMohamed, Abdul R. "The Economy of Manichean Allegory: The Function of Racial Difference in Colonialist Literature." *Critical Inquiry* 12 (1985): 59–87.

———. "Sexuality on/of the Racial Border: Foucault, Wright, and the Articulation of 'Racialized Sexuality.'" In *Discourses of Sexuality: From Aristotle to AIDS,* edited by Domna Stanton, 94–116. Ann Arbor: University of Michigan Press, 1992.

Jann, Rosemary. "Sherlock Holmes Codes the Social Body." *ELH* 57, no. 3 (Autumn 1990): 685–708.

Jayasuriya, Shihan de Silva. "The African Diaspora in Sri Lanka." In *The African Diaspora in the Indian Ocean,* edited by Shihan de Silva Jayasuriya and Richard Pankhurst, 251–88. Trenton, N.J.: Africa World Press, 2003.

Jayasuriya, Shihan de Silva, and Richard Pankhurst, eds. *The African Diaspora in the Indian Ocean.* Trenton, N.J.: Africa World Press, 2003.

Joseph, Manu. "India Faces a Linguistic Truth: English Spoken Here." *New York Times,* February 16, 2011. http://www.nytimes.com/2011/02/17/world/asia/17iht-letter17.html?_r=0.

Judson, Olivia. "Microbes 'R' Us." *New York Times,* July 21, 2009. opinionator.blogs.nytimes.com/2009/07/21/microbes-r-us/.

Kant, Immanuel. *Anthropology from a Pragmatic Point of View.* Translated by Victor Lyle Dowdell. Edited by Frederick P. Van De Pitte. Carbondale: Southern Illinois University Press, 1996.

Kapila, Shuchi. *Educating Seeta: The Anglo-Indian Family Romance and the Poetics of Indirect Rule.* Columbus: Ohio State University Press, 2010.

Kaplan, Jonathan Michael. "When Socially Determined Categories Make Biological Realities: Understanding Black/White Health Disparities in the U.S." *The Monist* 93, no. 2 (2010): 281–97.

Kiberd, Declan. *Inventing Ireland.* London: Jonathan Cape, 1995.

Kipling, Rudyard. *Plain Tales from the Raj.* London: Macmillan, 1910.

Kirby, Vicki. *Quantum Anthropologies: Life at Large.* Durham, N.C.: Duke University Press, 2011.

———. *Telling Flesh: The Substance of the Corporeal.* New York: Routledge, 1997.

Kolb, Bryan. *Brain Plasticity and Behavior.* Mahwah, N.J.: Lawrence Erlbaum, 1995.

Kraidy, Marwan. *Hybridity, or the Cultural Logic of Globalization.* Philadelphia: Temple University Press, 2005.

Kunzru, Hari. *The Impressionist.* London: Penguin, 2003.

Lahiri-Dutt, Kuntala. *In Search of a Homeland: Anglo-Indians and McCluskiegunge.* Calcutta: Minerva, 1990.

Lazarus, Neil, ed. *Cambridge Companion to Postcolonial Literary Studies.* Cambridge: Cambridge University Press, 2004.

Leder, Drew. *The Absent Body.* Chicago: University of Chicago Press, 1990.

Lévi-Strauss, Claude. *A View from Afar.* Translated by Joachim Negroschel and Phoebe Hoss. Harmondsworth: Penguin, 1987.

Lewontin, R. C. *Biology as Ideology: The Doctrine of DNA.* New York: Harper, 1991.

Lionnet, Françoise. *Autobiographical Voices: Race, Gender, Self-Portraiture.* Ithaca, N.Y.: Cornell University Press, 1989.

Lippit, Akira. *Electric Animal: Toward a Rhetoric of Wildlife.* Minneapolis: University of Minnesota Press, 2000.

Lloyd, David. "Race under Representation." *Oxford Literary Review* 13, no. 1–2 (1991): 62–94.

Loichot, Valérie. "Creolizing Barack Obama." In *American Creoles: The Francophone Caribbean and the American South,* edited by Martin Munro and Celia Britton, 77–96. Liverpool: Liverpool University Press, 2012.

Lopez, Barry. *Of Wolves and Men.* New York: Scribner, 1978.

Lycett, Andrew. *The Man Who Created Sherlock Holmes: The Life and Times of Sir Arthur Conan Doyle.* New York: Simon & Schuster, 2007.

Lyotard, Jean François. *The Differend: Phrases in Dispute.* Minneapolis: University of Minnesota Press, 1988.

Macaulay, Thomas Babbington. "Minute on Indian Education." In *Selected Writings,* edited by John Clive and Thomas Pinney, 237–51. Chicago: University of Chicago Press, 1972.

Malabou, Catherine. *The Future of Hegel: Plasticity, Temporality and Dialectic.* Translated by Lisabeth During. New York: Routledge, 2004.

———. *What Should We Do with Our Brain?* Translated by Sebastian Rand. New York: Fordham University Press, 2008.

Mampilly, Zachariah Cherian. "The African Diaspora of the Indian Sub-continent." *The-south-asian.com,* September 2001. http://www.the-south-asian.com/Sept2001/IndoAfrican_Diaspora.htm.

Manto, Saadat Hasan. "Toba Tek Singh." Translated by Frances W. Pritchett. www.columbia.edu/itc/mealac/pritchett/00urdu/tobateksingh/translation.html.

Marcuse, Herbert. *Eros and Civilization.* London: Sphere Books, 1969.

Martin, J. R. *The Influence of Tropical Climates on European Constitutions: Including Practical Considerations on the Nature and Treatment of the Diseases of Europeans on Their Return from Tropical Climates.* London: John Churchill, 1856.

Masani, Zareer. "English or Hinglish—Which Will India Choose?" *BBC News Magazine,* November 26, 2012. http://www.bbc.co.uk/news/magazine-20500312.

Masters, John. *Bhowani Junction.* New York: Ballantine, 1954.

Mauss, Marcel. "Techniques of the Body" (1934). Translated by Ben Brewster. *Economy and Society* 2, no. 1 (February 1973): 70–88.

Memmi, Albert. *Racism.* Translated and introduction by Steve Martinot. Minneapolis: University of Minnesota Press, 2000.

Memon, Ayaz. "Twenty Million People, Just a Handful of Pools." *Hindustan Times,* May 6, 2012. http://www.hindustantimes.com/india/twenty-million-people-just-a-handful-of-pools/story-yiCgVa0NjaToQBqZBWxuLM.html.

Menninghaus, Winfried. *Disgust: The Theory and History of a Strong Sensation.* Translated by Howard Eiland and Joel Golb. Albany: State University of New York Press, 2003.

Merleau-Ponty, Maurice. *Phenomenology of Perception.* Translated by Colin Smith. London: Routledge & Kegan Paul, 1962.

Mijares, Loretta. " 'You Are an Anglo-Indian?' Eurasians and Hybridity and Cosmopolitanism in Salman Rushdie's *Midnight's Children.*" *Journal of Commonwealth Literature* 38, no. 2 (April 2003): 125–45.

Mill, James. *The History of British India.* 3rd ed. Vol. 2. London: Baldwin, Cradock, and Joy, 1826.

Miller, Jacques-Alain. "Extimité." In *Lacanian Theory of Discourse: Subject, Structure, and Society,* edited by Mark Bracher, Marshall W. Alcorn, and Francoise Massardier-Kennedy, 74–87. New York: New York University Press, 1994.

Mitchell, W. J. T. *Picture Theory.* Chicago: University of Chicago Press, 1994.

———. "Translator Translated: Interview with Cultural Theorist Homi Bhabha." *Artforum,* March 1995, 80–84. http://prelectur.stanford.edu/lecturers/bhabha/interview.html.

Mitter, Partha. "Greece, India, and Race among the Victorians." In *African Athena: New Agendas,* edited by Daniel Orrells, Gurminder K. Bhambra, and Tessa Roynon, 56–70. Oxford: Oxford University Press, 2011.

———. *Much Maligned Monsters: A History of European Reactions to Indian Art* (1977). Reprint, Chicago: University of Chicago Press, 1992.

Mizutani, Satoshi. *The Meaning of White: Race, Class, and the "Domiciled Community" in British India, 1858–1930.* Oxford: Oxford University Press, 2012.

Müller-Doohm, Stefan. *Adorno: A Biography.* Translated by Rodney Livingstone. Cambridge: Polity Press, 2005.

Naipaul, V. S. *India: A Wounded Civilization.* London: Picador, 1977.

Nair, Rukmini Bhaya. *Lying on the Postcolonial Couch: The Idea of Difference.* Minneapolis: University of Minnesota Press, 2002.

Nietzsche, Friedrich Wilhelm. *Ecce Homo: How to Become What You Are.* Translated by Duncan Large. Oxford: Oxford University Press, 2007.

———. "On Truth and Lying in an Extra-Moral Sense." In *Friedrich Nietzsche on Rhetoric and Language,* edited by Sander L. Gilman, Carole Blair, and David J. Parent, 246–57. New York: Oxford University Press, 1989.

"Not All Caucasians Are White: The Supreme Court Rejects Citizenship for Asian Indians." http://historymatters.gmu.edu/d/5076/.

Oldfield, Roger. *Outrage: The Edalji Five and the Shadow of Sherlock Holmes.* Cambridge: Pegasus Press, 2010.

"Oprah's India Special Comes under Fire." *Huffington Post,* July 24, 2012. http://www.huffingtonpost.com/2012/07/24/oprah-winfrey-india-special-own-criticism_n_1699581.html.

Orwell, George. *The Road to Wigan Pier* (1937). Reprint, London: Secker & Warburg, 1959.

Pallasmaa, Juhani. *The Eyes of the Skin: Architecture of the Senses.* Boston: Wadsworth, 2009.

Pankhurst, Richard. "The Ethiopian Diaspora to India: The Role of Habshis and Sidis from Medieval Times to the End of the Eighteenth Century." In *The African Diaspora in the Indian Ocean,* edited by Shihan de Silva Jayasuriya and Richard Pankhurst, 189–221. Trenton, N.J.: Africa World Press, 2003.

Parry, Benita. *Postcolonial Studies: A Materialist Critique.* London: Routledge, 2004.

———. "Problems in Current Theories of Colonial Discourse." *Oxford Literary Review* 9 (1987): 27–58.

———. "Signs of Our Times: Discussion of Homi Bhabha's *The Location of Culture.*" *Third Text* 28–29 (1994): 5–24.

Pascoe, Peggy. "Miscegenation Law, Court Cases, and Ideologies of 'Race' in Twentieth-Century America." *Journal of American History* 83, no. 1 (1996): 44–69.

"Policy for Admission of Persons of Mixed Race." A5827 Vol. 13/Agendum 406 1964. National Archives of Australia, Canberra. http://vrroom.naa.gov.au/records/?ID=19244.

Prabhu, Anjali. *Hybridity: Limits, Transformations, Prospects.* Albany: State University of New York Press, 2007.

Pratt, Mary Louise. *Imperial Eyes: Travel Writing and Transculturation.* London: Routledge, 1992.

Preuss, Todd M. "The Human Brain: Rewired and Running Hot." *Annals of the New York Academy of Sciences* 1225, no. 1 (2011): E182–E191.

Ramachandran, V. S. "Mirror Neurons and Imitation Learning as the Driving Force behind the Great Leap Forward in Human Evolution." *Edge,* May 31, 2000. http://edge.org/conversation/mirror-neurons-and-imitation-learning-as-the-driving-force-behind-the-great-leap-forward-in-human-evolution.

Redmond, Dennis. Online translation of Adorno's *Negative Dialektik.* http://members.efn.org/~dredmond/ndtrans.html.

Regnault, Felix. "Les attitudes du repos dans les races humaines." *Revue Encyclopedique* (1896): 9–12.

Risinger, D. Michael. "Boxes in Boxes: Julian Barnes, Conan Doyle, Sherlock Holmes, and the Edalji Case." *International Commentary on Evidence* 4, no. 2 (2006): 1–94.

Robb, Peter, ed. *The Concept of Race in South Asia.* New Delhi: Oxford University Press, 1995.

Roberts, Celia. *Messengers of Sex: Hormones, Biomedicine, and Feminism.* Cambridge: Cambridge University Press, 2007.

Roberts, D. F. "The Pervasiveness of Plasticity." In *Human Variability and Plasticity,* edited by C. G. Nicholas Mascie-Taylor and Barry Bogin, 1–17. Cambridge: Cambridge University Press, 1995.

Roediger, David. *The Wages of Whiteness: Race and the Making of the American Working Class.* London: Verso, 1991.

Rony, Fatimah Tobing. *The Third Eye: Race, Cinema, and Ethnographic Spectacle.* Durham, N.C.: Duke University Press, 1996.

Roy, Parama. *Alimentary Tracts: Appetites, Aversions, and the Postcolonial.* Durham, N.C.: Duke University Press, 2010.

———. *Indian Traffic: Identities in Question in Colonial and Postcolonial India.* Berkeley: University of California Press, 1998.

Roy, W. T. "Hostages to Fortune." *Plural Societies* 7 (Summer 1974): 55–63.

Rushdie, Salman. Draft of *Midnight's Children,* Box 16, Folder 2; Box 16, Folder 218; Box 16, Folder 221. Salman Rushdie Papers. Rose Library, Emory University.

———. "The Empire Writes Back with a Vengeance." *The Times,* July 3, 1982, 8.

———. *The Ground beneath Her Feet.* New York: Henry Holt, 1999.

———. *Imaginary Homelands: Essays and Criticism, 1981–1991.* London: Granta, 1991.

———. *Midnight's Children* (1981). Reprint, New York: Penguin, 1991.

———. *The Moor's Last Sigh.* London: Jonathan Cape, 1995.

———. *The Satanic Verses.* New York: Viking, 1989.

Said, Edward. "Always on Top." *London Review of Books* 25, no. 6 (March 20, 2003): 3–6.

Sangari, Kumkum. "The Politics of the Possible." In *The Nature and Context of Minority Discourse,* edited by Abdul R. JanMohamed and David Lloyd, 216–45. New York: Oxford University Press, 1990.

Scarry, Elaine. *The Body in Pain: The Making and Unmaking of the World.* New York: Oxford University Press, 1985.

Schiller, Friedrich. *On the Aesthetic Education of Man, in a Series of Letters.* Edited and translated by Elizabeth M. Wilkinson and L. A. Willoughby. Oxford: Clarendon Press, 1967.

Scott, Darieck. *Extravagant Abjection: Blackness, Power, and Sexuality in the African American Literary Imagination.* New York: New York University Press, 2010.

Sealy, I. Allan. *The Trotter-Nama: A Chronicle.* New York: Viking, 1990.

Sen, Kshirod Chandra. *The Gita and the Castes: Being an Exposition of the Social Degeneration of the Hindus, Caused by the Corruption of Varna into Jati, and by the Tyranny of Custom, Confirmed by the Policy of Laissez-Faire, Ennobled by the Pious Appellation of the Policy of Non-Interference, Followed by the British Government in India.* Published by the author, Madaripur, Faridpur, 7th July 1920. IOR P/T595, India Office Collection, British Library, London.

Sen, Sudipta. *Distant Sovereignty: National Imperialism and the Origins of British India.* New York: Routledge, 2002.

Servan, Joseph Michel Antoine. *Discours sur L'Administration de la Justice Criminelle.* Geneva, 1767.

Shaler, N. S. "Historical Races as Products of Isolation." In *Introduction to the Science of Sociology,* edited and with an introduction by Robert E. Park and Ernest W. Burgess, 257–60. Chicago: University of Chicago Press, 1921.

Shih, Shu-Mei. "Comparative Racialization: An Introduction." *PMLA* 123, no. 5 (October 2008): 1347–62.

Shohat, Ella. "Notes on the 'Post-Colonial.'" *Social Text* 31–32 (1992): 99–113.

Shope, Bradley. "Anglo-Indian Identity, Knowledge, and Power: Western Ballroom Music in Lucknow." *Drama Review* 48, no. 4 (Winter 2004): 167–82.

Siddiqi, Yumna. *Anxieties of Empire and the Fiction of Intrigue.* New York: Columbia University Press, 2008.

Sikirov, B. A. "Primary Constipation: An Underlying Mechanism." *Medical Hypotheses* 28, no. 2 (February 1989): 71–73.

Simmel, Georg. "Sociology of the Senses: Visual Interaction." In *Introduction to the Science of Sociology,* edited and with an introduction by Robert E. Park and Ernest W. Burgess, 356–61. Chicago: University of Chicago Press, 1921.

Sinha, Jadunath. *Indian Psychology: Emotion and Will.* Delhi: Motilal Banarsidass, 1986.

Skipton, Horace. *Our Reproach in India.* London: A. R. Mowbray, 1913.

Smith, Andrew. "Migrancy, Hybridity, and Postcolonial Literary Studies." In *The Cambridge Companion to Postcolonial Literary Studies,* edited by Neil Lazarus, 241–61. Cambridge: Cambridge University Press, 2004.

Sollors, Werner. *Neither Black nor White Yet Both: Thematic Explorations of Interracial Literature.* Cambridge, Mass.: Harvard University Press, 1999.

Spillers, Hortense J. "Mama's Baby, Papa's Maybe: An American Grammar Book." *Diacritics* 17, no. 2 (July 1, 1987): 65–81.

Spivak, Gayatri Chakravorty. *A Critique of Postcolonial Reason.* Cambridge, Mass.: Harvard University Press, 1999.

———. "Three Women's Texts and a Critique of Imperialism." *Critical Inquiry* 12, no. 1 (Autumn 1985): 243–61.

Spurr, David. *The Rhetoric of Empire: Colonial Discourse in Journalism, Travel Writing, and Imperial Administration.* Durham, N.C.: Duke University Press, 1993.

Sreedharan, E. *A Textbook of Historiography, 500 B.C. to A.D. 2000.* New Delhi: Orient Longman, 2004.

Stark, Herbert Alick. *Hostages to India; or, the Life-Story of the Anglo-Indian Race.* Calcutta: Star, 1936.

Steger, Manfred B. "Mahatma Gandhi on Indian Self-Rule: An Instrumentalist, an Ethno-Symbolic, or a Psychological Discourse of Nationalism?" In *Emancipating Cultural Pluralism,* edited by Cris E. Toffolo, 129–46. Albany: State University of New York Press, 2003.

Stocking, George. *Race, Culture, and Evolution: Essays in the History of Anthropology.* Chicago: University of Chicago Press, 1982.

Stoddart, David Michael. *The Scented Ape: The Biology and Culture of Human Odour.* Cambridge: Cambridge University Press, 1990.

Stoler, Ann Laura. *Carnal Knowledge and Imperial Power: Race and the Intimate in Colonial Rule.* Berkeley: University of California Press, 2002.

———. "Sexual Affronts and Racial Frontiers: European Identities and the Cultural Politics of Exclusion in Colonial Southeast Asia." *Comparative Studies in Society and History* 34 (July 1992): 514–51.

Stone, Alfred. H. "Conflict and Accommodation." In *Introduction to the Science of Sociology,* edited and with an introduction by Robert E. Park and Ernest W. Burgess, 631–38. Chicago: University of Chicago Press, 1921.

Sussman, Herbert. *Victorian Masculinities: Manhood and Masculine Poetics in Early Victorian Literature and Art.* Cambridge: Cambridge University Press, 1995.

Taussig, Michael. *Mimesis and Alterity: A Particular History of the Senses.* New York: Routledge, 1993.

Thapar, Romila. *India: Historical Beginnings and the Concept of the Aryan.* New Delhi: National Book Trust, 2006.

Trautmann, Thomas R. *Aryans and British India.* New Delhi: Yoda, 2004.

U.K. High Commissioner in New Delhi to Cabinet Office, IOR POL 9198/47. India Office Collection, British Library, London.

Viswanathan, Gauri. *Outside the Fold: Conversion, Modernity, and Belief.* Princeton, N.J.: Princeton University Press, 1998.

Visweswaran, Kamala. *Un/common Cultures: Racism and the Rearticulation of Cultural Difference.* Durham, N.C.: Duke University Press, 2010.

Walcott, Derek. *Collected Poems, 1948–84.* New York: Noonday Press, 1986.

Wilson, Elizabeth. *Neural Geographies: Feminism and the Microstructure of Cognition.* New York: Routledge, 1998.

Yeats, W. B. "The Thinking of the Body." In *The Collected Works of W.B. Yeats,* edited by Richard J. Finneran and George Bornstein, 212–13. New York: Scribner, 2007.

Young, Robert J. C. *Colonial Desire: Hybridity in Theory, Culture and Race.* London: Routledge, 1995.

———. *The Idea of English Ethnicity.* Oxford: Blackwell, 2008.

———. *White Mythologies: Writing History and the West.* London: Routledge, 1990.

Young, Robert M. "The Linguistic Turn, Materialism and Race: Toward an Aesthetics of Crisis." *Callaloo* 24, no. 1 (2001): 334–45.

Younger, Coralie. *Anglo-Indians: Neglected Children of the Raj*. Delhi: B. R. Publishing, 1987.

Yule, Henry, and A. Burnell. *Hobson-Jobson: The Anglo-Indian Dictionary*. Ware: Wordsworth Editions, 1996.

Žižek, Slavoj. "Hegel and Shitting: The Idea's Constipation." In *Hegel & the Infinite: Religion, Politics, and Dialectic,* edited by Slavoj Žižek, Clayton Crockett, and Creston Davis, 221–31. New York: Columbia University Press, 2011.

———. *Looking Awry: An Introduction to Jacques Lacan through Popular Culture*. Cambridge, Mass.: MIT Press, 1991.

———. "Love Thy Neighbor? No, Thanks!" In *The Psychoanalysis of Race,* edited by Christopher Lane, 154–75. New York: Columbia University Press, 1998.

———. *Tarrying with the Negative: Kant, Hegel, and the Critique of Ideology*. Durham, N.C.: Duke University Press, 1993.

———. *The Ticklish Subject: The Absent Centre of Political Ontology*. London: Verso, 1999.

———. "Tolerance as an Ideological Category." *Critical Inquiry* 34, no. 4 (2008): 660–82.

INDEX

DEEPIKA BAHRI is professor of English and core faculty member in comparative literature at Emory University. She is the author of *Native Intelligence: Aesthetics, Politics, and Postcolonial Literature* (Minnesota, 2003) and coeditor of *Between the Lines: South Asians and Postcoloniality* and *The Realms of Rhetoric: The Prospects for Rhetoric Education.*

www.ingramcontent.com/pod-product-compliance
Lightning Source LLC
LaVergne TN
LVHW010732020926
846742LV00029B/66